Thank You IRELAND

Some phenomenal success stories of the Irish in North America

By FRANK KEANE & PATRICK LAVIN

Published by GARRYOWEN, INC.
White Rock, B.C. Canada

Canadian Cataloguing in Publication Data

Keane, Frank
Lavin, Patrick
      Thank You Ireland -- some phenomenal success stories
        of the Irish in North America.

      Includes bibliographical references
      ISBN 0-9697806-0-5

      1. Irish -- United States -- Canada -- History -- 18th - 20th
        centuries
      2. Irish -- emigration and immigration -- history -- 18th - 20th
        centuries
      3. Irish -- biographies

First published in 1994

Published by Garryowen, Inc., 14946-20A Avenue, White Rock,
British Columbia V4A 8G2   Fax (604) 581-1519

Printed in Canada
Printing by Mitchell Press, Vancouver, British Columbia
Binding by North-West Bindery Limited, Surrey, British Columbia

Thank You
IRELAND

Thank You Ireland

"Keep ancient lands, your storied pomp!"
cries she, With silent lips,
"Give me your tired, your poor,
Your huddled masses yearning to breathe free,
The wretched refuse of your teeming shore;
Send these, the homeless, tempest-tost to me,
I lift my lamp beside the golden door!"

When Emma Lazarus wrote those stirring words for the pedestal of the Statue of Liberty, she must have had the Irish in mind. Millions of starving, poverty-stricken, exiled Irish made their way to North America during the nineteenth century.

In time, they made their mark in the New World, contributing in many ways to the development and expansion of two great democratic societies -- the United States and Canada. Since World War II, North America has been blessed by new generations of Irish immigrants -- entrepreneurs and business leaders -- who are displaying their executive skills in the boardrooms of corporate America.

While we are grateful to the New World for accepting the "huddled masses," we would also like to say "Thank You Ireland" for sending us your best.

We would especially like to thank those who stayed behind to keep the home fires burning and the kettle on the boil for those of us who return now and then.

Other people see things and say: "Why?" ... But I dream things that never were and say: "Why not?"

-- George Bernard Shaw

Contents

FOREWORD

The history of the Irish in North America is the story of ordinary people achieving extraordinary prominence in the land of their adoption. This book is a tribute to those sons and daughters of Erin who made the North American continent their home while keeping a special place in their hearts for the green and misty isle from whence they came. It reveals their tenacity and dogged determination to embrace the liberty and opportunities offered by their adopted lands and it focuses on the immense contribution they made along the way.

Through research and interviews, a pattern of success is documented which astounds the imagination. The combination of hope, confidence, determination and unlimited opportunities stirred an ambition that lifted the Irish immigrants to heights of wealth, power and influence far beyond anything they had previously experienced or even dreamed about

It would be impractical to cover in one volume, or for that matter in several volumes, the stories of all of the sons and daughters of Erin who played a significant part in making the great North American dream a reality. Instead, the book focuses on the variety of the Irish experience.

The book is divided into sections to increase coherence. The general introduction on the Irish diaspora covers the causes and effects of the exodus. Each part begins with specific background to that particular field of endeavor; the personal stories follow arranged in historical and/or thematic order.

The authors are grateful to many individuals for helping to make this book possible. First and foremost we wish to acknowledge the cooperation and the recollections of the persons we interviewed. Their stories make our work come to life.

The authors wish to thank the editor, Joan Lavin, who labored endlessly over the manuscript. Her discerning eye, astute judgement and editorial wisdom made our work a lot less difficult. The authors are grateful to Edith Lavin who helped with the mammoth task of typing the book and spotting errors, and to Carol Freeman for the photography work. A special thanks goes to Dr. Ruby Cram who gave selflessly of her time to review the book and for her invaluable help and numerous useful suggestions relating to the enhancement and clarity of the text.

The Irish Diaspora

Historian Lord Macaulay, writing about the Irish Diaspora, said "There were Irish of great ability, energy, and ambition, but they were to be found everywhere except in Ireland: at Versailles, and at St. Ildefonso, in the armies of Frederick and in the armies of Maria Teresa. ..."

Today this is more evident than when Lord Macaulay made his observation. An estimated seventy million people throughout the world claim Irish roots. That same ability, energy and ambition for which they were famous in the past has stayed with them. While the European courts they loyally served and the battlefields on which they valorously fought have long since gone, their impact is more spectacular today as political leaders and as chief executives of financial and industrial institutions.

Recent census figures reveal more than forty million Americans claim Irish ancestry. North of the border, another three and a half million Canadians affirm their Irish lineage. Although far removed from their roots in Ireland, many still cling to their heritage.

The First Wave

The Irish have been leaving Ireland for some fifteen hundred years, first to evangelize and later to escape persecution and poverty.

The first significant wave of emigration from Ireland began at the end of the seventeenth century. In the aftermath of the Williamite wars, which ended with the Treaty of Limerick in 1692, a major exodus occurred. Those exiles were Ireland's Catholic nobility and fighting men who fled to Europe rather than join the British forces at home. More than 11,000 officers and soldiers left Ireland for France where they formed the French army's famous Irish Brigade. This Brigade, and others formed in Spain and Austria during the next century, were reinforced by tens of thousands of Irishmen. It is estimated that more than a third of a million Irishmen died fighting for France during the years between the Treaty of Limerick in 1692 and the Battle of Fontenoy in 1745.

1

These immigrants, better known as the "Wild Geese," distinguished themselves by their gallantry on many of the battlefields of Europe.

Many of those who fled, and their descendants, achieved fame and fortune. Limerick-born Marshal Count Brown achieved distinction serving in the Imperial Service of Austria. Count Peter de Lacy, also Limerick born, distinguished himself in the Grand Army of Peter the Great of Russia and was later appointed Governor of Livonia. Don Alexander O'Reilly, born in Ireland in 1725, was appointed commander of the Spanish Armies and later became Governor of Louisiana, which he captured from the French in 1761. Don Ricardo Wall became Prime Minister of Spain.

Brig. General Hugo O'Conor left County Roscommon in 1763 to join the Spanish Army. A long-time mercenary serving the King of Spain in the New World, O'Conor is credited with being the founder of the city of Tucson in Arizona. Hugo later became Governor of Chile and subsequently returned to Ireland.

Another Roscommon man, General Jacque Moran from Elphin, had the distinction of being the only Irishman to have his name inscribed on the *Arc de Triomphe*. He died in the French Revolution by the usual method of guillotine decapitation.

Ambrosia O'Higgins, born in Ballinary, County Sligo in 1720, fled Ireland as a youngster for Spain. He was educated in Cadiz, later making his way to Chile, where he engaged in trade between Europe and South America. He later became Governor of the Spanish Province of Chile in 1789. His son, Bernardo O'Higgins, born in Chile in 1778, led a revolt against the Spanish which succeeded in Chile becoming an independent country. Bernardo O'Higgins became known as the Father of Chile.

These and many others like them were the involuntary exiles whose fondness for Ireland was so aptly expressed in Emily Lawless's poem, *With the Wild Geese*:

War-battered dogs are we,
Fighters in every clime;
Fillers of trench and of grave,
Mockers bemocked by time.

War-dogs hungry and gray,
Gnawing a naked bone,
Fighters in every clime --
Every cause but our own.

The Second Wave

Early in the eighteenth century the Irish began heading for the shores of North America. Most were of Ulster Protestant stock who, unlike those who headed for the continent of Europe, left voluntarily to settle mostly in England's North American colonies. A flourishing flax-seed trade between Ulster ports and the Carolinas made passage easily available on the returning ships. Their numbers increased significantly throughout the 1700s with more than half a million settling in the middle colonies of Maryland, Virginia and the Carolinas. They were the frontiersmen and pathfinders of a yet to be born nation. Among them was Francis Makemie, the founder of American Presbyterianism. Makemie, born in Rathmelton, County Donegal, immigrated to the colonies where he was ordained into the Presbyterian ministry. In 1706, he founded the Presbytery of Philadelphia, the first in America.

Some Irish Catholics also immigrated to the American colonies during the 18th century. It was not as easy for them since the same English laws restricting Catholic worship and ownership of property at home were sometimes in force in the colonies. Maryland, in 1704, levied a head tax on indentured servants from Ireland to prevent the importing of too great a number of Irish papists. Those who did emigrate were mainly the well-to-do professionals and merchants. Others were indentured servants.

Notwithstanding, several Irish Catholic families have been identified with the colonial period. Among them were the McCarthys. Daniel McCarthy, a native of County Cork, was sent out to the Colonies after the signing of the Treaty of Limerick in 1692. He settled in Virginia and became a large landholder. He represented Westmoreland County from 1705 to 1751 in the House of Burgesses, and he occupied the important post of Speaker of the House from 1715 to 1720. Daniel's son, Denis

McCarthy, married Sarah Ball, a first cousin of Mary Ball, who was George Washington's mother.

There were also the Carrolls, who emigrated from Queen's County to Maryland in 1688. Charles Carroll of Carrollton, Maryland, born in 1737, attained the unique distinction of being the only Catholic and the wealthiest of the signers of the Declaration of Independence. Daniel Carroll, his cousin, was a delegate to the Constitutional Convention. Another Irish Catholic participant in the Constitutional Convention was Thomas FitzSimmons, a wealthy Pennsylvania businessman.

The Irish were also among the earliest settlers of the English-speaking Canadas and for a period they outnumbered the French, English and Scots. As early as the eighteenth century, Newfoundland was a destination for many Irish immigrants, mainly from southeastern Ireland. Between 1770 and 1836 some 35,000 Irish, largely Catholics from Wexford, Kilkenny, Waterford and Wicklow, settled in Newfoundland. However, immigration to Newfoundland lessened as economic possibilities declined and the island was bypassed almost completely during the famine years. Immigration to Prince Edward Island was almost all pre-Famine and many of the immigrants were Catholics from County Monaghan.

In the aftermath of the British victory over the French in 1760, many Irish immigrants settled in Nova Scotia as a result of England's efforts to establish loyal settlements there. In 1760, a County Donegal man, Alexander McNutt, was given a large grant of land on condition that he would settle Irish people in the colony. McNutt's venture only applied to Protestant Irish, and while his efforts were initially successful, he never fully realized his plan. The English government resisted, fearing it would lead to the depopulation of the Protestant communities of Ireland.

In the early 19th century, Irish Catholics from Cork and Waterford settled in New Brunswick's Miramichi Valley. Many immigrants journeyed inland by steamer to Ontario. The earlier immigrants settling in Ontario were better-off Protestants from Munster and Leinster who were fleeing economic depression in Ireland. There were several pre-famine Catholic settlements in Ontario as well, including Peterborough County and the Ottawa

4

Valley. Ulster Presbyterians became a significant element in the settlement of Ontario as the nineteenth century progressed.

The Seeds of 19th Century Emigration

The seeds of 19th century Irish immigration to North America were sown shortly after King William's victory over Catholic King James at the Battle of the Boyne in 1690. Both British and Irish Parliaments, responding to Protestant demands that the "seditious" Irish Catholics be punished for their disloyalty, enacted the Penal Laws abolishing civil rights and outlawing Catholic worship. Catholic bishops were exiled and the movements of secular clergy were restricted. Irish Catholics could not vote, sit in Parliament, serve as government employees, establish schools, practice law, possess weapons or purchase property. In fact, the Catholic Irish were relegated to subcitizen status at a time when they constituted seventy-five per cent of Ireland's population.

Adding to the severe impact of the Penal Code was a phenomenal population explosion which began about 1785 and continued for the next fifty years. In 1754, Ireland's population was 2.3 million. In less than a hundred years prior to the Great Famine, it had nearly quadrupled to 8.2 million. During roughly the same period, the world's population, according to best estimates, increased by about thirty-three percent. By 1821, Ireland's population of 6.8 million represented half the population of the British Isles and the density of population was greater than in any other European country.

The rapid rise in population severely increased the wretched conditions of the country's laboring and peasant classes, most of whom were subsisting mainly on a potato diet. Further perpetuating the problem was the fragmenting of land holdings by an age-old practice. Upon the death of a father, his holding was divided up among his surviving sons. As one generation succeeded another, this practice led to progressively smaller holdings and the inheritors grew successively poorer.

Ireland also caught the full impact of the post-Napoleonic War economic recession. In 1815, the Battle of Waterloo brought an end to the war, and the end of the war brought a severe decline

5

in the economic prosperity that was experienced throughout Britain and Ireland during the war years. In Ireland, agricultural prices, inflated during the war years, slumped after Waterloo and employment for wages virtually ceased to exist. Adding to this, repeal of the Corn Laws in the 1840s made tillage farming less profitable for the landowners, which brought about a shift in Irish agriculture from tillage to grazing. This change led to wholesale evictions of small tenant farmers and economic disaster for many.

Early 19th Century Emigration Trade

It was the rise of Britain's timber trade with her Canadian colonies, following the Napoleonic Wars, that opened the way for the mass exodus of Irish to North America in the 19th century. This trade also brought about a significant shift in that Irish Catholics replaced Irish Protestants as the dominant emigrating group. Owners of timber ships needed cargo for the trip to North America. Since the Canadian colonies were undeveloped and thinly populated, with fewer than a million inhabitants, one solution was to offer low fares to emigrants seeking to settle there. Thus began the business of conveying emigrants; cargo ships carrying timber eastward to Britain found it profitable to carry a full load of emigrants on the westward trip. The low fares and few restrictions enabled the poorer emigrants, mostly Catholic tenant farmers and farm laborers, who previously could not afford the fare, an opportunity to escape and build a new life -- for those who survived the trip. The voyage took from four to ten weeks and the human suffering was unrelenting. Many died before journey's end, many others upon arrival, from cholera and other diseases.

Among the tens of thousands who set sail from Europe for North America following the Napoleonic Wars, the Irish formed the largest group. Between 1815 and 1846, the thirty-year period before the Great Famine, it is estimated that one million Irish crossed to permanently reside in North America. Many of these early 19th century immigrants settled in rural areas of central and eastern Canada. During this period the Irish immigration to Canada outnumbered that of the English and the Scots. The cheap passage to Canadian ports also helped passengers heading for American destinations. Between 1831 and 1841, it is estimated that 189,255 of the 214,000 immigrants that left Ireland for North America landed in Canada, and many of these later went on to the United States. By 1842 Canada had 122,000 Irish born settlers.

The emigrants who left Ireland for Canada in the early part of the 19th century were not a representative cross-section of the Irish population. Some came with modest capital. Many of them, like earlier immigrants to the American colonies, were Protestant. Unlike those who followed during the height of the Famine, usually they came with trade skills or a good knowledge of farming methods. The Irish immigrants before the famine came to Canada in search of land. Unlike their counterparts in the United States, they were less likely to congregate in the cities. Many who came from Munster and Leinster made their homes in Ontario in settlements such as Peterborough, Renfrew and Carleton. Orangemen from Ulster mainly settled in the Toronto area.

The closing years of the "emigrant trade" era converged with the Great Famine. The Famine emigration was the end of mass Irish immigration to Canada and the beginning of a new phase of expansion of Irish communities in the United States. By 1855, Irish immigration to Canada had declined to a few hundred a year, and for the rest of the century it remained insignificant, relative to the flow into the United States.

The Famine Exodus

The mid-19th century saw a dramatic increase in Irish immigration to North America. Beginning in the late 1840s, traffic in the North Atlantic Ocean was intense. Ships sailing westward were filled with emigrants. These were the Famine emigrants, ninety percent of whom were from classes which were wholly dependent on the potato crop that had failed. Desperately fleeing poverty and starvation at home, they crossed the Atlantic under conditions regarded as beyond human endurance. These, for the most part, were poverty-stricken tenants shipped out by their landlords in crowded and unsafe vessels. Many of the vessels sank and thousands of emigrants perished along the way. Thousands more perished upon arrival at the quarantine stations from cholera and typhus.

In 1847, over 100,000 diseased and destitute Irish were off-loaded at Grosse Ile quarantine station in the St. Lawrence River near Quebec. It is estimated that 20,000 of them died in Canada within a year of arriving -- 5,300 never made it off Grosse Ile.

More than 1.7 million left Ireland for North America between 1845 and 1864. The all-time peak was reached in 1851 when 216,000 flooded the shores of North America, mainly to the United States. The Irish population of the United States was rapidly growing and was nearing fifty per cent of all foreign-born Americans. In all, during the hundred years following 1820 when statistics were first gathered on foreigners entering the United States, almost a quarter of the ten million emigrants who arrived were from Ireland.

Unlike most who emigrated before them, almost all the Famine emigrants began and many ended as unskilled laborers in construction camps -- building factories, docks and streets, wherever Irish muscle was a primary need. Poverty kept them in the eastern cities; ignorance of improved or large-scale agriculture methods kept them from settling in rural areas. Probably many associated farming with their homeland experience of insecurity, turbulence and unrest. Good wages in the cities were more attractive.

The Irish Came and Stayed

The influx of uneducated and impoverished Irish immigrants, during the period between the Famine and the Civil War, initially caused serious problems of prejudice and discrimination. But discrimination was nothing new to the Irish. They had long experienced the injustice of discrimination in Ireland and they had learned to cope with their lot. They established themselves within the American Catholic Church and in due time transformed it into a powerful Irish-Catholic religious institution.

The 19th century Irish immigrants, as a group, made no measurable impact on American life before the middle of the century. By the late 1800s, however, they had become a settled and important element in American society and their presence was being felt in areas such as politics, sports and entertainment.

8

They were now the largest of the dominant ethnic groups. By 1870, there were 1,855,827 native-born Irish compared to 1,690,410 native-born Germans, the next highest group.

The Road to Success

Maybe it was the Irishman's sensitivity about status that drove him so hard to rise from impoverished immigrant to successful partner in a new venture. In their adopted countries of North America, the Irish worked hard and progressed quickly. First they moved into the ranks of skilled labor, dominating trades like bricklaying and plumbing, and soon established themselves as leaders in trade unions. Next they infiltrated the police, fire fighting and many other services associated with county and city government. In due course, they reached the pinnacle of success in many fields -- politics, the military, trade unions, literature, entertainment, sports and industry. Theirs is a success story that challenges comparison. William Shannon, in *The American Irish -- A Political and Social Portrait*, said "In Ireland, the Irish had inherited history and suffered it. In America they became the makers of history."

Their Impact on North America

Irish soldiers were considered the backbone of Washington's troops in the American Revolutionary War. John Barry, considered by many to be the father of the United States Navy, came from County Wexford. Among the signatories of the American Declaration of Independence were Limerick-born Matthew Thornton, Dublin-born James Smith and Charles Thomson, Tyrone-born Edward Rutledge, and Galway-born Thomas Lynch.

Nowhere did the Irish achieve so much as in politics. With their political *savoir-faire*, their leadership talents and their strong command of the English language, they built strong political bases which helped elect them to political office, first at the city level, next at the state level and finally at the national level. Many of the United States presidents were of Irish ancestry, beginning with the seventh president, Andrew Jackson, whose father and mother emigrated from Ireland. More recently,

Presidents Kennedy and Reagan are descendants of immigrants from Counties Wexford and Tipperary who left Ireland in the mid-1800s. Thomas D'Arcy McGee fled Ireland to avoid being arrested for treason by the British and became a Father of Canadian Confederation. Brian Mulroney, the grandson of Irish immigrants, became Canada's eighteenth prime minister.

In the Civil War, the Irish served with distinction on both sides of the line. Some became legends in their own time. County Cork-born Major-General Patrick Cleburne, of the Confederate forces, was regarded by the leaders of the Confederate States as second only to the great General "Stonewall" Jackson. Major-General Phil Sheridan, the son of County Cavan immigrants, distinguished himself with the Union side, as did County Wexford-born Major-General Thomas Meagher.

The Irish have dominated the upper echelons of the Catholic Church in America from the second half of the nineteenth century. Of the sixty-nine Episcopal offices that existed throughout the country in 1886, thirty-five were held by Irish, fifteen by Germans, eleven by French and eight by English. John Joseph Hughes, born in County Tyrone in 1797, became the first archbishop of New York in 1842. John McCloskey, whose parents emigrated from County Derry, succeeded Hughes as archbishop of New York and became the first American cardinal in 1875.

In the fields of entertainment, literature and the arts, the Irish have made major contributions. People such as George M. Cohan, Eugene O'Neill, Frank O'Hara, John Ford and numerous others became legends in their fields.

The American labor movement owes its creation and growth to the Irish. From the early militant miners under Queens County-born John Siney, to Terence Vincent Powderly who built the Knights of Labor, to Phil Murray of the Congress of Industrial Organizations (CIO), and George Meany who had served as president of the American Federation of Labor -- Congress of Industrial Organizations (AFL-CIO) for thirty years before his retirement in 1986, the Irish have been in the forefront of transforming an array of widely scattered unions into a powerful labor organization.

10

The Irish impact in industry has not been as conspicuous as in the other fields, probably because the industrial revolution was late in reaching Ireland. Notwithstanding, there were many individual Irishmen who made fortunes in banking, mining and retailing, from Andrew Mellon of Pittsburgh, whose immigrant father founded the Mellon Bank; to Henry Ford, the man who put America on wheels; to Joe Kennedy, the grandson of emigrants from County Wexford, who built a family fortune in banking and motion picture production and was a millionaire many times over by the time he was thirty-five; and Timothy Eaton, who founded the T. Eaton Company that became Canada's largest retail enterprise.

The stories that follow are about ordinary Irish men and women whose remarkable combination of hope, confidence and imagination propelled them to extraordinary peaks. Inspired by the abundance of opportunities, these immigrants and their descendants seized the opportunities that came their way. Some are modern success stories. In the interviews which follow, one learns what made these people different and how they achieved so much success. They tell how they went about getting a job (their approaches were varied) and they reveal one common thread -- an ambition and determination to succeed.

Any partisan political views expressed are strictly the views of the persons interviewed. The authors do not claim that the book is all encompassing, the sheer volume of historical data on the Irish in North America precludes such coverage. This book is meant solely as a tribute to the men and women of the Irish Diaspora who made their homes in North America. Others may wish to elaborate on any of the stories.

In the words of President John F. Kennedy, speaking to a welcoming crowd at Dublin Airport on June 26, 1963, "No country in the world, in the history of the world, has endured the hemorrhage which this island endured over a period of a few years for so many of her sons and daughters. These sons and daughters are scattered throughout the world, and they give this small island a family of millions upon millions who are scattered all over the globe, who have been among the best and most loyal citizens of the countries that they have gone to, but have also kept a special place in their memories, in many cases their ancestral memory, of this green and misty island, so, in a sense, all of them who visit Ireland come home."

Wildcatters and Sourdoughs

The mining business in North America early in its history did not require highly skilled or educated individuals. What it did require was people who were prepared to challenge the ice, snow and cold of the mountains and the northern isolation in Canada; or the search for gold, silver, copper, lead and zinc in the deserts of the southwest, where temperatures often reached well over one hundred degrees.

Many Irish became itinerant miners, following the gold rushes from California to the Yukon. A lot of placer mining was undertaken in the early days of American settlement. This kind of mining allowed the novice to work for himself as the cost of entry was often just a shovel and a pan. Groups often banded together for safety and to share the cost and the work effort needed when placer mining got a little more complicated, needing sluice boxes and shallow shafts to extract the gold or silver.

Some Irish worked in the underground mines of Montana where Irish copper kings Clark and Daly owned most of the big copper producing mines, which made places like Butte and Helena famous mining towns. The town of Anaconda was founded in 1883 by Marcus Daly who had built his Washoe Smelter and Reduction Works to smelt the copper concentrates from the many mines in the area. Daly, born in Ballyjamesduff, County Cavan owned the Anaconda Mine with George Hearst, father of newspaper magnate Randolph Hearst. The Hearst family fortune was created by the Anaconda Mine. William Clark was a third generation Irishman whose family came from County Tyrone. He was an elder of the Presbyterian Church and a Mason. There was intense rivalry between Clark and Daly which was fed by their religious differences and by the fact that Daly was a Democrat and Clark was a Republican.

Marcus Daly and William Clark ran most of the economic and political life of the Butte area. They were involved in most of the area's disputes and they influenced all aspects of decision-making involving ownership of the mines and working conditions of the miners. They even influenced the location of the State

Capital. Butte had the largest Catholic population, where St. Patrick's Catholic Church had 7,000 parishioners in 1900. Helena, which eventually became the State Capital, was William Clark country and mostly Protestant.

The great majority of the Anaconda mine workers were Irish and, interestingly enough, you could get a pint of Guinness draft in Butte as far back as 1887. Between 1893 and 1919, nine of Butte's mayors were Irish. Thirty-two of the first thirty-six mine workers union presidents were also Irish.

Daly died in 1900 and after his death, control of the Anaconda group of companies was bought out by Rockefeller's Standard Oil Company. William Clark at first opposed the Standard Oil takeover, but later threw in his lot with them.

Others, like the McDonough brothers, sought their fortunes in mining. The McDonoughs mushed into remote Red Lake in the Ontario wilderness, starting the 1926 gold rush to that camp. Others followed by dog sled, canoe and airplane to Red Lake. Several gold mines were developed, some of which are still producing today. The Red Lake camp boasted such gold producers as Dickenson Red Lake, H. G. Young Mines, Howey Gold Mines, Campbell Red Lake and Foley Red Lake Mines.

Another famous Irish brother act was that of the Byrne family, headed by the adventurous Jerry Byrne. The Byrnes ventured 1,000 miles northward to Great Bear Lake in Canada's Northwest Territories, where they discovered and brought to production the high-grade Discovery Gold Mine in the Giaque Lake area. The Byrnes discovered and developed twelve mines in the forty-odd years they were active in the Canadian north country, including Rayrock Mine, Tundra Gold Mine and La Forma Mine. The Byrnes were also involved in developing several of Canada's uranium mines.

John Mackey, born in Dublin in 1831, immigrated to New York in 1846 at age fifteen. Two years later, he headed west to Virginia City, Nevada and with fellow-Irishman James Fair, developed several small mining properties. Needing more capital, Mackey and Fair brought in three partners -- a wealthy Virginian and two Irish saloon keepers from New York, James Flood and William O'Brien. In 1873, they discovered the Bonanza Gold Mine

14

and became multi-millionaires overnight. Mackay bought out the Virginian and he became the most important member of the partnership. He later moved back to New York and invested his money in telegraph lines and a transatlantic cable company. His son, Clarence Hungerford Mackay, is best remembered as the father-in-law of Irving Berlin. James Flood built the last of the great mansions on Nob Hill in San Francisco.

Then there was Gaelic speaking Michael MacGowan, born in the village of Cloghaneely, County Donegal in 1865. With no work in Cloghaneely, Michael, at age fifteen, and a few of his friends went to Scotland where they worked as tatie-hookers. After five years working in Scotland, Michael set sail for America, still speaking only Gaelic.

In those days, all one needed to get to America was the £4.10 fare and a good strong pair of legs to get one the fifty miles or so to Derry to catch the boat. Michael set off, with buddies Tom Ferry and Jimmy Doherty, to make his fortune. Michael had some relatives in the Bethlehem area of Pennsylvania working in the steel mills. After landing in New York, they still had to get the one hundred or so miles to Bethlehem, so they did what many immigrants before them had done, they rode the rods just like the hobos.

After a year in the steel mills, they took Horace Greely's advice to "Go west young man" and headed for the silver mines of Montana. After a six-day train ride, they arrived at the Granite Mountain Mine, located at an elevation of some 7,000 feet in the American Rockies. There were already six Irishmen from Donegal working underground, so Michael was able to get hired. He worked there for seven years without making his fortune. Then the price of silver dropped to forty cents an ounce and the mine closed.

About this time, stories were circulating about the fabulous riches which were being mined in the Klondike. But the Klondike was thousands of miles from Montana and the seven Irishmen from Donegal did not have enough money to get all of them to the Yukon. They pooled their meager earnings, sending MacGowan and two others on their way to the Klondike with the promise that when they had made sufficient money, they would send for the others or share whatever they made in the gold diggings with those left behind.

To avoid going over the dreaded Chilkoot Pass, MacGowan and his buddies sailed from Seattle to the mouth of the Yukon River (a thirty-two-day trip) and from there caught a boat up the Yukon River to get to the nearest point of the diggings. After fifteen days on the river, the boat became stranded when it ran into a sandbar. When ordered off the boat by the captain, the boys demanded their fare back. After an argument, in which the captain threatened to shoot them if they didn't get off, MacGowan and his friends left the boat and walked the rest of the way to the diggings. MacGowan eventually dug up enough gold to return to County Donegal, build himself a fine house and marry.

His story was picked up by Radio Eireann where Michael related his experiences in Gaelic over the air. Valentine Iremonger translated the story into English and had it published as a book, *The Hard Road to Klondike*. In 1958, the story won the award of the Irish Book Club. Michael MacGowan died on November 29, 1948.

There was Patrick Hughes, who left his native Ireland to work in Canada's north country. Patrick, a bricklayer and construction worker, built the first bank in Uranium City in northern Saskatchewan in the late 1950s. In those days, the uranium boom was just getting underway. The area around Uranium City was likely prospecting ground. However, uranium was considered a strategic material so the government had placed a moratorium on its exploration. Later, when the moratorium was lifted, the Atomic Energy Commission began issuing licenses to small Canadian mining companies to produce uranium for military and power production uses. Patrick Hughes and his partners were in there fast and staked a large parcel of claims. They then sold these claims for $100,000 to a company called Violamac Mines. This gave them the stake they needed to get into the mining business in a serious way.

When they heard that mining activity was making a comeback in Ireland, Patrick Hughes sent his geologist, Gerry McGinn, back home to try to secure some worthwhile properties. The outcome of this venture was the discovery of the major Tynagh

16

lead-zinc deposit in County Galway on the land of farmer Eamon O'Reilly. Hughes had formed a Canadian company, Northgate Explorations, to explore in Ireland and when the Tynagh discovery was made, the price of the Northgate shares increased tenfold, putting Pat Hughes and his partners on easy street. The Tynagh discovery resulted in the construction of a major port in Galway to handle export of the lead-zinc concentrates to Europe. Hughes' people also developed the Gortrum, County Tipperary copper-zinc deposit and the Hughes Tara lead-zinc mine outside Navan.

The discovery of the first commercial oil well in North America -- Oil Springs in Enniskillen Township, Lambton County, Ontario -- in the 1850s, is credited to Irishman Hugh Nixon Shaw. With a stake of fifty dollars, Shaw started hand digging and pretty soon his fifty dollars was gone. He persisted, scrounging the rest of the funds needed from friends and neighbors. On January 16, 1862, Shaw's well blew in at a rate calculated at 2,000 barrels of oil per day. The well flooded adjacent farmland and roads and caused great excitement. By the end of 1862, another thirty oil wells had been completed within a square mile of Shaw's discovery. This was the beginning of the oil boom which spread all over North America.

The Ontario discoveries helped create several small exploration companies. Several of these small companies were merged and the resulting company was called Imperial Oil, which went on to become Canada's largest fully integrated oil and gas company. Imperial, later taken over by Exxon, continues to operate under the Imperial name in Canada.

Exploration of western Canada is also credited, in a small way, to another Irishman, John George (Kootenay) Brown, a sometimes guide, packer, adventurer and oilman. Brown, the story goes, talked some Stony Indians into tasting a concoction of molasses and coal oil he had lumped together. His directions to the Indians were, "If you come across anything that smells like this or tastes like this, let me know." The Indians located something that looked and smelled like Brown's concoction at Cameron Creek, near present day Pincher Creek in Alberta. An Irishman, John Linehan, drilled the first well in Cameron Creek. The well site is now known as Oil City and is a historic site.

The Connells of Conwest Petroleum developed the natural gas fields in Lake Erie and John Doyle, through his Bison Petroleum, drilled hundreds of oil and gas wells in Alberta and Saskatchewan. Eddie Galvin, who started off as a wildcatter in western Canada, went on to become president of Canadian Industrial Gas & Oil, which operates pipelines, produces oil and gas and has operations in many countries.

The following stories of Charlie O'Sullivan and the McDonough brothers illustrate just how thin the line is between phenomenal success and just making a good living. The Nellie Cashman story touches the heart, as she must have touched the hearts and brightened the lives of the miners she befriended.

The stories of Frank McMahon and Cameron Milliken catch one up in the excitement of the hunt for oil and the frustration and nail biting that ensued before their visionary plans became successes. The Smilin' Jack Gallagher story depicts a man who had it all and lost it.

Montana's Irish Copper Kings -- Marcus Daly (above) and William Andrews Clark. (Photos courtesy of the Montana Historical Society)

Charles Noel O'Sullivan
Prospector, Mine Finder, Geophysicist
and Seasoned Sourdough

C harles Noel (Charlie) O'Sullivan is first and foremost a
prospector, with the essence of the Barren Lands in the
Canadian far north in his nostrils and try as he might, he seems
doomed, like the Flying Dutchman, to wander the tundra
endlessly searching for mineral deposits. Although he has found
economic deposits, he still gets the stirring of the blood every
spring when the snow line retreats and the lichen starts to peep
from the frozen ground.

There is a poem by some old prospector that describes the
prospecting fever that guys like Charlie get:

The Prospector
The men who daily risk their lives in ships
       that go to sea,
Are not by far, as brave or bold, or so it
       seems to me,
As he who roams the wilderness, where white
       man never trod,
Where dangers lurk around him and his only
       help is God.

He faces countless hazards in every
       river run.
His rooftree is uncertain skies, or else
       the blazing sun.
He knows the forest denizens from Whiskyjack
       to bear,
And fosters their companionship, there
       is no other there.
His day is one long vigil, he seeks the
       precious thing
That sways the power of empires and provides the
       playboy's fling.

20

His nights are filled with music, from woodland,
    lakes and bogs.
He has an unpaid orchestra, the night birds
    and the frogs.

His is a vision splendid, his dreams are
    ages old.
Tomorrow he is sure to find that mother
    lode of gold,
And should perchance he find it and deem
    his labors done,
Small recompense is often his, although he
    fought and won.
              -Anonymous

Almost a Widow

Mona O'Sullivan has had several close calls as the wife of mining man Charlie O'Sullivan. "Often," she says, "I wish he was in some safe job, like a policeman or a race car driver." One fairly harrowing experience she does not want to go through again was the time in December of 1968 when Charlie decided to fly out of Coronation Gulf in the Northwest Territories (NWT) with hell-raiser and legendary bush pilot Jim McAvoy who was, and is, one of those stubborn sourdoughs who has no time for the advancement of law and order into his beloved North. Jim never bothered with maintenance on his planes -- too sissy he figured, and he never bothered getting a license. Once, for a bet, he flew his plane low enough to leave his ski marks in the snow on the roof of the Yellowknife Post Office, while crowds lined the main street cheering him on. They had streamed out of the bar of the Yellowknife Hotel to watch this dare-devil feat.

Charlie had a crew of twenty working on his claims and when the Douglas DC-3 came to take them out, Charlie decided he would fly out with McAvoy and Charlie's helper, a Metis Indian named Arden. They took off for Yellowknife, the capital of the NWT and a blizzard came up, reducing visibility to zero. To try to find their way, McAvoy took his plane, *The Found*, down to treetop level. However, this was a tricky maneuver as *The Found* had no lights on the instrument panel. This small inconvenience was overcome by Charlie holding a flashlight on the panel and shouting out the speed and altitude to McAvoy.

The blizzard became so bad they were forced to put down on Duncan Lake, about sixty miles from Yellowknife. They built a roaring fire and got their sleeping bags out -- their only survival gear was a box of chocolates. Charlie managed to get warm enough, despite the December weather, and was in a sound sleep when he was shaken awake by McAvoy. "I can see stars," he yells at Charlie. "The weather has lifted and we are going to take her up again."

They got airborne, and Charlie suggested they get high enough so they would be able to see the lights of Yellowknife, but stay within sight of their campfire so they could land again if they had to. They climbed to 1,000 feet, with Charlie still shining his flashlight on the instrument panel, but there were no lights to be seen. They then climbed to 2,000 feet, but still there were no lights. Now panic set in and McAvoy decided to set her down again. Getting down in the dark with no instrument lights was a little precarious. Charlie had to open the door of the plane to physically guess their altitude, all the time keeping his light on the altimeter and speedometer, while at the same time shouting above the roar of the plane's engines, "200 feet, 85 miles an hour; 120 feet, 60 miles an hour" and then screaming, "50 feet and 50 miles an hour." There was a horrible bang and clatter as the kite hit and skid across the deck with bumps and grinds and screeches. The plane finally came to rest with everybody sweating blood and the Metis yelling, "You're not taking this freaking thing up again as long as I'm alive."

Eventually, daylight came and McAvoy coaxed Charlie, the Metis and the plane back into the air. They arrived in Yellowknife just in time to meet a rescue party about to set out to look for them, to the everlasting relief of Mona O'Sullivan.

From the Kingdom County He Came
Charlie O'Sullivan was born in County Cork. His family moved to County Kerry when he was just three months old. He had the traditional Irish education from the Christian Brothers.

22

Charlie received his post-secondary education at University College Cork, getting a Bachelor of Science degree, but no instruction in business. "We did not even know how to analyze a balance sheet," mused Charlie. His disciplines were geology, experimental physics and mathematics, but nary a course on how to set up and run a business.

This meant, in Charlie's case as with thousands of other Irish graduates, that you had to leave the country to get work. Most small and medium businesses were passed from father to son. This practice left educated sons and daughters with few opportunities in the business community. Just about all of the entrepreneurial and professional talent went abroad to find outlets for their skills and energy.

The Luck of the Irish

Graduating from University College Cork in 1965, and not being able to find a job, Charlie O'Sullivan went back to take postgraduate studies. In October of 1965, Charlie got a call from the Professor of Physics telling him there was a company looking for someone with a background in geology, with some experimental physics and mathematics, to train as a geophysicist. As luck would have it, there were only four in Charlie's class with the called-for qualifications. In 1965, University College Cork had only 1,400 in its whole student body -- now there are about 12,000.

Charlie met Dr. Harry Seigel, the father of the Induced Polarization (IP) technique. Newmont Mining, with large copper deposits in the southern part of Arizona, had provided Dr. Seigel development money to make use of the IP technology to outline ore bodies on their copper properties, which were covered with overburden and did not outcrop. Using the IP technologies, ore bodies down to 300 feet could be outlined and drill targets could be spotted with the expectation that ore could be found. Although he did not know it at the time, being hired by Dr. Harry Seigel was to lead Charlie O'Sullivan into high adventure across North America and would shape the rest of his life.

An upsurge in mining in Ireland had brought Dr. Seigel and his IP technology to Ireland to try to discover more ore bodies.

Ireland seemed a logical place for IP as the country is mostly pasture land with very little outcroppings to indicate ore bodies. By the mid-1960s, mining companies using IP technology had discovered the Tynagh deposit in Galway, the Gortdrum deposit in Tipperary and the extensions of the Silvermines deposit. Also discovered was the Tara deposit at Navan in the early 1970s. Charlie was paid $300 a month to start, which was big money in those days. He received a week's training on the IP system outside Naas, Co. Kildare and then he was on his own.

At the same time, Jan Baird, who had just graduated from the University of Toronto and had been trained by Dr. Seigel to use the IP technology in Canada, discovered the great pyramid ore body on the south shore of Great Slave Lake in the NWT. This discovery caused one of the great mining and stock market booms in Canada. Geophysicists trained in the IP technology were in high demand and Dr. Seigel offered Charlie a fifty per cent increase in salary if he would come across to Canada for a year to eighteen months.

Off to the Canadian North

So Charlie Noel O'Sullivan, like millions before him, left Ireland to seek his fortune in the wilds of Canada. Wide-eyed, Charlie got an early lesson on how clout works. He presented himself at the Canadian Embassy in Dublin, expecting to have the usual immigration hassle. To his surprise, he was cleared in a week. The Embassy people told Charlie, "We have been waiting for you, wondering who you are, as our instructions are to clear you immediately." In those days Canada needed such highly skilled people and was prepared to smooth the way.

Charlie landed in Toronto in January in the middle of a Canadian snow storm. He was met at the airport by Harry Seigel. Harry was always interested in his employees and thought nothing of making the trip to the airport to pick up Charlie. In those days, Seigel's company was quite small and Charlie was only the fourth geophysicist to be employed by them. Now it is one of the biggest geophysical companies in the world. Most of the early staff were youngsters like Charlie who worked in the Canadian bush for six months or more. Every time they came into Toronto, Harry

Seigel was there to welcome them. "He was like a father to us youngsters," Charlie recalls.

After Charlie was over his awe at the Canadian winter, he was sent along to an Arctic outfitter. Here he was lumbered up with parkas, boots, hats and big snowshoes. Booking into the posh Lord Simcoe Hotel in Toronto, Charlie was quite a conversation piece. Toronto is about 2,000 miles from the Northwest Territories -- like going from Dublin to the Middle East, so the sight of a sourdough was an unusual event. (A sourdough is anyone who has wintered north of the sixty degree parallel. The name comes from making bannock bread in a frying pan).

From Toronto, Charlie took off for Edmonton and wandered into the lobby of the McDonald Hotel with his accouterments -- complete with snowshoes. About this point, Charlie was longing for the familiarity of Tralee and the boys at the local pub. From Edmonton he set out for Hay River in the NWT, where the temperature was about fifty degrees below zero and the only place to get in out of the cold was the beer hall. With fifty below outside, the bar was always full with guys sleeping in the halls, on the stairs, on the tables, under the tables and in just about every unoccupied spot -- a custom still in vogue in the far north where leaving a person outside is like sentencing him to death. There were about one hundred men and two women working on exploration work in the Pine Point camp. The only entertainment was heading for the bars in Hay River and doing a lot of stomping and drinking.

Placer Development, one of Canada's major mining companies, had optioned a huge tract of ground in Pine Point on the south shore of Great Slave Lake, around the Pyramid discovery. Charlie's job was to conduct the IP survey on the properties. For Charlie, this was a test of his mettle. The ground was frozen solid. To carry out the IP surveys, probes were driven into the ground through the frost so that the electrical charges could penetrate into the ore below (if there was ore below).

Charlie's first spell in the bush lasted for six weeks. He had a crew made up of Cree Indians, Metis and Inuit. None of them could understand Charlie's brogue and, of course, Charlie could not understand them. He had to manage by doing --

showing them that he wanted the probes to go below the frost, and he showed them how to set up the survey system. Charlie accomplished this by using a sledge hammer to break through the ice and frost. Another major hazard was that Charlie was injecting about a thousand volts of electricity into the ground and he was worried about frying some of his crew. Charlie did give the crew a couple of jolts, inadvertently, but they soon got the message. Eventually, the survey party was extended to eighteen crews and Charlie became one of the head honchos, checking out false alarms and making sure nobody got lost in the bush. They surveyed miles and miles of bush for Placer Development and other companies and found no deposits.

The Wandering Begins

Harry Seigel's first contract in British Columbia was at the Jericho Mine in the famous Highland Valley copper belt. A Bolivian geologist, Enrico Arteaga, was running the show for Seigel. Enrico's wife and kids were still in Bolivia and did not want to go into the British Columbia hinterland, so Enrico decided to go home and Charlie was given his job.

Enrico left at a fortuitous time for him. Lightning had struck the IP equipment and everything had been blown apart. After Charlie fixed the equipment, the IP survey outlined an anomaly. After it was drilled, they had a mine which later became the Highmont Copper Mine.

Charlie's next venture was for Homestake and Superior Oil. They had a property in the Poison Mountain area of British Columbia. As Charlie was working on this property, the drills were right behind. As fast as he was outlining anomalies, the drill crew would come in and poke holes in the ground. For a twenty-three-year-old not long out of the wilds of County Kerry, it was a big responsibility and lots of pressure.

During that period, around 1966, there was a huge demand for copper from Japan. The Japanese had financed a number of large open-pit copper mines in British Columbia and a kind of staking and drilling frenzy took place. Many world class copper mines were discovered as a result of the exploration. The IP technology played a large part in outlining the ore bodies. After finishing at Poison Mountain, Charlie went to McLease Lake in British Columbia where Gibraltar Mines had the makings of another large copper mine.

In the winter of 1966, Charlie headed back home to Ireland for a break. On his return, he was shipped out to Princeton, British Columbia. There he supervised the geophysics for Newmont's Similkameen copper deposit -- also a very big copper mine. Similkameen was one of Charlie's more interesting mining experiences. The IP geophysical survey outlined a deposit which lay underneath the Hope-Princeton Highway, the main highway connecting Vancouver with the Interior of British Columbia.

The old mine was across the canyon on the opposite side and Charlie's job was to find the extension of the ore body. Charlie's instruments told him the center of the ore body was right underneath the highway. Charlie did not want to believe his instruments, telling himself that the responses he was getting were from the hydro lines or telephone lines under the highway. He checked with B.C. Telephone and with B.C. Hydro, but they told him there was nothing there.

Finally, after about a week, Charlie told the mine manager that his ore body was right under the highway. Of course the mine manager didn't want to hear that, as it would mean diverting a main highway. If you drive up the Princeton Highway, you can see where Charlie O'Sullivan's IP forced the Department of Highways people to move a major highway to make way for a copper mine. "I can tell you, I was one happy Irishman when the drills confirmed that the ore body was under the highway," says Charlie.

Charlie's next assignment took him to the United States. In Nevada, he flew the Humboldt Mountains for United States Steel. This was in the early days of airborne exploration using the Airborne Magnetic method, where the mechanism, or "bird," was hung from a cable below the plane. Sometimes, flying became a little tricky as the "bird" would bang against the side of the plane, giving the pilot a major thrill as he tried to figure out if his kite was falling apart or if Charlie had fallen out. Often it became so hazardous that the mechanism had to be jettisoned and another "bird" had to be sent out from Toronto. It was not considered good form to try to land at the airport with the "bird" swinging about, endangering those around.

From Arizona, Charlie went to southeast Texas looking for uranium for Humble Oil, a subsidiary of Standard Oil. In Texas, Charlie learned all about local politics. He was in "Landslide Johnson" country, the home of the 36th president of the United States -- Lyndon Johnson. Johnson got the nickname "Landslide Johnson" because his first election to the Senate was by a margin of less than 100 votes. During the recounting of votes, the schoolhouse in Duval County burned down. Johnson got nearly every vote in that county. There could not be a recount as the ballots were destroyed in the fire.

To get any work done in Texas, Charlie had to go through the same people. They controlled the grazing rights, the oil rights, the mineral rights and the hunting rights, and every one of them had to be satisfied. To traverse the ground to follow up on the aerial surveys, he had to go to the courthouse to get the keys to allow him into the various parcels of land. Each gate had five or six locks on it and a payment had to be made to get the key for each lock. It was great fun going through the tumbleweeds and watching for rattlesnakes! Uranium was found, but not in commercial quantities.

Going North Again

Charlie's next stint for Harry Seigel was the Coppermine area of the NWT where legendary mine finder Murray Watts was working on a copper prospect. This was somewhat of a bust as the copper showings were just surface floats and did not extend to depth. The only excitement there was a blizzard in August, which had the crew eager to get the hell out of there for fear of being stuck for the winter.

On his way out of Coppermine, Charlie O'Sullivan made a stopover in Yellowknife. He was burned out from years in the Arctic, in the bush, in the Nevada desert and in the wilds of Texas. While sitting in the bar in Yellowknife commiserating with himself, two men started a conversation with him. One of them, Gren Thomas, was a mining engineer at Giant Yellowknife Mines and the other was Paul Conroy. Both happened to be fed up with

28

what they were doing and had decided to work for themselves. Charlie was interested in joining them, but first he had to go back to Toronto to make out his reports. Seigel saw how blown away Charlie was and told him to go back to Ireland to get unwound. He had ten grand walking-around money. Seigel sent him first to the World Fair at Montreal, then Charlie took the *Empress of Canada* out of Montreal to Liverpool. It was on its last trip of the season before the St. Lawrence River froze for the winter.

After about two months in Ireland, Charlie's ten grand was spent and he returned to Canada. In March of 1968, Charlie and his two newly found buddies started their own mining and consulting company -- Anglo-Celtic Exploration Ltd. They went to work staking claims and offering geological and geophysical expertise to mining companies and prospectors operating out of Yellowknife. The company was soon grossing about one million dollars a year and Charlie was on his way as a mining man.

Claim Staking in the Barren Lands

In 1968, Charlie O'Sullivan started staking claims in the Coronation Gulf area of the Barren Lands in the NWT. At times he was employing a crew of thirty to forty people, staking claims, mapping, sampling and line cutting. During this period, he traveled all over the North West Territories from Hudson Bay to Great Bear Lake and from Great Slave Lake to the Arctic Islands. He staked claims and explored the area at Coronation Gulf for the first time. One of Charlie's best geological hunches was in the Queen Maud Gulf at a place called Perry River. A man named Fleming had gone bankrupt and left behind a fantastic geological library. Charlie and his partners bought the library from the receiver.

Gren Thomas was reading the material when he came across a report by ornithologist Peter Scott, son of Scott of the Antarctic. Peter Scott was one of the best known wild life experts in the world, as well as being a very good watercolor artist. Gren was reading a report on the Ross Goose. It is one of the largest of the species and very rare. In those days people were only just becoming environmentally and ecologically aware, so the report itself was hardly of passing interest. What did fascinate Gren and

Charlie was the spectacular type of rocks mentioned in Scott's reports.

Ore samples taken from the area were high in nickel and the rock types were the same as those at Sudbury, Ontario, site of the world famous Inco and Falconbridge mines. The partners kept the information on the discovery quiet and the next spring flew into the area, landing on an ice floe about eight miles from the rugged shore. They managed to get their inflatable boat to the shore and found the outcrops mentioned in the diary. Nine weeks were spent prospecting, mapping and staking claims in the area.

Thinking and half hoping that they had another Sudbury on their hands, the partners prospected an area of about five hundred square miles, trudging through tundra and across streams. When they came to muskeg and swamps, they took off their clothes to cross. To dry themselves, they ran around the tundra. They had two separate camps and would move every week or so. Gren Thomas and Frank Ipakohak were in one camp. Charlie and Dave Nickerson -- who later became the Member of Parliament for the NWT -- were in the other camp. They kept radio contact with each other every night.

They slept in a squawpole tent contraption with a pole across two uprights. As the weather got colder, Charlie would cut six inches off the uprights, bringing the tarp down to hold in the heat. Before they left, the tent was so low they had to crawl inside. Their rations consisted of frozen meat; to keep it from going bad they would dig a hole in the perma-frost and use that as a freezer. Charlie learned a great medical fact from his nine weeks: eating off a frying pan and using dishes which still had soap suds from the last time they were washed gave him a dose of the runs. His body had been rapidly losing its salt, so when he hit Yellowknife, the first place he headed for was the pub to load up on beer, a kind of automatic reaction to his dehydrated body. This is why the northern bars are always full of prospectors.

When Charlie's crew came out of the tundra, they had with them some phenomenal ore samples. These samples enabled them to make a deal with Cominco, a major mining company, which recovered all their investment money and left them with a good piece of the property. Had a mine been found, they would have made another big score. However, the word got out about the Ross Goose and this put a stop to all mining exploration. The land was later turned into the Perry River Bird Sanctuary, which killed all mining in the area.

In the mid-1970s, when the uranium boom was hitting Saskatchewan, Charlie staked about one million acres around the fabulously rich Key Lake Mine. The discovery of Key Lake started a major staking rush in the wilds of Northern Saskatchewan and Charlie, being an old Northern Canada hand, managed to pick up a lot of in-close ground. He sold off most of this ground to French government owned Acquataine, German government owned Uranex and to an Italian government owned uranium company. This gave Charlie his first serious money from all his years in the mining business in Northern Canada's ice, snow and wilderness.

Charlie and the Tomcat

Around the middle of 1977, Charlie O'Sullivan formed Hemisphere Development Corporation, a publicly traded company, to consolidate his many prospecting ventures. Soon after, the oil and gas business started heating up and Charlie was lucky enough to get involved in a deep gas play in Oklahoma. He didn't know it at the time, but when he took a piece of the Tomcat Well, he became part of American oil-and-gas folklore.

On January 27, 1981, the Tomcat Number One, the largest deep gas well ever drilled on the continental United States, blew in with a deafening roar, blowing away the "blowout preventer." Gas whistled through the hole at a rate of 115 million cubic feet per day. The well was out of control, forcing the evacuation of the town of Eakly for a week and shooting a flare over three hundred feet into the air. The flame could be seen for miles and the Tomcat became a tourist attraction.

An investor who put up $140,000 for a one percent interest in the well could expect to get back $100,000 a month for the fifteen year life of the well. Charlie O'Sullivan had a two percent interest, so he was looking at getting $200,000 a month or $2.5 million a year for fifteen years. Because of the gas shortage at the time and with government incentives for deep drilling, the

Tomcat could get eight dollars per one thousand cubic feet for its gas compared with about one dollar and fifty cents per thousand cubic feet for gas from normal wells. This was during President Jimmy Carter's so-called energy crisis.

Overnight, investors in the Tomcat, such as Charlie, saw themselves becoming millionaires from the gas sales and also from the jump in the price of their stocks. Washington Gas & Light Co., listed on the New York Stock Exchange, saw its share price jump from $21.75 to $37.25. Charlie O'Sullivan's Hemisphere, listed on the Vancouver Stock Exchange, jumped from five dollars a share to around sixteen dollars.

Investors were lined up outside the offices of Ports of Call, the Oklahoma City company which had drilled the well, wanting to sign up for the next wells. Bankers were offering money to the participating companies in the millions of dollars for development drilling of the rest of the land. In 1981, because of the excitement caused by the Tomcat well, investment for oil and gas drilling in Oklahoma went to an unbelievable $4.6 billion, with most of the money going to deep wells.

The Tomcat was never completed as a production well. The well had cave-ins and blow-outs and was never brought under control. After a while, the price of gas for deep wells came down to the real market price and the Tomcat was uneconomical at such prices. While it lasted, it was a dandy. Hemisphere is still getting about $10,000 per month from oil and gas wells in Oklahoma in which it retains interests.

The Billion Dollar Sunrise Deposit

Having established a name for himself as an expert in the North country, Charlie O'Sullivan formed numerous joint ventures with multinational companies to explore various areas of the Northwest Territories.

In the 1980s, Charlie spent a lot of time, money and effort exploring for gold in the Contwoyto and Courageous Lake areas of the NWT. The year 1986 was a bad year -- drilling results at Contwoyto were disappointing. Sitting around the campfire one night, late in the season at Contwoyto, Charlie and Gren Thomas decided they would send four geologists to explore a volcanic belt

32

along the Beauleau River. They prospected by canoe, coming ashore at whatever promising ground they came across. They found what they thought at the time was an interesting quartz vein with some chalcopyrite in it. Subsequent assaying showed up to an ounce of gold from this showing.

On the basis of this discovery and the area's favorable geology, and spurred by competitive activity in the area, the joint venture began staking claims on speculation in the Sunrise Lake region which, according to Charlie, had only received cursory exploration for gold and base metals in the past. They invited a number of international companies to join them in a joint venture, but got no takers, so they decided to continue exploring on their own.

In mid-1987, a geological/geophysical program located a VLF-EM conductor. "The story sometimes gets told that we were looking for gold and drilled for gold and it's not far off the mark, but we did recognize the target we were going after and we very specifically tailored it to that," recalls Charlie. A limited drilling program was made on the discovery in October of 1987. The first hole tested the area of the gold-copper showing, and intersected encouraging stringer-type mineralization. This prompted the drilling of the second hole 400 feet further north along the conductor. This time a hit was made -- nineteen feet of sulfides grading 18.3% zinc and lead combined, and twenty-seven oz./ton silver along with minor gold and copper values. A second hole was drilled immediately right under the first find. Then they put a lid on everything and went on a land acquisition program. They acquired about twenty-five miles of the belt primarily to the north where they knew from previous assessment reports there were a string of airborne conductors. The thinking was that these types of deposits do not occur in isolation; they occur in groups.

Further drilling proved up about two million tons of good grade ore -- a one-billion-dollar ore body, which has yet to be fully delineated. This deposit is about eighty miles northeast of Yellowknife and will eventually become an operating mine.

Since the mid-1960s, Charlie O'Sullivan has been watching the parade of mining companies come and go in the last great frontier of mining in North America -- the Coronation Gulf area of the NWT. Canada's north country encompasses about fifty per cent of the country's land mass and except for a few sporadic attempts, its mineral wealth has been untouched. In the past, some government efforts have been made to entice mining explorers into the area, but as those governments were defeated, or lost interest in the north, exploration more or less dried up. However, Charlie, who really has "Sourdough Fever" -- an affliction which affects those who spend any length of time in the Arctic -- keeps coming back year after year.

Charlie's current and burning interest is in his Continental Pacific Resources (CPR) company which holds about two hundred and twenty square miles of mining properties in Coronation Gulf. His fever has got such a grip that he has spent over two million dollars in the area. This money has been well spent as it has resulted in locating some twenty-one mineral structures within CPR land holdings.

In the spring of 1993, Charlie consummated a deal with Metal Mining Corporation, a subsidiary of German mining conglomerate Metallgesellschaft. Metal has to pay Charlie's company $400,000 in cash and spend five million dollars to get a sixty per cent interest in just two of the mineral occurrences.

A study made public in March, 1993 showed that it was feasible to ship ore concentrates by sea from Coronation Gulf to Europe or Japan. This method will result in substantial saving for the mines as it eliminates the need to build roads and railways and docking facilities in the south to take the ore to market.

Charlie O'Sullivan was the prime mover in having the Canadian government consider the idea of using ships to move ore from Coronation Gulf. Having operated in Canada's North for about twenty-five years and having several promising mineral properties in his portfolio, Charlie realized that without some means of getting the supplies in and the ore concentrates to market, he was looking at a very long wait before he could capitalize on his dream of becoming a major player in the mining business. Convincing the powers that be in Ottawa took three trips. By then the government was convinced that finding a transportation route through the Northwest Passage would create a major mining industry for Canada and open this huge territory,

The different worlds of Charlie O'Sullivan. Above, Charlie and family at daughter's graduation from the University of British Columbia. From left, Charlie, his daughters Hilary, Tamara and Charlotte and wife, Mona. Below, Charlie (right) in the Barren Lands with fellow mine seekers Lou Covello (left) and Doug Bryan (center).

about one-third of Canada's land mass, to trade and commerce. As a result of Charlie's efforts, a consortium was formed which includes the mining companies and the governments of Canada and the Northwest Territories. The results of a study released in March 1993 confirmed the feasibility of shipping concentrates out and supplies into Coronation Gulf.

The major mining companies started looking at the area with renewed interest and, thanks in large part to Irishman Charlie O'Sullivan, the last remaining major mineral belt in North America was opened up to development. Charlie is now working on the Snofield property in Coronation Gulf, expounding on its similarity to the great gold mines of Hemlo in Ontario. This man really has Sourdough Fever!

The McDonough Brothers
Mining Men All Nine of Them

Back in the early days of the century when Canada's mining industry was still in its infancy, Irishmen were involved all over the country staking claims and working in the few mines which were then in existence. Foremost among the mine seekers in Ontario and Quebec were the "McDonough Boys," all nine of them. Their story is remarkable. They were left fatherless and motherless at fairly early ages, but they stuck together, nine brothers and Mary, the only girl in the family.

They set up house in the various mining camps, with Mary keeping house for them until they were old enough to fend for themselves. From 1908, when they joined the Gowanda silver rush, until the late 1920s, when they started the gold rush into Red Lake in northwestern Ontario, the McDonough brothers were responsible for the discovery of several mines and mining camps. Red Lake, where brother Joe McDonough was president of major gold producer Madsen Red Lake, eventually had fourteen producing gold mines and is still a producing camp today.

During their active exploration life, the McDonough brothers -- Charles, Peter, Patrick, Joseph, John, Michael, Albert, Eddie and Tim -- could be found in mining camps throughout Quebec and Ontario. When the Porcupine Camp in the Ontario bush was caught in the 1911 forest fire which wiped out three small towns and caused a tidal wave on the lake, Charlie and Joe McDonough were prospecting in the bush. It was erroneously reported they burned to death. The fire was so fierce that miners who sought refuge down the mine shafts suffocated and died when the fire sucked all the oxygen out of the shafts. Many more drowned in the lake when the dynamite train exploded, causing the tidal wave. Others prospecting in the bush were never accounted for. Fortunately, Charlie and Joe McDonough had been prospecting west of the fire and escaped unharmed, but their cabin and all their equipment were destroyed.

Joe and Pete McDonough explored the Kirkland Lake area in 1912, camping for the winter on property which later became the Sylvanite Gold Mine, but they were unsuccessful. It was a few years later before the Kirkland Lake gold camp, with such mines as Lakeshore and Wright Hargreaves, became world-famous.

In the famous Rouyn camp, the McDonoughs staked the Waite Amulet copper mine. Joe had 500,000 shares of the stock which he sold for twenty cents a share. The stock later took off and if Joe had held on, he would have been a multimillionaire. The McDonoughs were involved in some of the well-known Ontario and Quebec mines such as Waite Amulet, Opemiska Copper, East Malartic Gold Mines, United Siscoe, Cochenor Willans, McKenzie Red Lake Gold Mines, Ultra Shawkey and the family controlled Madsen Red Lake. At one time, there was a saying in the mining country, "behind every bush lurks a McDonough." The government even named a township for the brothers.

The McDonough family came to Canada in the 1850s, not long after the Famine. Today, there are just two of them left -- Kervin (usually called Kevin) and Emmett, sons of Joe McDonough. Kervin lives in St. Catharines, Ontario and is still active in the mining business. The McDonough brothers' grandfather, Jack McDonough, was born in County Sligo and their grandmother, Margaret Tyman, came from County Mayo. The family settled in the Gatineau Valley and became part of what was known as the Ottawa Valley Irish.

Paddy, Eddie, Tim and Pete McDonough and fellow prospector John Jones and several local Indians photographed outside the Hudson's Bay Company store in Red Lake, Northern Ontario during the 1926 Red Lake gold rush. By the time the camp was developed, there were fourteen producing gold mines at Red Lake. One wag noted that you couldn't shake a bush in the North Country without flushing out a McDonough. The township of McDonough in the Red Lake area was named for the McDonough brothers.

39

Nellie Cashman
Angel of the Sourdoughs

Long before women's liberation, an Irish lady named Nellie Cashman asserted her independence in some of the most primitive and inhospitable environments in North America. Nellie waded in, as the saying goes, where angels fear to tread. She did her good deeds with a sense of compassion and good humor which endeared her to everyone with whom she had contact. Nellie was one of those highly competent, high-spirited women, the kind that a father used to wish had been a boy.

Nellie was born in Queenstown, County Cork around 1851. Nellie and her sister set sail for Boston in 1868. Seeking adventure, they set out on a trip across America on the newly constructed transcontinental railway and arrived in San Francisco in 1869. Nellie's sister fell in love with Irishman Thomas Cunningham and settled down to married life. Satisfied that her sister no longer needed her, Nellie let her wanderlust take over and she started visiting the romantic and exciting gold mining camps she had been reading and dreaming about.

She was called the "Angel of the Sourdoughs" by the Irish miners in the Cassiar area of British Columbia when she, at her own expense, arranged to have a shipment of potatoes and other vegetables delivered to the camp, saving the trapped miners from being caught in an outbreak of scurvy. Cassiar was supposed to be the next big gold strike after the Cariboo diggings were worked out. Instead, all the miners found in that godforsaken country in the winter of 1877 was heavy snowfalls. There were no roads in or out, leaving the miners trapped. Adding to their predicament, there was no gold to be found. Nellie saved the camp from disaster, earning the eternal gratitude of the miners.

As these miners went after other gold rushes, Nellie went with them. The Chilkoot Pass was the most dangerous and only land access to the Klondike gold fields. Nellie traversed this pass in the fall of 1898. She looked after the miners, setting up bunkhouses and restaurants to feed them and hopefully to make a strike of her own. She grubstaked prospectors. During her sojourn in Dawson City in Canada's Yukon Territory during the Klondike gold rush, Nellie ran Donovan's, a combined store and boarding house. Nellie went out to Bonanza and Hunker Creeks, the rich placer creeks, and got the miners to donate gold dust and nuggets towards the building of the Sisters Hospital in Dawson. After the Klondike was played out, Nellie went farther north, up towards the Arctic Circle, still chasing that elusive big strike.

Next, Nellie tried her luck in the great silver rush into Virginia City in Nevada. When that camp was played out she went on into the wilds of Arizona, where she took up residence in Tucson. In 1879, Tucson was more or less a Mexican pueblo. You could count the number of women on one hand and there were plenty of desperadoes. She opened the Delmonico restaurant in Tucson and personally took charge of the cooking.

When Nellie's brother-in-law Thomas Cunningham died, leaving her sister with five young children to look after, Nellie took off for San Francisco and brought her sister and the five children back to Tombstone, Arizona to live with her. Nellie was operating the Russ House restaurant in Tombstone at that time. About three years later, Nellie's sister died, leaving her with the five youngsters to feed, clothe, educate and bring up in a rough frontier town. Nellie did this job as efficiently and lovingly as any mother could have done. All the children reached maturity. One of the boys, Michael Cunningham, went on to become president of the Bank of Bisbee and later president of the Bank of Lowell, Arizona.

Nellie Cashman had a fierce sense of fair play and believed in taking action when she felt a wrong was being perpetrated on any one. During a bitter mining strike in Tucson in 1884, she smuggled the visiting superintendent of the Grand Central Mining Company out of town in her buggy when she heard the miners were planning to kidnap and hang him. Another time, she arranged for a number of her friends to tear down a grandstand that had been erected by a get-rich-quick operator. He had erected the grandstand with the idea of selling seats to the townspeople to view the hanging of five desperadoes. She also made sure that the victims got a decent burial and that their remains were not used for medical experiments, as had been planned.

On an ill-fated exploration venture into Mexico in search of gold, Nellie and a party of prospectors became stranded in the desert in desperate circumstances. Nellie managed to secure food and water from a Catholic mission which saved their lives. There were additional hardships. On their return trip, a drunken captain on a ship which was to take them across the Gulf of Mexico had them arrested and thrown into a Mexican jail. Somehow, Nellie managed to get them all safely home to Tucson.

Nellie Cashman never married; she seemed to have saved her love for the poor. Many of her good deeds were done spontaneously and went unnoticed. Others were more visible as she carried out many fund raising ventures. In 1882, she raised the funds to build the Catholic Church in Tombstone. She put up much of the money herself.

In the summer of 1924, while in Alaska, Nellie became very ill with double pneumonia -- so ill that she had to be taken "outside." The doctor would not allow her to travel alone so a woman friend accompanied her on a thousand mile journey by small boat to Fairbanks, Alaska. Determined to make her way back to Arizona, Nellie and her companion set out by boat. On arriving at Victoria, British Columbia, she was taken to hospital and she died there on January 4, 1925.

Nellie Cashman, who lived through the growing years of the American and Canadian gold mining industry, is buried in the Catholic cemetery in Victoria, British Columbia.

Irish-born Nellie Cashman, affectionately called "Angel of the Sourdoughs" by Irish miners. Nellie staked claims, led mining expeditions and operated restaurants and boarding houses for miners from Tucson to the Yukon. She died in Victoria, British Columbia in 1925 on her way home to Tucson from Alaska.

Frank McMahon
Canada's Legendary Wildcatter

Francis Michael Patrick (Frank) McMahon was one of those legendary wildcatters who drilled a lot of dusters and saw many of his companies crater during his career exploring for oil and gas in western Canada. In the end, he realized his life-long dream of building Canada's first major natural gas pipeline from British Columbia's Peace River country to the United States border. Between his beginnings and his happy ending lies a tale of hope, despair, frustration and nail-biting. Eventually, he was inducted into the Canadian Business Hall of Fame.

Born in the small mining town of Moyie in southeastern British Columbia in 1902 to Francis Joseph and Stella McMahon, Frank was the oldest of three sons and he grew up more or less looking after himself and his two brothers, George and John. Frank's dad and his dad's brother, Pat, owned a small hotel-saloon in Moyie where the miners hung out spinning their tales of gold strikes in far away and impossible places.

The elder Frank and his brother Pat had the wanderlust. They followed the gold discoveries across the west, without too much luck. Both had washed gravel on the gold creeks of the Dawson area during the Klondike gold rush of 1890. When the mine at Moyie, the town's main support, ran out of ore, Frank and Pat sold the hotel and moved, leaving the McMahon boys fatherless.

The son, Frank McMahon, managed to make out on his own and even got high enough marks and money to attend Gonzaga University in Spokane, Washington, Bing Crosby's Alma Mater. Bing and Frank became lifelong friends. After university, Frank got a job as a driller for a mining company and soon had enough money put aside to buy his own drilling equipment and start his own company. Determined to become a millionaire, he was able to convince the lovely Isobel Grant that his prospects were good and in 1928 they were married.

Frank McMahon was the kind of person who seemed to be more interested in the chase than in the spoils. He was active at the very birth of Canada's oil and gas industry, and even though it was a long and painful birth, Frank saw his baby come in healthy and roaring with the discovery of the Leduc Oil Field in 1947. Frank and his brother George were in the thick of the rush, picking up a quarter-of-a-million acres in central Alberta and a chunk of land close in to the historic find made by Imperial Oil.

The McMahons vended in their property to a new company they had formed. The Atlantic Oil Company, listed on the Vancouver Stock Exchange, went on to make a sizable stake. The Vancouver Stock Exchange was, and is, a venture capital market where oil and gas and mining promoters can raise risk money to finance their ventures.

Frank spent some twenty years drilling dry holes and chasing rainbows, using Vancouver listed companies to raise capital, before his luck changed. His first hit of any note was in Turner Valley, one of Alberta's first commercial oil finds. With his last hundred dollars, Frank managed to pick up thirty acres from the Canadian Pacific Railway agent. Frank and Isobel drove the thirty odd miles from Vancouver to Abbotsford in a driving snow storm, with Isobel scraping the ice and slush off the windshield of the old jalopy, to pick up the option on the thirty acres. He also had to keep a sharp eye out for the huge water filled ditches which were part of the joys of driving in British Columbia in those days.

Armed with that option, Frank went out and acquired options on another six hundred acres, this deal financed by a group of Vancouver investors. Following the time honored procedure, Frank vended in the options to another new company, West Turner Petroleums Ltd. He then picked up another fifty acres and that also went into the West Turner pot. Knowing that down the road he would eventually have to fund the exploration on the acres he had picked up, he formed yet another company, British Investment Company Ltd. The British bit gave the impression that there might be serious money and British investors involved in the company.

He started drilling his Turner Valley well, as usual on a shoe-string, and soon ran out of money. It looked like another tale of woe until his buddy, Norman Whittall, also an investor in the project, convinced Imperial Oil to finish the well and take their costs out of production, if there was any. Finally, Frank was beginning to see some of the "Irish" luck which was supposed to be the "birthright" of all Irishmen. His West Turner #1 was brought in on April 17, 1930 as one of the biggest wells in Turner Valley, flowing over 1,300 barrels of oil a day. By the end of the year, his company had three producing oil wells in Turner Valley. While this production would normally be great news, it looked like Frank's Irish luck was deserting him. So prolific was Turner Valley that its 40,000 barrels of oil a day was screwing up the oil market, which only needed 17,000 barrels to fill the demand. The glut of oil sent the prices down to around $1.20 a barrel.

Not a man to sit around and bemoan his plight, Frank McMahon went out and picked up more acreage around Turner Valley and put that land into another new company, British Pacific Oils Ltd. -- the British name inference was obviously impressive at the time. While relatively content with his oil discoveries, Frank still was pursuing his lifelong dream, to develop the huge Peace River gas potential and ship it by pipeline to the United States market. He made a trip to England to try to raise money for his gas pipeline proposal. Unfortunately, while he was over there hustling the British, the government of British Columbia put a moratorium on gas exploration in the Peace River country and he came up empty.

The Beginning of Pacific Petroleum

Stymied on his natural gas project and with his stocks going into the dumpster on the Vancouver Stock Exchange due to the low prices for oil, Frank McMahon did what Vancouver promoters have been doing since the year one. He declared what has become known as an "Irishman's Dividend." Under this procedure, a company or several companies have their shares consolidated and the shareholders are given a lesser number of shares in a new company. This new company acquires the assets of the old companies, but, as it will have less shares outstanding, it can expect to raise more money than if it tried to finance through the tired old company. West Turner Petroleum was selling for around a nickel so Frank merged it with British Pacific Oils into a new company called Pacific Petroleums Ltd.

46

The outbreak of World War II looked like a big break for the oil business, with the expectation that the war would increase the demand for oil and prices would rise substantially. However, the Canadian government imposed wage and price controls, keeping the oil price low. Frank kept plugging away with Pacific Petroleum, but his board of directors started looking at the way he was spending money picking up land and drilling dry holes, so they gave him and his brother the bum's rush.

Pushed out of the company he had founded, Frank McMahon and brother George started a new business for themselves, and when Standard Oil of California made an oil strike at Princess in Alberta, they were in like Flynn, picking up land around the find. They formed a host of new companies to hold this acreage and to raise money on the Vancouver Stock Exchange to explore the lands.

Frank hooked up with Sun Oil, selling them some of the leases for $250,000, which gave him some walking around money to carry on exploring. Frank took the Sun Oil money and went back to his dream of exploring Northeast British Columbia for gas to supply his as-yet-to-be-built pipeline. In 1945, the British Columbia government finally opened up the Peace River Country for gas exploration, and Frank McMahon and his friends applied for leases on 260,000 acres and reservation permits on another one million acres.

Meanwhile, over in Leduc, other excitement was brewing. Imperial Oil, which had been drilling dry holes for years, much like Frank, made the discovery which was to put Western Canada firmly on the oil map of the world. When the Leduc #1 discovery well came in in February, 1947, it set off the biggest land rush ever in Canada, and the McMahon brothers were in the thick of the rush. They picked up about 250,000 acres in central Alberta and a parcel of land close to the Leduc discovery well.

Pacific Pete, a company originally formed by Frank McMahon, took a piece of the action. The McMahon interest was vended into a new company, Atlantic Oil Company, which then became a public company. Later, the McMahons were invited back into Pacific Pete through a deal which saw Pacific Pete acquire a stake in the McMahons' Atlantic Oil Company for a block of

Pacific stock, making the McMahons the largest shareholders in Pacific Pete. This transaction coincided with the issuing of permits by the British Columbia government to a new company, Peace River Natural Gas, set up by the McMahons.

Atlantic's #3 well in Leduc blew in out of control, with flows of oil estimated at 15,000 barrels per day and natural gas ranging up to 150 million cubic feet per day. Texas experts in mastering out-of-control wells had to be brought in to control the well. This one well produced so much oil that it made the McMahons financially secure and able to finance their other ventures.

As a kind of side deal, Frank McMahon hooked up with brothers Jack and Lou Diamond and formed Alberta Distillers Ltd. to make whiskey in an old discarded plant in the Calgary area. When the whiskey did not take off, they decided to make vodka, then the drink of the "in" crowd, and they prospered.

Pacific Petroleum, now fairly flush with cash, started drilling for natural gas in Alberta and in northeast British Columbia in anticipation of getting approval for the pipeline. It took over six years from the time of their first application to build the pipeline until they got Canadian government approval to export the gas from the provinces, and a parallel approval from the Canadian National Energy Board.

Then they had to try to get approvals from the United States to export the gas to the States. This process took another few years and a lot of lobbying with Howard Hughes (who was big in the production of oil and gas equipment) and Clint Murchinson, a Texas wildcatter of note and owner of Delhi Oil, a large United States natural gas producer. Despite all of the high priced help, the Federal Power Commission turned down the Westcoast deal and Pacific Pete stock, which was the major shareholder of Westcoast, dropped from twelve dollars a share to six dollars on the American Stock Exchange, and Canadian Atlantic dropped to three dollars and fifty cents a share from seven dollars.

Late in 1954, Frank McMahon made a deal with one of the American companies which had been lobbying against Westcoast's attempt to ship Canadian gas into the States and the regulatory wars came to an end. Frank finally saw his dream near

Frank McMahon and his son, W. G. (Billy) in 1975. Billy now runs Battery Master, Inc. in Calgary, Alberta. (*Photograph courtesy of Billy McMahon)*

realization. The building of the Westcoast pipeline was one of the world's greatest construction feats. The lines had to cross several mountain ranges, including the Rockies and the Cascades, and various rivers, ravines and some 650 miles of very rough terrain. The Westcoast mainline now covers some 870 miles from Fort Nelson in Northern British Columbia to Huntington at the international border and sells its gas to United States pipelines such as Northwest Pipeline Corporation at the border and to B.C. Gas and Centra Gas in British Columbia. Pacific Petroleum, which had in the meantime become a fully integrated independent oil and gas company, with its own refinery and gas stations, was bought by Phillips Petroleum and then purchased by Petro-Canada, the Canadian government owned oil company, for $1.6 billion.

Frank McMahon used some of his oil money to build McMahon Stadium for the Calgary Stampede football team. Frank and his brother George put up $300,000 and underwrote a bond issue for $650,000 to provide the financing for the stadium.

All the McMahons, except for son Billy who still lives in Calgary, have passed away. Billy recalls his brother telling him that the family originally came to Canada from County Cork, settling first in Ontario and then wandering west following the mining and oil exploration.

Cameron Millikin
Horse Trader, Roughneck, Stuntman,
Mud Salesman and Political Spin Doctor

Cameron Millikin's introduction to North America was his first lesson in the sharpness of the Yankee trader. Americans are noted for their business acumen, but most of them are more honest than the agent Cameron used in his deal to ship a load of brood mares to Kentucky. When he went to New York to collect his commission on the deal, the agent had "gone south," as they say.

The brood mare deal was Cameron's first entrepreneurial venture on his own account. He had grown up with horses and in a horse breeding family. His grandfather, John White, of Liffybank, Dublin was a well-known horse dealer and his horses were famous all over the world wherever horse racing was undertaken. Cameron worked on selling the horses, shipping them all over the world and delivering them.

His horse riding skills even got him a job as a stunt man in the film business. Back in the early 1950s, 20th Century Fox was shooting a movie at Lutterellstown Castle in Ireland and Cameron got a job riding around as an extra. Then one of the stunt men was killed and the director asked for a volunteer to take his place. Cameron was used to falling off horses every day and being bucked off, so being a stunt man and getting well paid for what he normally did for nothing was a bit of a surprise for him. Cameron was given a contract as a stunt man and he went to Spain with the film crew, performing stunts in the *Black Knight* with Alan Ladd and Patricia Medina, in the *Vikings in Norway* with Kirk Douglas and Tony Curtis, and in a series of other movies where he kept falling off horses.

After his stunt days, Cameron decided to strike out on his own and that was the time when he got "stiffed" by the New York agent. Near broke, Cameron hitchhiked to Toronto and to conserve his meager capital -- all of fifty dollars -- he checked into the YMCA on Carlton Street. With not much to do, he took to reading the Y's bulletin board. One notice caught his eye. A man had posted a notice asking for someone to drive him and his car to Western Canada. This seemed to be tailor-made for Cameron as he remembered being told by Ambassador Gill at the Canadian Embassy in Dublin that there were tremendous opportunities, especially for roughnecks, in the Alberta oil fields if one were big and strong. Cameron was both, six feet seven inches tall and he weighed 230 pounds.

The man who had posted the notice was an Italian barber who had lived in Canada for more than thirty years. He had a brother in Western Canada that he hadn't seen for over thirty-five years and he wanted to see him before he died. He needed a driver because he had never learned to drive. Not only did he want a driver, he wanted someone to teach him to drive. Cameron and the barber picked up a new Ford car in Oakville; you could buy one cheaper there and it was on their way out west. The journey was fairly uninteresting in that the Italian barber had his problems learning to drive and it was a long haul across the country.

It became more interesting after the barber said good-bye in Saskatoon, Saskatchewan, in the heart of the Canadian prairies, and left Cameron and all his gear on the side of the highway. Cameron's luck held out, however, and he was picked up by a Holy Roller who preached to him all the way to Medicine Hat, Alberta. After dropping him off in a parking lot, he made Cameron get down on his knees and thank the Lord for his good fortune in meeting an angel of mercy.

From Medicine Hat, Cameron made his way to Calgary, Canada's oil capital, where he hoped to get work. However, 1958 was not the best time to be looking for work in the oil business -- the industry was going through one of its worst recessions and trained geologists were driving taxis, selling cars and peddling storm doors and windows.

Determined to get a job, Cameron decided on a tactic which only a big man with a lot of blarney would attempt. He sat outside the office of Peter Bawden, president of Peter Bawden Drilling Ltd. and remained there for two days before Peter Bawden, in exasperation, called him in and hired him as a roughneck -- a helper around a well drilling site. After all, you can't get too obstreperous with a six foot seven inch Irishman!

After he got his feet wet with Peter Bawden Drilling, Cameron moved on to the McMahon operations. Frank McMahon and his brother, George, had single-handedly founded an oil and gas pipeline giant in Alberta and British Columbia, operating as explorers, producers, drillers, refiners, gas retailers and natural gas producers and distributors through Westcoast Transmission.

According to Cameron, one day while thumbing through a technical magazine, he got a lucky break. "I had been reading about a drilling fluid down in California that someone had invented and perfected and I thought it would suit our drilling conditions up in Canada. I wrote for additional information and passed it on to my boss. He took it upstairs to the boardroom, but he didn't know enough about it to properly explain it. Frank McMahon was a tough guy and demanded to talk to the person who was familiar with the information. So I was ordered up to the boardroom and I explained all I knew about it. I was on a plane to California at two o'clock that afternoon and I was able to get a contract signed. Frank McMahon made an awful lot of money off that. Anyway, I got promoted to the head of that department and I eventually ended up as his Executive Assistant."

Getting Involved in Politics

John Diefenbaker, the Progressive Conservative Prime Minister of Canada in the late 1950s and early 1960s, had no real love for the United States and was not above taking a potshot at the mighty neighbor to the south whenever the opportunity arose. In this case, it was by way of a stiff tariff against Cameron's drilling mud imports which had a negative impact on Westcoast's drilling budget. Looking for a way to protest the tariff, Cameron joined the young Liberals, the party in opposition to the Progressive Conservatives. He went to work politically for the mayor of Calgary, Harry Hayes. Harry won the seat for South Calgary for the Liberal Party and became the Agricultural Minister in the new Liberal government. Cameron became his political aide.

This big Irishman soon attracted the attention of some bigwigs in the Liberal Party and Cameron found himself involved as a political advisor to the Office of Prime Minister Lester B.

Pearson. Over the years he has kept his political lines open and has worked as an advisor to other Prime Ministers such as Pierre Trudeau and John Turner. Cameron Millikin operates from his Calgary office to Ottawa, Canada's capital, scurrying back and forth for political strategy meetings. He is still very active in the Liberal Party.

Back to Business

In 1966, Cameron was back working full-time with the McMahon Group, this time working out the details of establishing a potash slurry pipeline from Esterhazy, Saskatchewan down to the Imperial Minerals and Chemical (IMC) plant in Chicago. Saskatchewan has one of the world's largest reserves of potash and it seemed to make sense to ship the stuff by pipe to fertilizer manufacturer IMC.

Cameron worked for over a year negotiating with the governors and state officials for the rights-of-way through several American states. He got his end of the job done, which took a year to complete, then the bottom fell out of the potash market and the deal was shelved.

After the aborted potash pipeline deal, Cameron went out on his own. With David McLean, he started a company called Erinmore, which he named after a brand of tobacco he smoked before leaving Ireland. Erinmore built several apartment buildings. The company also built a motel in Jasper in the Canadian Rockies and did several business deals. He sold out of Erinmore and used the money to invest in an FM radio station -- CHFM in Calgary.

Millikin's next move was the acquisition of a position in the television cable industry through a company called Cablecasting. Shaw Cable, one of the premier cable television companies in Western Canada, bought out Cablecasting. Still restless, Cameron Millikin became involved with Art Henuset in a company called Canadian Siberian Oil, which built a sixty-million-dollar (68.5 kilometer) oil pipeline in Siberia.

Big Rock Brewery

Cameron Millikin was a founding director and shareholder in Big Rock Brewery in Calgary. It all came about when he and

Irish-Canadian Ed McNally, a Calgary lawyer whose grandfather came from County Cork, got caught up in the micro-brewery fever. Cameron Millikin did the consultant work and handled the marketing chores.

Big Rock is doing very well for a small brewery, keeping forty people in jobs and shipping its beer into British Columbia, Manitoba and the United States. A fairly major expansion has increased capacity to 100,000 hectoliters a year. Big Rock has a major break on its shipping costs into California, making the brew very competitive. The refrigerator trucks from California which haul produce to Canada and which would be back-hauling empty are used to take Big Rock beer to that market. Big Rock is a public company trading on stock exchanges in the United States and Canada.

The Millikin Family

Born in Long Acre Baily near Howth, Dublin, Cameron Millikin has come a long way. He has a great attachment to Ireland. Cameron is the founding president of the Calgary chapter of the Canada Ireland Fund, which supports a wide variety of causes in Ireland, including community and reconciliation programs. Cameron is married to Susan Coulcher, whose mother came from Sligo town. They have three sons, Rory, a twenty-four-year-old, works for the company distributing Big Rock beer; Craig is a bond dealer in Dallas, Texas; and John attends Athol Murray College at Notre Dame in Wilcox, Saskatchewan.

About himself, Cameron says, "I'm a founding member of the Calgary Irish Rugby Club. I'm Chairman of the Laurier Club of Canada, the Liberal Party's fundraising arm in Alberta. I'm past director of Rowing Canada, the sponsor of the Canadian Olympic crew which won the gold medal at Barcelona in 1993. Best rowers in the world! They won twelve gold medals.

"I go back to Ireland about once a year. I have uncles and aunts in Ireland, but my mother and father are dead. I have a brother, Chesley, in Austin, Texas who goes back more often; he's in the music business. I was so fortunate to be born in Ireland. It gave me a head start when I came over here. I always thank my lucky stars that I was born, bread and buttered in Ireland."

Smilin' Jack Gallagher
The Last Great Buccaneer

In the 1970s, in the wake of the Organization of Petroleum Exporting Countries (OPEC) oil price hikes and threatened shortages, the price of oil shot up to forty dollars a barrel. There were long line-ups at the pumps and panic in the industrialized world. Canada, an oil producing nation with vast unexplored areas, determined to become oil sufficient to protect its national interest. Pierre Trudeau's government made huge sums of money available to companies who were prepared to explore in the so-called "frontier" areas -- the Beaufort Sea in the Arctic and in the ever turbulent Atlantic Ocean off Newfoundland. Companies involved in exploration in these areas also qualified for generous tax write-offs.

Jack Gallagher (Smilin' Jack) was one of those legendary characters who come along once every century or so and who happen to be in the right place at the right time and have the vision to realize it. He had been a geologist with Shell Oil and with Exxon (Standard of New Jersey) from where he had been furloughed. He was hired by Dome Mines to work with their oil and gas subsidiary, Dome Petroleum, a small (about fifteen million dollars in assets) oil and gas explorer. Under Smilin' Jack, Dome took off using the huge grants and tax write-offs the Federal government had made available to Canadian exploration companies. From a minor player, Dome became a multibillion-dollar oil and gas conglomerate and its stock was the darling of Wall Street and Bay Street.

Jack Gallagher was the ultimate promoter and his smiling face could, and did, get money from the stone-faced investment dealers, bankers and even from his own employees. The drunken sailor could have taken lessons from Jack Gallagher when it came to spending, and instead of being chided for his spendthrift ways, Jack was urged on to bigger and bigger spending.

From his headquarters in Calgary, Jack Gallagher spun a magic web of ever increasing profits for the stockbrokers and made tax experts dizzy with the size and the flood of tax shelters and write-offs. With money pouring in faster than most gushers spurt oil, Jack accumulated such a conglomeration of assets that it began to look as if he would own the whole Canadian industry. In its heyday, Dome had 17,000 producing wells, 160 gas processing plants, oil reserves of 263 million barrels, five Arctic drilling systems (including islands Dome built to drill from), eighteen ice breakers and support vessels, 3,903 billion cubic feet of natural gas reserves, 9.2 million acres of oil and gas lands, and 4,260 miles of pipelines. Dome had oil production of about 80,000 barrels a day -- five per cent of Canada's production. Dome also produced eight per cent of Canada's sulfur and seven per cent of the country's natural gas.

Bankers were falling all over themselves to give Smilin' Jack money and Jack was not bashful about taking it. Everything was going smilingly well for Smilin' Jack, that is until the western producers caught up with OPEC production output, and the price of oil dropped from forty dollars a barrel to twenty a barrel and natural gas dropped from around five dollars per 1,000 cubic feet to two dollars and fifty cents.

From being the darling of the government and the investment community, Jack Gallagher became a pariah and people were screaming for his blood. His ventures in the Beaufort Sea, where he drilled eleven oil wells, were now looked upon as the actions of a mind out of control. Jack Gallagher, son of an Irish immigrant who worked on the railroad in Winnipeg, saw his star reach its zenith and die out all in the space of a few short years.

When Jack's Dome Pete was scrutinized after its fall from grace, the company owed nearly eight billion dollars, and the stock which had traded in the mega-dollar range had skidded to pennies. Smilin' Jack Gallagher, after he had his fifteen minutes in the limelight, had the good grace to pass away and not hang around to be pilloried.

What was left of the once mighty Dome Petroleum was taken over by Amoco Canada in 1986. It had reported a loss of $2.2 billion in 1985 and its debt rivaled that of many third world countries. Like Smilin' Jack, Dome Pete disappeared from the face of the earth.

Entertainment, Literature and Culture

Music and the Theater

Back in the days when the signs "No Irish Need Apply" were displayed in some American eastern cities, Irish entertainers took to the stage in "black face." Theater owners would not allow black performers to go on stage but when Irish entertainers blackened their faces, they were accepted. These entertainers took advantage of the opportunity to perform.

Later, comedians such as Gallagher and Sheen did their very successful "Irish Washerwoman" routine in the 1890s and gradually the Irish comic genius came to the fore. Acts like the Seven Little Foys carried on the tradition. With the advent of movies and television, the Irish became a major force in American entertainment.

Tom Maguire arrived in San Francisco with the first wave of forty-niners. He operated San Francisco's most famous saloon and gambling house, the "Parker House." In 1850, he turned the top floor of his establishment into the Jenny Lind Theater. When the theater was destroyed by fire the next year, he constructed in its place the largest theater on the west coast, with seating capacity for two thousand patrons. The Jenny Lind Theater ran into financial trouble and later became the new San Francisco City Hall. Maguire then built a smaller San Francisco Theater and established a resident stock company. He was a successful and popular man who remained active in cultural affairs all his life.

Introduced to America by Irish immigrants, step dancing and Irish music had a major influence on the development of country music and the American hoe-down. Tap dancers such as Gene Kelly and Donald O'Connor owed much to the Irish tradition of jigs, hornpipes and reels.

Many country songs and songs of the trail were Irish in background. Elvis Presley's "Love Me Tender" is the old Irish air "Aura Lee," "Kisses Sweeter Than Wine" is the "Old Dun Cow tune," "Streets of Laredo" comes from "Bold Phelim Brady the Bard of Armagh," and the "Yellow Rose of Texas," the most popular song of Texas, is an old Irish melody.

George M. Cohan was a legendary songwriter and play-wright who earned the Congressional Medal of Honor for his World War I composition "Over There." Other great songs he composed are, "You're a Grand Old Flag," "Give My Regards to Broadway" and "Mary." Few can forget movie actor James Cagney who played the tough-guy role in many great films. Cagney won the Oscar for best actor in the movie *Yankee Doodle Dandy*, which immortalized the life of George M. Cohan.

Great Irish tenors such as Count John McCormack and Dennis Day found fame in America, and Frank Patterson from Tipperary is following in their footsteps. Irish groups such as The Chieftains, The Wolfe Tones, U-2 and the Irish Rovers have enjoyed great popularity in Canada and the United States. They are loved by all who hear them, not just the Irish. The Irish treasure this connection with home. Other immigrants must feel as lonely as the Irish do, but they are not as vocal about it. Somehow, when Irish songs are happy, everyone feels happy, but the poignancy in the sad songs touches the inner core of everyone away from home, be it from Europe, Britain, Ireland or across this immense continent of North America.

The story of the Irish Rovers and the interview with Will Millar is a case in point. The Irish Rovers have enjoyed a wide popularity and Will Millar is only too happy to talk about the hard times, the loneliness and their phenomenal success.

The stage has seen such Irish greats as Helen Hayes, Hugh Cronin and the Barrymores (who owe their Irishness to the Drew side of the family). Jackie Gleason and Art Carney made their mark in radio and television in the *Honeymooners*.

Hollywood was and is a favorite haunt of the Irish. Movie stars such as John Wayne, whose real name was Marion Morrison, Victor McLaglen, Irene Dunne, Margaret O'Brien, Maureen O'Hara, Barry Sullivan and Walter Brennan are among the all-time greats. Barry Fitzgerald and his brother, Arthur Shields, came from Dublin's Abbey Theater. Bing Crosby, equally famous for his voice and his acting, Stephen McNally, Gregory Peck and Pat O'Brien all had Irish blood.

Pat O'Brien owes his success in no small way to the great Howard Hughes, even though he never met the man.   In

December of 1930, Pat received a call from Howard Hughes' agent telling him that Mr. Hughes wanted him for a part in the movie *Front Page*. Hughes paid the producer of the play in which Pat was rehearsing the princely sum of $10,000 for Pat's contract and the rest is history.

Pat O'Brien went on to star in several of the movies of the 1930s and 1940s with such Irish stalwarts as Spencer Tracy, James Cagney, Bing Crosby, Frank McHugh and Ronald Reagan. Pat served in the United States Navy in World War I. During World War II and the Vietnam War, he entertained the troops in many of the war zones.

The Irish on Pat O'Brien's mother's side came from the McGoverns of County Galway and on his father's side from County Cork. The McGoverns left Ireland during the Famine period. Margaret and William McGovern, with their four daughters, Agnes, Katherine, Mary and Margaret and two sons, Philip and William, settled in Waukesha, Wisconsin. The family later moved to Milwaukee, then a city of wooden sidewalks and gas lights.

Pat's father and mother lived in two tiny rooms over O'Donnell's Saloon in Milwaukee, where William Joseph O'Brien (later called Pat) was born. He was called Pat in deference to his grandfather, a peace loving man who had tried to stop a fight in a saloon. He was shot between the eyes by one of the combatants and died on the spot.

Pat's movie career took off when he starred in the movie based on the life of Knute Rockne, the famous Notre Dame football coach. After being selected to play the part of Knute Rockne, Pat was approached by a young Ronald Reagan, asking him to intercede with the director to get Reagan the part of George Gipp (the Gipper). Reagan had been a sportscaster and had studied and knew everything about the life of Rockne and the Gipper. Pat was instrumental in Ronald Reagan getting the part. During his career, Pat O'Brien played in over one hundred movies.

Pat and his wife, Eloise, had four children -- Terry Kevin O'Brien (always known as TKO), Brigid, Sean and Movourneen. Movourneen was given that name by Pat out of love for his mother who used to sing the old Irish songs to the family when he was young.

Then there was Spencer Tracy who drew patrons to the movie cinemas for more than thirty years and won Oscars for his roles in *Captains Courageous* and *Boys Town*. And who can forget Barry Fitzgerald who won the hearts of movie goers everywhere with his impish roles in such great movies as *The Quiet Man* and *Going My Way*. Daniel Day Lewis, of *Robin Hood* and the *Age of Innocence*, is Irish, as are Warren and Ned Beatty. Shirley McLaine is Warren Beatty's sister.

Grace Kelly, a third generation Irish-American girl, was born in Germantown, Pennsylvania into a family of talented sportsmen, entertainers and businessmen. Grace Kelly became a real life princess when she married Prince Rainier of Monaco on April 19, 1956. The Kelly clan in America originated with the Dowager, Grace's grandmother, who had emigrated from County Mayo. The Dowager had ten children, most of whom attained fame and fortune in America.

Grace's father, John Kelly, was a successful building contractor and a well-known athlete. He won the single and doubles sculls in the 1920 Olympics. Her uncle George was an actor and playwright who wrote several Broadway hits. Both John and George Kelly served in the United States armed forces in World War I.

Her Uncle Walter was a vaudeville star and an actor in the early days of the movies. The family lived in Philadelphia and made many contributions to the cultural life of that city. After Grace's father died in 1960, the city renamed the Playhouse in the Park the John B. Kelly Playhouse in his memory.

Grace Kelly became one of Hollywood's best loved stars, sharing the screen with such big names as Gary Cooper in *High Noon*, Clark Gable in *Mogambo*, Ray Milland in *Dial M for Murder*, James Stewart in *Rear Window*, William Holden in the *Bridges at Toko Ri*, Frank Sinatra in *Country Girl* and Cary Grant in *To Catch a Thief*.

The John Ford story which follows is a legend in Hollywood success stories. As a director, Ford became famous for his Western and Civil War movies. His versatility was amazing. He was a genius at getting to the heart of a story and at getting the best performance from his actors.

Literature and Newspapers

Irish writers have made a major contribution to the American field of literature. F. Scott Fitzgerald, the author of such great American classics as *This Side of Paradise* and *The Great Gatsby*, was the grandson of County Fermanagh born Philip Francis McQuillan, who built a thriving grocery business in St. Paul, Minnesota. John O'Hara, who wrote *Butterfield 8, Ten North Frederick Street* and *A Rage to Live*, belonged to distinguished Pennsylvania Irish families on both his father's and his mother's sides. Eugene O'Neill, America's greatest playwright, was the son of James O'Neill who was born in Kilkenny in 1846. O'Neill was very proud of being Irish and was offended by the comic "song and dance Irishman" portrayals. His classic and probably his best play, *Long Day's Journey Into Night*, is his own life story, based on the theme that if one does not learn from the past, one is condemned to repeat it.

James T. O'Farrell wrote about the world of the working-man in South Chicago. His great books include *Studs Lonigan, A World I Never Made, No Star Is Lost* and *Father and Son*. Poet Edgar Allen Poe was the grandson of an Irish immigrant.

Brian Moore, a native of Belfast, is the author of seventeen books covering a wide spectrum of subjects and locales. His latest book, *No Other Life*, is set in the mythical country of Ganae and tells the story of a Catholic priest who becomes president of that country. The book is based loosely on Father Aristide, who was president of Haiti and was overthrown. *The Luck of Ginger Coffey* and *The Revolution Script*, based on the FLQ October Crisis in Quebec, are both set in Montreal. He wrote about French Canadian missionaries in *Black Robe*. *Judith Hearne* was made into a movie with Maggie Smith playing the title role. Moore lived in the Montreal area for several years and was at one time looked upon as a Canadian writer.

Moore has lived in California for about thirty years. He went there initially to work with Alfred Hitchcock on the script of the movie *Torn Curtain* and has continued to live there, although he retains Canadian citizenship.

Forefront among current Irish writers is William Patrick Kinsella. His interview reveals the modern journey of a creative man who had to beat his head against the wall to get his work published, then the heady success of having one of his stories made into a movie which received three Academy Awards.

Prior to the great writers and playwrights, Irish writers were publishing newspapers. The story of Francis Collins, founder of the *Canadian Freeman*, brings to life the struggle for freedom of the press in its coverage of the poor in York (now Toronto), Canada. He wanted all people to be free to pursue their fortune in any manner that their talents led them, unfettered by a created aristocracy who wanted all avenues of wealth and prestige reserved to themselves.

There was Bartholomew Dowling who was born in Listowel, County Kerry in 1823. He immigrated to Canada with his parents as a young boy. Following his father's death, he returned to Limerick where he became a clerk to the treasurer of the Corporation of Limerick and a contributor to the *Nation*. In 1857, he immigrated to America and engaged in mining in California. In 1858, he became the editor of the *San Francisco Monitor*. He died in San Francisco on November 20, 1863.

Three Women with Pioneering Spirit

The delightful story of Ma Murray is a humorous tale of an unorthodox newspaperwoman in British Columbia in the early 1900s. Equally unusual is the story of two Irish girls, Norah Denny and Dorothy Goeghegan, who opened a boarding and day school for girls in the town of Duncan on Vancouver Island. Margaret O'Grady Orange, a more modern pioneer woman, is an artist. With her two small daughters in tow, she followed her husband into the wilds of the Northwest Territories in Canada. All three stories provide insight into the lives of women with courage and ambition and these stories show how they each achieved success.

Will Millar
And The Irish Rovers

The Irish Rovers have been together for about thirty years and have never gone a year without touring. During this time they have had many strange and wonderful experiences on the road. To cover them all would encompass a whole book. We include a few of Will Millar's favorite stories.

Will recalls his first experiences with Irish audiences from his father's gigs at dances in Ballymena. His dad played the button accordion at a place called the "Struggle." "It was," says Will, "a struggle to get in, a struggle to dance and a struggle to get out. The shenanigans used to start when the bus would pull in from Belfast, loaded up with boyos who themselves were half loaded." As soon as they came in the door, Will's dad and the rest of the band would scamper under the stage and continue belting out the music from there, while the bottles and fists flew overhead.

At one of the Rovers' first outdoor fairs, the New York State Fair, "The act that went on before us," says Will, "was a bunch of bloody chimps." As if that wasn't bad enough, the act before the chimps had this mad Irishman who blew himself up every night. "This bloody Paddy," Will remembers with a grin, "would put himself in a coffin with a stick of dynamite. The coffin would lie on the race track in front of the grandstand. Then there would be this god-almighty explosion and your man would stagger out of the coffin in tatters with his face all black."

The Rovers had a road manager for the show named Sherman Walker. He was a great big guy who wore a black karate outfit, the strangest character one could ever hope to meet. He had a beard and a fearsome look, like one of those heavies who always beat up on Popeye in the cartoons. It was Sherman's job, as soon as the chimps were finished, to run onto the stage with the guitars and the accordions and set up for the Rovers.

There was a big old chimp -- the old grandfather chimp -- who would sit on a high stool while the others performed. He caught sight of Sherman in his big beard and black suit. "Now, whether he fell in love with him, or wanted to challenge him be-

64

cause there were females on the stage, I don't know," says Will, "but he took one look at Sherman and his eyes opened wide. I could see the whites," Will laughs. "He was like a cartoon character and before anyone knew what was happening, this bloody monkey went berserk, tore himself loose and tried to attack Sherman. The female chimps performing on the high wire started shrieking and fell into a heap on the stage in a great bundle. The wee Italian man who was running the chimp show was yelling 'Momma mia, sonnma bitch, whatte happen.' The chimps were all over the place, running into the audience and going crazy. They broke up the audience and disrupted the show for half an hour, and we had to follow this act," Will adds hilariously.

Another time in Truro, Nova Scotia, their show was in an ice arena with the ice still in place. The arena staff had placed some boards over the ice surface for the patrons to sit on. The back end of the place was still bare ice. It was a real hillbilly makeshift arrangement with noisy patrons drinking out of brown paper bags to get around the "no booze" regulations. The Rovers, used to the rough and tumble of touring, were getting into their fourth number, the very lively "Black Velvet Band," when this half-drunk Nova Scotian jumps over the boards and starts doing an enthusiastic wild jig on the ice, accompanying himself with a loud discordant voice. With that the Rovers' promoter, a big Irishman, grabs hold of your man around the neck and tells him, "You're disrupting the show" and for good measure, he gives him a clout on the head. Right away about twenty of the loud Nova Scotian's mates start after the promoter, and soon the whole place was looking like something out of the Keystone Cops, with people slipping and sliding all over the ice. And the boys played on!

How The Rovers Got Together

Will Millar started his musical career operating out of Calgary, working his way across Canada and the United States singing and playing in clubs and bars. Will got hired by Phil's Pancake House, a small restaurant chain that had four outlets in various parts of Calgary. They were clients of Les Weinstein who later became the Rovers' manager. It was an unlikely place for Will to perform, especially as Will was bearded and a bit wild

65

looking. However, it worked out well as Will was and is a real charmer, and great with kids. He was a crowd pleaser par excellence.

Will played the pancake houses in Calgary and Banff. From the pancake houses he was invited to do guest spots on radio. He was offered the opportunity to take over the children's program which aired daily from four to five o'clock, five days a week on Channel 4 in Calgary, part of the CTV network.

While working the pancake houses and doing the television program, Will's younger brother, George, and Jimmy Ferguson came out from Toronto to visit. Will had them as guests on his show at the Pancake House and at clubs in the Calgary area. George and Jimmy returned to Toronto. Will was saddened at their departure and talked to manager Les Weinstein about forming a group. Before you could say *céad mile fáilte*, the two boys were back in Calgary. Cousin Joe Millar joined them a month later and the Irish Rovers were in business.

Full of hope and glory, they piled into a beat-up old jalopy and drove down to California, telling each other what great things lay ahead and how they were, with fingers crossed, going to take the United States by storm. Of course, it did not really work out like they had hoped. The car broke down in a little backwater town called Valleyford in California.

While Will scoured the town for a mechanic, the others found this little Italian pub called De Nuchi's. Inside were two Irishmen who had arrived from the Ould Sod just a month before and had bought the pub. They gave the boys an opportunity to sing for their supper, after which they passed around the hat, had a few pints and they were allowed to sleep upstairs. In true Hollywood style, a customer stopped for a cold beer and spotted our heroes. This customer had a friend who was a booking agent in Santa Rosa, in the wine making area of California. The agent came over to De Nuchi's, saw the Rovers and arranged for them to audition at San Francisco's Purple Onion Club. They were hired on the spot.

They opened at the Purple Onion on New Year's Eve, 1964. They were booked for two weeks and were so popular they were held over for another twenty weeks. The Purple Onion is the spot where the Smothers Brothers got their start. Phyllis Diller and other top flight American entertainers were headliners. Steve Martin, the now famous comedian and movie star, used to open for the Irish Rovers at the Purple Onion.

Wilcil McDowell joined the Rovers shortly after they had recorded "The Unicorn." Wilcil was a member of a Ceili band which the Rovers had previously used to produce an album called the *Sound of Ireland.* The Rovers had brought them over from Ireland, together with some Irish dancers.

Before "The Unicorn" actually made it, cousin Joe Millar, at that time the only married member of the group, used to send home grocery money to his wife and sons in Toronto. It was becoming increasingly difficult for Joe's wife to be a working mother and look after two growing boys. As there did not seem to be much success on the horizon for the Rovers, Joe's wife more or less gave him an ultimatum -- three months to make it or lose his family. Joe chose to go back home and he got a job in Eaton's in Toronto. Timothy Eaton, who also happened to come from Ballymena, had always followed a policy of hiring first the people from Ballymena and then the other Irish. Joe's timing was priceless -- he left around Christmas 1967, just as "The Unicorn" was beginning to take the charts by storm. As Joe tells the story, "I'm working in the shipping room with a few other guys when lo and behold they unpacked the first of the Irish Rover albums. Of course, my picture was on the label and I said to the guys, 'That's me!' One of the guys replied, 'Yes, and I'm the president of the United States.' "

How The Rovers Met the Unicorn

Will Millar loved the song "Puff the Magic Dragon," but he wanted something different for his own television show. After scouring the music libraries, he found a record by Shell Silverstein, a song called "The Unicorn." Will loved the song. At the time, he didn't know much about copyright, taking liberties with lyrics, or what have you! He rewrote the whole song to suit his style and used it on his television show.

The owner of the Pancake House in Calgary where he entertained loved the song. He told Will he would pay for a recording and they had a school choir back Will on the record. They made ten thousand of those plastic give-away records as a promotion. That was how "The Unicorn" came about.

During one of the shows at the Purple Onion, a tourist from Calgary was in the audience. He yelled out, "Sing 'The Unicorn'!" Will was the only member of the Rovers who really knew the song, the rest of the group faked it. It was a smash hit with the audience, so the boys added "The Unicorn" to their act.

The Rovers used to perform at the Ice House in Pasadena. While there, they decided that they should produce a live "in concert" album. Agent Les Weinstein had a friend, Wally Heider, who had just started his own studio. Wally had a mobile unit he was anxious to test so the fee was reasonable. Wally Heider is now one of the more famous names in record production. The Rovers did the concert and after editing the tape, Les and Wally started calling people in the record market place. They were turned down with great regularity, or they were offered weird deals from hustlers and fly-by-nighters.

Frank O'Connor, who was with Universal Studios, an affiliate of MCA, happened to catch the Rovers on the *Art Linkletter Show*. He got them an interview with Bud Dant, a former musical director of the NBC Orchestra. Bud Dant listened to the tape and recommended the Rovers be signed to a contract with Decca-MCA. MCA paid the Rovers what they had invested in the tape, plus a reasonable performance fee. For the first time, they had money in the bank. Robert Wachs, a lawyer hired by the Rovers, made the contract language with MCA understandable. As a result of this contract the Rovers are still, twenty-five years later, getting royalty cheques from MCA.

Later, during the promotion of their album, Will told Bud Dant that they had this silly little song which seemed to be a great hit with every audience. Bill Dant was enthusiastic about "The Unicorn" and made it the lead song on the album. They called the album *The Unicorn* and released the lead song as a single. A station in Albuquerque, New Mexico aired "The Unicorn" for the first time on the graveyard shift. The switchboard lit up like a Christmas tree. It sold over three million copies in the United States and was a major hit in Canada, Europe, Australia and New

Zealand. The song made dozens of charts in the United States. It was number three in *Record World*, number four in *Cashbox* and number seven in *Billboard*. It continues to sell well all over the world to this day

As soon as "The Unicorn" took off, Les Weinstein got a call from Shell Silverstein's publisher. He was ecstatic, Les recalls. Al Bracken, the publisher, came up to Montreal where the Rovers were playing and spent two days with them. Al did not have a chance to discuss the matter with Shell Silverstein as Shell was on a nine month vacation in Tahiti and knew nothing about the hit his song had become. Neither did he know about the liberties Will Millar had taken with the words and music. Les convinced Silverstein's publisher that Will Millar's arrangement had made a hit of an otherwise forgotten song which had been sitting on the shelf for eight years. Les did such a good selling job on the publisher that he actually volunteered royalty payments to the Rovers for Will's "improved" song for five years.

The Rovers Take Off

The Irish Rovers have had gold and platinum records in Australia, New Zealand, Canada and the United States. Their hits include "Wasn't That a Party," "The Unicorn" (which sold three million copies in the United States) and *The Irish Rovers Collection* put out by *Reader's Digest* for the Rovers' twentieth anniversary collection. They have written several original songs and modernized many old favorites. As a group, the Rovers have sold thirty albums and have never missed a year touring. They have stayed together since the beginning and even their manager, Les Weinstein, has been with them from the start.

In 1975, the Rovers won the ACTRA Award for best television variety show in Canada. They participated in several World Fairs on behalf of Canada, including Expo '67 in Montreal, Expo '70 in Osaka, Japan, Expo '75 in Okinawa and Expo '86 in Vancouver. The only complaint was by Irishman Pat Reid, who was Canada's Commissioner at the World Fairs. His beef was that whenever he was looking for the Rovers, they were usually in the Irish Pavilion. After a guest spot on a Canadian television show in 1970, they were asked to do their own show. They agreed to a series of six half hour shows in 1971. By the end of the second show CBC expanded the series to eighteen shows. Since then the Rovers have performed 175 half-hour television shows and twenty-five one-hour specials.

The Rovers played in Gaelic Park in New York, with twelve thousand mad Irishmen (from north and south of the border) all singing "Kevin Barry" and other rebel songs. They played to sell out performances in Carnegie Hall in New York, at Boston Symphony Hall, at Nashville's Grand Old Opry and at Montreal's Place d'Arts. They appeared in several segments of the television series *The Virginian*. The Rovers' Jimmy Ferguson explains their success and appeal this way, "We're very happy people, enjoying what we're doing."

The Nightmare

In 1983, the Irish Rovers went back to Ireland with a Canadian film crew, into the streets of Belfast to film a documentary called *Children of the Gael*. The purpose of the tour was to look at the trouble in Northern Ireland through the eyes of its children. The Rovers were representing UNICEF at the time and for Will Millar, who loves kids and has produced several shows for children, it was a very touching and disturbing kind of experience. The Rovers had, on many tours, been asked "What the hell is wrong in Ireland? What is it all about?" This trip back home was a chance to find out.

The Rovers went into Protestant schools and Catholic schools. The trip for Will Millar was to have been a revisiting of his childhood where he had grown up on a small farm knowing nothing about Catholic and Protestant hatred, or of bombings and knee-capping. Instead, it was a nightmare.

"Up in Belfast," Will recalls, "I had this little ten-year-old blond-haired, blue-eyed boy look straight into the camera and say to me, 'If they are not out of the country when I'm fourteen, I'll take up the gun.' This was no Arab terrorist, or street tough," says Will Millar. "He was just an ordinary child, just like anybody's son.

"I met the same characters in the Protestant ghettos -- one wee boy had a rubber bullet through his leg and another little boy

70

had been blinded by a rubber bullet. He had been shot by a nervous young British soldier who had just arrived in Ireland. This soldier looks out from his bunker and sees a group of young boys running up the hill towards him. They were just racing as young boys do. The young soldier thought they were coming for him so he fired off a rubber bullet, but instead of bouncing the bullet off the ground as he was supposed to do, he hit the little boy right between the eyes and blinded him."

Will Millar tells of a visit to a youth club and hearing two young girls talking about their evening out. One young one says to the other, "Are ye going to the riot tonight?" The other one answers, "Yes, I am, and what are you going to wear?" Things like that stick forever in the mind, says Will.

The Irish Rovers did several tours of Ireland for the Canadian Broadcasting Corporation (CBC), Global Television of Toronto and Irish Television. They played the pubs of West Clare and Kerry. They did a show out of Bunratty Castle and the pub next door -- Dirty Nellie's, and they downed a few pints in famous playwright John Keane's pub in Listowel.

These tours were a great success and when they were played back on television in Canada, they brought a taste of the old country to the millions of Irish in North America. For the Rovers there was also another benefit. They got the rights to their television series from the CBC and these are being repackaged in a video called *All Our Yesterdays*.

Another Side of Will Millar

The Will Millar seen by the public might give the impression that he is just a performer full of song and blarney but like most people, he has several other sides. Will Millar lives in a beautiful home on the Saanich Peninsula ocean front, near Victoria in British Columbia. His home is part library, part museum and part recording studio.

An Irish buff, Will's home is full of books and paintings about Ireland. His recording studio has all the bells and whistles found in major recording studios and the Rovers use it to tape their own music. The studio is also used by many other musicians and groups.

Will is working on a pet venture, *The Last Leprechaun*, an animated video for kids. Will is using this popular medium to introduce the legends and myths of old Ireland to children. Celtic heroes and villains, such as Balor of the Evil Eye, Fionn MacCool and Cuchulain and the Red Branch Knights are all to be found in *The Last Leprechaun*. Concurrently, he is working on *Russell's Philosophies*, a book full of blarney and homilies, combining Will's own adventures and those of a long ago uncle who lived in New Zealand. (Will previously wrote and had published *Children of the Unicorn*.)

Will's collection of paintings include *Young Ulster With Its Back to the Wall* by T. Bond Walker. This painting shows a twelve-year-old boy, the artist's son, with his back to the wall and a defiant look on his face. The boy was later killed at the Battle of the Somme in World War I. A painting by Anthony C. Hall, called *Clifton*, shows an Irish country scene. Hall was a student of the Group of Seven -- a famous Canadian group of painters. Will Millar swapped Lord O'Neill's trap (as in pony and trap) for the painting. The trap had the original harness and was over four hundred years old. He also swapped a Rover car for a painting by W.H. Mintwood.

Will Millar is an accomplished painter in his own right and has painted hundreds of pictures. His picture of his late mother tending her garden is his favorite.

Will Millar's Favorite Joke

Your man Murphy and his wife lived in the mother-in-law's house for a long time. The woman was nice -- the mother-in-law was a lovely woman. She got along with everybody, except Murphy. They were always arguing, always fighting. This one day they had a terrible argument. Murphy was so frustrated that he slammed the door, jumped into his car and took off down this country road in Ireland, going full pelt, cursing the mother-in-law a blue streak. He turned a corner and had to slam on the brakes for right there in the middle of the road was a huge funeral. There were 3,000 men walking behind the hearse. He couldn't get by them, so he parked the car and joined the procession. He talked to a wee man at the back of the crowd. "Who's dead?" he asked.

72

And your man says, "The person up there in the hearse."

"Fair enough," says Murphy. He is a curious man, so he pushes his way through the crowd, all the way through these three thousand men, until he gets up just behind the hearse. There he finds the chief mourner with a huge dog on a chain, bigger than an Irish wolfhound, with red bloodshot eyes and slavering mouth. Murphy says to the chief mourner, "Who's dead?"

The fellow says, "That's the wife's mother," and he hits the hearse a kick on the bumper.

"My God!" says Murphy. "What happened to her?"

The fellow says, "Do you see this dog? Well this dog bit her on the leg and she was dead in five minutes."

"Oh my God!" says Murphy. Then his eyes lit up and he says, "Do ya think I could borrow that dog for the afternoon?"

And the fellow says, "You can, but you'll have to join the back of the queue."

The Group

Will Millar leads the group. He is a man of many hats. Besides emcee, he is singer, composer, story-teller, poet, writer and musician (guitar, mandolin, banjo, steel drums, bodhran and tin whistle). His published works include *Tales to Warm Your Mind* and *The Children of the Unicorn* (a biography of the Irish Rovers). Will, his wife Catherine and their three children live in a beautiful waterfront home on Vancouver Island, to which he has just added a new recording studio to record Celtic music. Besides having produced his own solo albums, *Make Believe Days* and *Lark in the Clear Aire*, Will wrote and appeared in his Irish award-winning documentary *Children of the Gael*. Will has been extremely active in support of UNICEF and he has served as an honorary voice of UNICEF Canada in 1980-81, for which he was the recipient of the Danny Kaye Humanitarian Award.

Jimmy Ferguson, lead singer, comedian and irrepressible "life of the party" brings to the group the unique spirited vocals that add so much to "Party" and other hits. Jimmy lives in Vancouver and recently starred in a regional CBC comedy series. He devotes much of his spare time to local charities, which includes CKNW Radio Station's Orphans' Fund and Big Brothers.

73

His favorite sport is golf and he regularly visits friends in California to have a game or two.

George Millar, singer, composer and guitarist, co-writes the majority of the group's original material with brother Will. As a record producer, George won his first Juno Award for the Best Children's Album of the Year which he produced for his sister (and fellow Attic artist) Sandra Beech. He has a love for 1950s and 1960s Rock'n Roll and music trivia. He spends much of his time at home locked away in his computerized music studio. He and wife Betsy live in a lovely waterfront home on Vancouver Island where there is a non-stop procession of water birds, seals and whales traveling up and down the inside passage between the island and the mainland.

Joe Millar is featured on love songs and other ballads. He plays base, harmonica and button-key accordion and is also base harmony to the group vocals. While at home in Vancouver, Joe will most likely be found sharpening his skills on the golf course. At the nineteenth hole, on a day when he breaks eighty, Joe has been known to "stand a round for the house."

Wilcil McDowell, known for his accordion prowess (he was All-Ireland Champion Accordionist), is now dazzling audiences with a variety of keyboard instruments including a new electronic MIDI accordion complete with the latest sampling technology. In addition to his fine talents as a musician, Wilcil has a keen mind for business and is involved in developments here and abroad. Wilcil keeps a residence in Vancouver as well as two farms in Antrim, Northern Ireland.

Les Weinstein, who has managed the Rovers since they started, says there is no better remedy at the end of a tough day than to plug in a Rovers' tape and tap your toes and snap your fingers, to pick you up.

74

The Irish Rovers on tour in Ireland. From left, George Millar, Will Millar, Jimmy Ferguson, Joe Millar and Wilcil McDowell.
Below, Will Millar the painter. Will is an accomplished artist, as well as an Irish history buff.

John Ford
A Hollywood Legend

John Ford, one of Hollywood's great film makers, was a legend in his own time with such masterpieces as *The Informer, Stagecoach, Wee Willie Winkie, The Grapes of Wrath, How the West Was Won, Mister Roberts, The Quiet Man* and scores of other classics. He arrived in Hollywood at the outset of World War I, when the movie industry was taking off.

Over the next fifty years of film making, he directed over one hundred and fifty movies and received numerous awards, including eight Oscars for his work. He has been called a genius who was able to capture in his films the "situation which forced men to reveal themselves and become aware of what they truly were." According to Ford himself, this tool allowed him to find the exceptional in the commonplace.

From Connamara to Maine

John Ford was born John Augustine O'Feeney on February 1, 1895 in a farm house on Cape Elizabeth near Portland, Maine. He was the last child of a family of eleven born to Sean O'Fearna (O'Feeney) and Barbara Curran. Only three brothers and two sisters were surviving when he was born. The others had died in infancy.

The elder John was born in Spiddle, a Gaelic speaking area in the Connamara district of County Galway. His mother was from the Aran Islands. Both father and mother were Gaelic speakers and they used the Gaelic form of their name, O' Fearna.

In 1872, at age sixteen, the elder John immigrated to Maine. For a while he worked for the gas company in Portland. He met and married Barbara Curran, who had immigrated to Maine with her sister a short time before. John O'Fearna was an ambitious young man and he opened a saloon and restaurant with a partner in the Portland area. Maine was a partially dry state at the time and only beer, with a low alcohol content, was legally available. But saloon keepers did manage to keep, under the counter, something stronger for their regular customers.

Boyhood Days in Portland

Little Johnnie, as he was then called, attended Emerson Grammar and later Portland High School. He made the High School football team, where he was known as Bull Feeney for his ability to charge forward and block the tackle. English was his favorite subject and he had no difficulty graduating near the top of his English class; as for his other classes, he finished near the bottom. His first choice upon graduating from High School in 1914 was to be a sailor, but he failed to win an appointment to Annapolis. Instead, he went to the University of Maine on an athletic scholarship.

Heading for Hollywood

Johnnie's stay at the University of Maine was brief. After a few days on campus, he made up his mind that he would join his brother, Frank, in Hollywood. Frank, thirteen years his senior, had run away from home and enlisted to fight in the Spanish-American War. After his father had used some political influence to get him out of the army, he took off again and joined a circus. Next he joined a stage troupe and took the acting name Frank Ford.

When the new motion picture industry began attracting entertainment people from the east coast to California, Frank headed west and found work as a stuntman and actor in the early films. Soon he was working as a director, writer and actor for Carl Laemmle's own production company at Universal Studios.

Johnnie headed west by train to Los Angeles and began working for his brother as a laborer and assistant propman. It was at this time that he took the name Jack Ford to identify himself with Frank. In Hollywood, Jack Ford struck up a friendship with Nebraska cowboy Edmond "Hoot" Gibson. They worked together as stuntmen while Jack was picking up the movie making craft from his brother.

Jack Ford's first opportunity to direct came by accident in 1917. Laemmle was making the movie called the *Soul Herder* and one evening the film crew threw a party for him. The next morning, while the director and the main actors were sleeping off their hangovers, Laemmle gave Ford the job of directing because, says Laemmle, "He yells real loud. He'd make a good director."

When the United States entered World War I, Jack Ford volunteered for naval duty but was rejected because of his poor eyesight. Since he had learned to operate a camera, he applied to be a photographer in the new Naval Corps. His application didn't get approved until just before the Armistice of 1918.

A Rising Star

By 1920, Jack Ford had directed twenty-nine feature films for Universal, all but three of them westerns. Those included *The Soul Herder, Straight Shooting* and *The Last Outlaw*. Many of his early movies starred Harry Carey. At age twenty-five, he had become an experienced director. Jack Ford met and married Mary McBryde Smith, a Scots-Irish Presbyterian from North Carolina, in 1920.   A nurse by profession, she had been living in Annapolis before she headed to Los Angeles to look after an ailing aunt. There were two children by the marriage, Patrick born in 1921 and Barbara the following year.

The Rebel Stirring Within Him

When the Irish Republican Army went on the run against British forces in the fight for independence in 1920-1921, Jack Ford was determined that he would do his part for Ireland's freedom.   Leaving his young wife and baby behind, he headed east, first to visit his parents in Maine and then to Ireland. While he was in Ireland, he claimed that British spies followed him everywhere he went and searched his baggage at his hotel. Whether he connected with the rebels while he was there and if he did, how he managed to elude the British authorities is open to speculation.

The Legendary Ford

The first great epic Ford directed was *The Iron Horse* in 1924.   His first sound movie was *Napoleon's Barber*, which was about the French emperor stopping to shave on the way to Waterloo. He made a number of romantic Irish films. The first was the *Shamrock Handicap*, filmed in 1926.   In 1928, he made

78

John Ford in military regalia. Ford, rejected for active military service during World War I because of his poor eyesight, served instead as a photographer in the Naval Corps. (Photo courtesy of the John Ford Archive)

Mother Machree starring Victor McLaglen. His first Academy Award winning film was *The Informer*, also starring Victor McLaglen. Ford himself won both an Oscar and the New York Film Critics Award for *The Informer*, while Oscars were also voted to McLaglen, Dudley Nichols and Max Steiner. In 1952, Ford made the *Quiet Man*, the story of a Yank returning to live in Western Ireland. Ford won the last of his six Oscars for the *Quiet Man*, beating Fred Zinnemann's *High Noon*. Some of Ford's other classics include *Stagecoach* made in 1939, *The Grapes of Wrath* made in 1940, *Tobacco Road* made in 1941, *Mister Roberts* made in 1955, and *How the West Was Won* made in 1962.

Ford was always a family man who loved his home. His other affinity was boozing and card playing with his close knit family of cronies. Ford never drank while he was directing a movie and liquor was not allowed on the set. But when the shooting was over, he and his friends would settle in to have a few drinks. Ford's test of friendship usually involved inflicting humiliation. If a man could survive a series of degrading practical jokes, Ford would reckon he had the fiber to be a comrade. He ruled the set by the scapegoat principle of baiting and humiliating one of his people. Those who survived the blast of his terrible camaraderie began to form his group of regular actors and technicians. John Wayne was one; Victor McLaglen, George O'Brien, Frank Nugent and Ward Bond were others.

Ford was awarded the presidential Medal of Freedom, the nation's highest civilian honor, by President Nixon in 1973. After World War II, Captain Ford had been awarded the Legion of Merit for his four years of exemplary service with the Field Photographic Branch of the Office of Strategic Services.

Ford died of cancer on August 31, 1973 at age seventy-eight. On the roster of great American film makers, the name of John Ford is preeminent.

William Patrick (Bill) Kinsella
The *Field of Dreams* Man

William Patrick Kinsella found America's nostalgic zone with his *Field of Dreams*, the heart-warming, enchanting story of shoeless Joe Jackson and other immortals of America's favorite pastime -- baseball. The *Field of Dreams* is like something out of Irish myth and legend where fantasy conjures with the senses, where joy and despair and the happy ending take one back to childhood where fairy tales really do come true.

Bill Kinsella carries a noble and ancient Irish name, steeped in the history of Ireland. The Gaelic *Cinnsealalach* dates back to the ancient Kings of Leinster, in County Wexford, where Bill's grandfather, Patrick, was born. Like many Irish, Patrick immigrated to the New York area where he met and married Bill's grandmother, Ellen Murphy.

Bill Kinsella was born about sixty miles west of Edmonton, Alberta in Riviere Que Barre on May 25, 1935. He spent his first ten years getting his schooling by correspondence and cut off from the world. According to Bill, "It might as well have been 6,000 miles for all the contact we had with civilization." Blessed with an Irish imagination, where banshees and the little people are forever lurking in the mind in the still of a lonesome prairie night, Bill Kinsella had plenty of time to let his mind wander into the beyond of Tir N'Og and beyond the beyond until his head was full of the hundreds of stories he was later to spurt out, once he had learned the technique of writing. Bill credits his undergraduate mentor, Bill Valgardson, with putting him on the right track, enabling him to put his great store of accumulated literature before the public.

Bill Kinsella has the academic armory to go with his great imagination. He has a Bachelor of Arts degree from the University of Victoria and a Master of Fine Arts degree from the University of Iowa. He also has honorary doctorates from several universities, including the Laurentian University in Sudbury, Ontario, the University of Victoria, British Columbia and the Open Learning University in Vancouver.

One of Bill Kinsella's proudest boasts is that everything that he has written has been published. In addition to his *Field of Dreams* bestseller, his books include *Dance Me Outside*, *Scars*, *Born Indian*, *Shoeless Joe Jackson Comes to Iowa*, *The Moccasin Telegraph*, *The Thrill of the Grass*, *The Iowa Baseball Confederacy*, *The Fencepost Chronicles*, *Red Wolf*, *Further Adventures of Slugger McBatt*, *The Miss Hobbema Pageant*, *The Rainbow Warehouse*, *Two Spirits Soar*, and *Box Socials*.

Bill has been showered with awards and honors, including the Houghton Mifflin Fellowship, Alberta Achievement Award for Excellence in Literature, Books of Canada First Novel Award, Canadian Authors Association Lifetime Prize for Fiction, Writers Guild of Alberta Medal, Stephen Leacock Medal of Humor and Author of the Year from the Canadian Booksellers Association.

The *Field of Dreams* movie received three Academy Award nominations, including Best Picture and Best Screenplay Adaptation. Bill Kinsella recently received the Order of Canada award, and was commended by the Senate of the State of Hawaii in 1990.

Kinsella lives in the White Rock area of British Columbia with his wife, the former Ann Knight, also a writer. They sometimes collaborate on projects and worked together on the *Rainbow Warehouse*, a poetry collection published by Pottersfield Press.

A full-time writer, Kinsella travels extensively, making some forty to fifty public appearances a year. Baseball, however, is his major love. He co-owns a fantasy team, the Memo Lunatics, in the fantasy Seattle Sixties Lezcano Ultimate Baseball Association. His Lunatics finished second in their league in 1991 -- which shows that Bill is still a fairly humble Irishman.

Meanwhile, Bill is dickering with movie producers and television people who have optioned some of his works and he is still pounding away, working that Irish imagination for all it's worth. He can often be seen engrossed in the newspaper at McDonald's in White Rock, a seaside town in British Columbia, oblivious to the world as he soaks up the news of the day.

*William Patrick (Bill) Kinsella, author of **Shoeless Joe Jackson**, from which the movie **Fields of Dreams** was made, photographed at home in White Rock, British Columbia. Kinsella was awarded the Order of Canada in 1993 for his writings.*

Francis Collins
Founder of the *Canadian Freeman*

Francis Collins arrived in York (Toronto), Upper Canada in 1818, joining a small Irish Catholic community of poor emigrants who had fled the penal laws in Ireland. He became the spokesman for this community, boldly defending the rights of the people and freedom of the press.

Collins was born in Newry, County Down in 1801. He came to Canada to seek his fortune when he was only seventeen years of age. He was a printer by trade and went to work for the *Gazette*, a paper founded by Upper Canada's Lieutenant Governor, Lord Simcoe. He became the first official stenographer for the speeches and proceedings of the Upper Canada Legislature. After he did this work for five years without pay, the Legislature voted him five hundred pounds per year for his services.

Francis Collins adamantly opposed the Family Compact, the political oligarchy that ruled Upper Canada at the time. He had first-hand knowledge of the injustices and tyrannies inflicted by the oligarchy leaders, under whose rule the commoner was no better off than he had been in Ireland.

The Family Compact had its beginnings in the Constitutional Act of 1791, which carved out Upper Canada (later Ontario) from Quebec to satisfy the demands of English and United Empire Loyalist settlers who moved there following the American Revolution. This Act created an independent, privileged class in Upper Canada that became known as the Legislative Council. These men became the Family Compact leaders, supported by Lieutenant Governor John Graves Simcoe. The elective House of Assembly was ineffective, strangled by the Legislative Council, appointed by the Crown.

While Simcoe was reputed to be a man of integrity and devoted to the interests of Upper Canada, he was always the aristocrat. He wanted to duplicate what he had known back in England -- a Canadian aristocracy, a landed gentry to whom was given enormous grants of land. He set up a State Church (Anglican) and a privileged clergy who supported the Family

84

Compact. This consolidated the wealthy Anglicans behind succeeding governors.

For nearly fifty years this Family Compact grew in strength and stubbornly resisted any reform. The leaders controlled the magistracy, the church, the legal profession, the banks and the majority of the newspapers. They had grabbed the public lands and had divided up amongst themselves all offices of trust and profit.

Collins felt this oligarchy was ruining the life and stunting the growth of the province. In 1825, at twenty-four years of age, he founded the *Canadian Freeman*. Like the *Colonial Advocate* of Wm. Lyon Mackenzie, the *Canadian Freeman* was violently opposed to the Family Compact.

As a result of Collins's critical editorials, his stipend of five hundred pounds as the official reporter for the House was cut off in 1829 and a charge of libel was brought against him for criticizing Attorney-General Robinson. Collins was found guilty and was sentenced by Judges Hagerman and Sherwood (both ardent Family Compact men) to a year in jail in York. He was also fined fifty pounds.

The citizens of York, whose battles he had been fighting, rallied to his side, paying his fine and petitioning for his release. Sir John Colborne, Upper Canada's Lieutenant Governor at the time, refused to free him in spite of the fact the House of Assembly had voted thirty-seven times to free him. Lieutenant Governor Colborne kept insisting that Collins give a personal security of four hundred pounds and provide two sureties of one hundred pounds each, which had the effect of leaving Collins in prison indefinitely. Collins did not suffer alone. Any paper or citizen who openly criticized members of the Family Compact or its policies was subjected to the same treatment.

That Collins should be convicted of libel for criticizing the Attorney-General, while the newspapers in the pay of the government were permitted to pursue malicious attacks with impunity, did not go unnoticed. The voice of Collins was not silenced, however; he continued to write scathing editorials from York Jail. A direct appeal to the Crown by Marshall Bidwell, Speaker of the Common House of Assembly, eventually led to his release.

Collins, his wife Anne and daughter Mary died within a week of each other in the terrible cholera outbreak of 1834. Collins left a sizable estate which shows that he regained his livelihood and became prosperous in the few short years that remained to him. A Mr. Maurice Scollard of St. Paul's Catholic Church was appointed trustee for the orphaned children, a trust he carried out faithfully.

Opposition to the ruling oligarchy grew. Three years after Collin's death in 1837, rebellion broke out in Upper Canada. William Lyon Mackenzie and several hundred armed supporters attacked the provincial capital in Toronto. However, government forces quickly defeated the rebels and Mackenzie and other leaders fled to the United States. Two of the rebels were hanged for treason. Political repression followed. Finally, the authorities at Westminster became convinced that reform was needed and the Family Compact was swept away forever.

Ma Murray
Newspaperwoman Extraordinaire

Margaret Theresa "Ma" Murray, one of Canada's most out-rageous and delightful characters, lit up the newspaper business like no one before or since. Her flamboyant approach to the English language blistered the hide of politicians and delighted the locals in the many northern outposts where she and her husband owned and operated always precariously financed community newspapers.

Ma Murray, the daughter of Irish immigrants, Patrick and Margaret Lally, was born on August 3, 1888 at Windy Ridge, Kansas. She was the seventh of nine children. The family eked out a living farming, raising a few cows and hogs and picking apples. Ma got through grade three at school.

At thirteen years of age, she went to work doing kitchen help in several houses in western Kansas. Dissatisfied with what she was doing, Ma took herself off to Nebraska where she attended school and "graduated" with typing, bookkeeping, filing and shorthand skills. However, she never did get the hang of putting a sentence together.

Returning to Kansas City she went to work as a bookkeeper for Shipby Saddlery Company. The bookkeepers, curious about life in Canada, would often enclose notes with the billings for saddles destined for Calgary, Alberta. There were many replies and pictures. Adventurous Margaret decided she wanted to go to Calgary, so she and her younger sister, Bess, boarded a train for Seattle. A year later, they went on to Vancouver, British Columbia.

She met her husband, George Murray, when he hired her to look after his books at a newspaper he had started in Vancouver. To stop Ma from leaving (George was a lousy bookkeeper and Ma was good at collecting the accounts), he married her. Ma and George had two children, Georgina and Dan. Both children were heavily involved in the newspaper business and both of them served in the Canadian armed forces during World War II.

Ma the Newspaperwoman

Ma made many forays to the Vancouver metropolis to hustle up advertising from the stores and businesses, taking with her as inducements such local produce as dressed turkeys, potatoes, apples and cantaloupe. On one occasion, she was too late to deliver two turkeys to an account so she had to take them with her to the Georgia Hotel in Vancouver where she was staying overnight. Unable to find a refrigerator, Ma tied them to the radiator and hung them out the window to keep them fresh. Next morning, scores of seagulls and crows were dive-bombing the window, causing such a racket that the hotel management was warning guests that some catastrophe was about to happen. Ma hauled in her two turkeys and after brushing over the teeth and claw marks, presented them to the client and walked away with a nice ad.

In the early years, George was able to keep a bit of a rein on Ma, picking up her dangling modifiers, tightening her run-on sentences and improving her grammar. Then George Murray entered politics, serving first as a member of the British Columbia Legislature and later in the Canadian Parliament, where he pushed for the opening up and the development of the Peace River area in British Columbia.

When he went into politics, Ma gave full vent to her spectacular destruction of the King's English. The attacked politicians could only gnash their teeth in rage at what Ma wrote about them. The message, while savage and vitriolic, was so garbled that any attempt to sue her would have been laughed out of court, adding to the chagrin of the victims.

Georgina Murray Keddell, writing about her mother in her book, *The Newspapering Murrays*, came as near as anyone ever has to describing the indescribable with the following: "She has always been sublime in her ignorance, and no doubt the vivid, poignant and sometimes lurid qualities in her writing would have been ruined by formal education."

While she detested the duplicity of politicians, Ma had a heart of gold when it came to her readers. One poor woman, who had no money to pay her subscription bill, but wanted to be kept on the list, paid with eight frying chickens. Ma was so touched that she gave the woman ten dollars saying, "Get a perm. It'll give that old man of yours something new to look at for a while."

Ma's weddings and obituaries were things of beauty. Every bride was blushing and lovely and the description of what she wore was straight out of Eaton's mail-order catalogue. One unfortunate housewife, who met an untimely end, had her obituary read: "She had, unknowingly, used airplane gas for cleaning clothes in the kitchen. She was blown out the side of the house."

Ma's unorthodox ways of selling subscriptions and her hilarious bookkeeping methods often cast doubts on her circulation figures. To combat the unbelievers, Ma printed on the masthead of one of her papers, "The Only Paper in the World That Gives a Damn About The North Peace" (referring to the Peace River area). On the masthead of the *Bridge River-Lillooet News* she had, "This Week's Circulation 1769, and every bloody one paid for."

Ma Murray is remembered as the lady who kept plugging away, trying to get the politicians to open up the north country.

Marjorie O'Grady Orange
A Woman of Courage and Talent

Part of what has been called the "Ottawa Valley Irish," Marjorie O'Grady Orange is a Canadian watercolorist who had a round-about way of pursuing her career. The daughter of a very protective father who sent his three daughters to a convent school, her life took on the characteristics of a Jack London novel after her marriage.

Marjorie became the wife of a government bureaucrat who brought his family to the Northwest Territories. He eventually became its Member of Parliament. She had a unique opportunity to relate to a culture and a climate unattainable for most Canadians. Her personal perspective of her country is wide and deep. Her love of nature was expanded from her origin in the Ottawa and Gatineau valleys to include a vast northern Canadian vista across the Canadian shield and the barren lands. This concept of isolation and space affects all those who live it.

Marjorie's early years were a total immersion in an Irish environment, the natural result of having four Irish grandparents. Her paternal grandmother, Ellen McCoy, had come to Canada from Newry, County Armagh around 1862 at the age of eight. On the crossing, her baby brother had died and was buried at sea, a heartbreak shared by so many of the Irish immigrants. The McCoys settled in Ottawa and her great-grandfather found employment on Parliament Hill.

A generation before, the O'Gradys had settled in Perkin's Mills, Quebec. When Marjorie's father was a child, the family moved to Ottawa and built a home in the Glebe.

On her mother's side, Marjorie's maternal grandfather, Dominic Fleming, was working for the E. B. Eddy Company in Wrightville, Quebec. The main industry there was lumbering, which provided employment for many immigrants. Grandfather Fleming decided that he could not provide for his growing family on his meager wages. He bought a farm in Cantley, Quebec, a few miles north along the Gatineau River and there he raised ten children.

Marjorie's mother, Bridget Alice Fleming, was born on that farm in 1900. She died at the age of eighty-five after a short illness. Her oldest sister, Mary Elizabeth Black, lived to be one hundred and two. On the adjacent farm to the Flemings lived the Birts, who were cousins of the O'Gradys. It was through this connection that Marjorie's parents met.

Her mother, it seems, was the source of Marjorie's creative talent. Her grace and love of beauty were qualities absorbed by her daughters. She had an innate sense of creativity which was ever present in their home environment. Marjorie's two sisters are teachers. Patricia Mulvihill is a teacher of the hearing impaired. Marilyn Ogilvie is a high school mathematics teacher. Garfield Ogilvie, her husband, is author of the recent book *Once Upon a Country Lane*, which tells the story of the Irish Catholics and Protestants in West Huntley, Ontario. The colorful jacket of his book is a watercolor rendition of a Corkery farm scene painted by Marjorie.

The Far North

On January 3rd, 1962, Marjorie and her two daughters, Diane and Deborah, moved from Ottawa to Frobisher Bay on Baffin Island in the "Far North." The community is now known as Iqaluit. Her husband, Robert (Bud) Orange, had recently been posted as Regional Administrator of the Eastern Arctic. Marjorie was six months pregnant on her arrival, it was forty-five degrees below zero and she had never before lived outside of Ottawa, her home town.

The Oranges were accommodated in Butler Buildings, gray warehouse type structures, standard government issue of the day. Despite the almost continuous January's winter darkness, after they were outfitted with parkas, duffel socks and kamiks, the family was ready to venture out for short spells. During the winter in the land of the long nights it was advisable to be home early in the afternoon before darkness fell. Whenever a "whiteout" occurred, all activity came to a standstill and anyone daring to go out could easily become disoriented and lost.

Diane, the eldest daughter, was twelve. She soon adjusted to Arctic life, making friends of the Inuit children as well as those like herself from "the south." Deborah, at age five, was less enthusiastic and more reserved. She described her new home to her Grandmother O'Grady the following summer with a sigh, "Nana, the wind never stops blowing there."

For an expectant mother, the medical facilities were quite basic. The baby was born on April 2nd, 1962. He was named Robert Harry Albert after his father and his two grandfathers. The newspapers noted that it was the first time "oranges" had been grown north of the tree line. Rob grew up to be a rugby player for the Ottawa Irish and he played more than once in Dublin. Today, although he is a Sun Life insurance agent, he still loves the game of rugby and is a current member of the Ottawa Irish Club.

For a young mother with three young children, life on Baffin Island was an unique cultural experience. Marjorie was alone a great deal of the time while she was raising her children. She had the support of a young Inuit woman, Peukliak, who used to carry Rob on her back in her own mother's amautik (parka with a back pack to hold a child).

Communication at that time was so poor and traveling conditions so perilous that Marjorie had many sleepless nights wondering whether she was ever going to see her husband again. In some ways it was a similar experience to the immigrant woman of old and like them she had a strong Irish will to keep things on an even keel.

Two years later in 1963, the family moved west to Fort Smith in the Northwest Territories, a small community just north of the Alberta border. Bud became the Administrator of the Mackenzie District which stretches to the Arctic ocean on the north and the Yukon Territory on the west. It includes communities such as Tuktoyaktuk, Inuvik and Yellowknife. They settled into a beige clapboard house with a picket fence, a garden, green grass and slender fir trees.

Running for Political Office

After a two year stint in Forth Smith, Bud Orange was approached to run for the Liberal Party under Lester B. Pearson in the federal election of 1965. At that time, the incumbent Member of Parliament (MP) was a Progressive Conservative. The constituency represented the entire Northwest Territories, one third the land mass of Canada. Today, two MPs represent the same area. The challenge proved impossible to resist.

The first election in particular was not one easily forgotten by Marjorie O'Grady Orange. She accompanied her husband on the hustings. Together they traveled by bush plane, bombardier, or any available ground vehicle, covering twenty-five thousand miles in the campaign. Most of the travel was by air.

There were a few hair raising experiences on the campaign trail. One trip, from Yellowknife to Baker Lake on Hudson Bay, which normally took about four hours, consumed seven. The fog was so thick the pilot was forced to fly dangerously low, just skimming the rocks of the Barren Lands. Marjorie, looking out the window of the small Apache, asked herself, "Why am I doing this? Any moment now I will have made orphans of my children." Eventually the little plane touched down at Baker, thanks to the expertise of Billy Sylvester, their young pilot.

Another time during that campaign, they were flying down the Mackenzie River meeting the people in the small communities. When they landed at Norman Wells, where an evening meeting had been scheduled, the weather began to act up. The advance man was out on the deck to meet them. However, pilot Dunc Matheson was worried about flying conditions and told Bud, "There is no time for a meeting. You can go on up for a few minutes. We have to get out of here and back to the base." They were flying with pontoons and the river was starting to freeze. They would be flying back to Yellowknife over frozen lakes.

Marjorie remained in the plane which was bumping around ominously in the rough waves. Her husband made a quick stop to speak to his organizers and hurried back to the plane. Trying to get the plane unhitched was a difficult job for the candidate. At last the plane was ready for takeoff. After successfully crashing and banging through the rough water at high speed, the plane mercifully was airborne. It was the last plane of the season to land on floats at the Yellowknife Wardair base; the time had come for skis.

Election day eventually arrived and Bud won the seat. The Oranges moved back to Ottawa and for the next seven years traveled throughout the north as often as they could, particularly when school was over for the summer break.

MP Bud Orange was constantly covering the largest riding in Canada. He ran once again in the 1968 June election under Pierre Elliot Trudeau. By now he was well known and his efforts respected. He was returned to office with a huge majority. Again his wife campaigned enthusiastically with him. This time they were joined by their eldest daughter, Diane, who was studying political science in university and putting it to good use.

The Budding Artist

While living in the north country, Marjorie started to paint. This was not an activity entirely new to her. She had enjoyed art in her early school days and had shown some promise. It was one of those pursuits shelved for the raising of a family. As the children required less of her time and as her husband's career required more of his, she felt the need to have something for herself. She needed a creative outlet and she turned to the visual arts. Her interest in painting was a wise decision. When her marriage of twenty-six years ended, she had a hobby which was to develop into a fulfilling career.

Marjorie has had extensive formal training from the beginning in Fort Smith. She studied at the Ottawa School of Art, the Mary Schneider School of Fine Arts in Actinolite, Ontario and attended an art school as far away as County Clare in Ireland. In 1987, she enrolled in the Emma Lake Workshop in Emma Lake, Saskatchewan, a rewarding and inspiring experience in meeting fellow artists and international guest lecturers and critics.

Once while studying in oils, she was startled to be told she should be painting in watercolors. It was at the Mary Schneider School. Her instructor had invited two experts from Toronto to critique the students' work. After looking at Marjorie's work, both commented, "This person is a watercolorist." Her instructor suggested she get out some watercolors and see what she could do.

It seems those experts were right. Since then, she has painted almost exclusively in that medium. She has had numerous solo exhibits, shown in galleries and with groups of artists. Her work has gone far afield.

Marjorie O'Grady Orange, Canadian watercolorist. (Below) "Baffin Island," one of her paintings.

95

In 1979, Marjorie visited Ireland for the first time. Her marriage had come to an end a couple of years before and she was completing a European junket on her own. Her feeling of belonging and self discovery was not realized until she walked off the pier at Dun Laoghaire when she was arriving in Dublin. She had often heard of the stirring of Irish roots, but her own experience left her convinced and very moved. This was the first of many trips to Ireland, painting the landscape, meeting the people and absorbing the feeling.

One of Marjorie's first commissions was from Maureen McTeer, wife of Joe Clark who was Prime Minister of Canada at the time. Maureen had seen a *vernissage* of her work at Old Chelsea, Quebec and had expressed an interest in it. "I was wondering if you would come over and paint Harrington Lake for me?" Maureen asked. "I would like to give one of your watercolors to Joe for Christmas." Harrington Lake is the summer residence of the Prime Minister. The arrangements were made, the painting was done and apparently well received.

Today, Marjorie lives in Ottawa and continues to paint in her studio on St. Laurent Boulevard as well as frequently in the outdoors. She is hoping to return to Ireland and paint the Irish landscape once again. Her greatest pride of achievement, she claims, is in her three children and the grandchildren, who now number four -- Bridget, Reid Adrian, Marley Anne and Kiernan Orange.

Norah Denny and Dorothy Geoghegan
Higher Learning in the Wilderness

Norah Denny and Dorothy Geoghegan, a pair of Irish girls, opened their boarding and day school for girls on April 1, 1921 in far away Duncan on Vancouver Island, with fourteen girls and one little boy. Today, their school, Queen Margaret's, is a thriving institution accepting boarders from all over the world. Their story is one worth mentioning as it is one of unwavering courage and faith.

Norah Denny had traced her ancestry back to before the Norman Conquest; an ancestor came over with William the Conqueror. Norah's father was born at Churchill, near Tralee, in County Kerry. A cousin of her father's, Sir Cecil Denny, was one of the first three hundred men who made up the Northwest Mounted Police. Norah Denny's family on her mother's side goes back to the time before the arrival of the Normans to Ireland. Norah was the eldest of a family of four boys and two girls. She moved to Duncan in British Columbia in 1919, where she met up with Dorothy Geoghegan.

Dorothy Geoghegan's family on her mother's side was Ottawa Valley Irish. Her mother was born in Ottawa and her father, born in Dublin, was one of sixteen children. Her grandfather had been brought up as a Catholic. In order to enter Trinity College however, he had to change his religion to Protestant as the Penal Laws were still in effect.

Dorothy's arrival in Canada came about as a result of a visit her father had made to Vancouver Island to see an old friend. Upon arrival, he was so taken with the place that he bought a parcel of land, built a house on it and then wrote to his wife telling her about her new home. The family moved to Duncan on September 13, 1912.

Creating the School

Queen Margaret's had a very inauspicious beginning. Dorothy and Norah bought six acres of farmland, paying $100 as a down payment -- the $100 was borrowed from Dorothy's dad,

Dr. Geoghegan. Later, they acquired an old building which they moved onto the property. The painting, decorating and fixing of the roof were all part of the students' and the staff's education.

As the years went by, Queen Margaret's developed its own farm of sorts, with a few cows, a pig or two, a bull, a donkey and several ponies. They called the farm "Innisfree."

Some of the daunting projects for an all-girl staff and student body included the construction of the basement which was needed to store the students' coats and game equipment. With shovels, picks, garden forks, hand trowels and wheelbarrows, they burrowed beneath the school building, saving the dirt removed as a foundation for the tennis courts -- which were also hand built, using the same tools and the same staff and students to do the work.

The Chapel and Candlelight Service Legend

One of the more special places at Queen Margaret's is its chapel. Constructed of logs, the chapel is a very modest affair. It was not supposed to be that way. When Norah and Dorothy started thinking about the chapel, they hired a very well known architect to design something grand, a most elaborate edifice. After he had done some original sketches for the chapel, the architect inquired about the funds for building the chapel. Miss Denny, with a glow of pride, told him not to worry about the money -- they had already raised thirty-six dollars towards the cost! A more utilitarian plan was produced and humble as it is, the chapel is a focal point of the school.

The chapel is used for weddings, christenings and on a daily basis by the students. But the magic moments are when the chapel is used for the service preceding the breakup for the Christmas holidays. During this service the lights are extinguished, leaving the chapel in total darkness. In this darkness the stained glass windows, with their saintly images, are faintly illuminated by the outside Christmas lights, while complete silence reigns over the congregation. Then a single candle is lit and from it the school choir girls light their candles and the whole chapel glows and flickers. The choir then breaks into song and Christmas hymns fill the air. The familiar *O Come All Ye Faithful* is picked up by the congregation and soon the little chapel swells and resounds to the pure ecstasy of the moment and the moment becomes a feast for the spirit.

As the congregation troops outside into the snow, it marches through a passageway formed by the choir. The night is filled with their young voices, creating a memory the students cherish for the rest of their lives.

Horses at Queen Margaret's

While it is now an established school with an international student body, traces of its Irish origins are to be found in the riding program, still a part of the curriculum. The girls at Queen Margaret's have been riding horses almost since the inception of the school. The ladies who founded the school knew that girls and horses are inseparable. The riding program is a big draw, with the students participating in riding events throughout Vancouver Island and in the British Columbia mainland.

Horsemanship as an elective subject is offered to the grade eleven and grade twelve students. The school runs about sixty horses and meets are a big deal at the school, attracting hundreds of parents, local riders and students.

Norah Denny passed away in 1983 after spending sixty-two years at the school. Dorothy Geoghegan died in 1991, well into her nineties, after an association with the school she helped found going back over seventy years. These gallant Irish ladies started their school on a shoe-string, worked at it all their lives and were determined not to die until Queen Margaret's had overcome its teething problems and was a flourishing institution. This legacy is their great memorial.

People Who Made a Difference

The Irish have often provided care givers and people who looked beyond their own welfare to the welfare of their adopted communities. Irish priests, nuns, nurses and doctors have provided leadership in religion, education, health and welfare for the poor. Since the very beginning of Federation in the United States and Confederation in Canada, Irish men and women have been in the midst of the fight for equality for all people.

The eight stories that follow provide a close look at the individual lives of some of those who have made a difference in the altruistic sense. Every effort has been made to let those who were interviewed speak for themselves and the views expressed are their own.

The vulnerability of a people with no rights brought indignation and outrage to Francis Collins in the early 1800s in York, Upper Canada. The story of his fight for freedom of the press and freedom of the individual to pursue his full potential has already been told. But Collins went beyond his fight through his newspaper. Collins visited the sick and destitute and demanded that religious and political leaders in York do something to alleviate the suffering. As a result of his visits, Collins, his wife and daughter contracted cholera and died.

Nellie McClung was a social reformer, novelist and fierce advocate for women's rights. As a reward for her efforts, she was appointed as a Canadian delegate to the United Nations where she was a member of the Fifth Committee which dealt with social legislation. Then there was Father Flanagan who took in homeless, neglected boys, demonstrating what love and care could do for what the public thought were delinquents.

There is Dr. Patrick McGeer who bent the rules a bit when he was a Cabinet Minister in British Columbia to bring the University of the Air to the outlying reaches of the Province. Patrick McGeer and his wife, Edie Graef McGeer, have discovered a treatment that arrests the progression of Alzheimer's disease, using a combination of off-patent drugs. Patrick McGeer's story is an eye-opener on how the established drug companies operate and how it takes a determined, maverick entrepreneur to produce a product that could conceivably help one-third of the total population.

Patrick Reid is a gregarious, popular man who has spent his life in the service of his adopted country, Canada. He played a major part in designing Canada's national flag. He has promoted Canada throughout the world through his role as commissioner of world expositions and he is currently working to convince the nations of Asia to use Vancouver as a main port of entry for their products, through his position as head of the Vancouver Ports Corporation.

The fire within Shellyn McCaffrey drives her to accomplish something worthwhile. She has a heightened sensitivity to the plight of oppressed people. She was in the unique position, as head of the International Bureau of the United States Department of Labor, of being able to do something for the Polish workers in 1989 when they led the revolution against communism. Her story describes how her "Irishness" became the driving force compelling her to help the Polish workers.

The DeLury story shows a father and son, each a leader in his field, fighting for worker safety and improved working conditions in the workplace -- the son, Bernie DeLury, as deputy commissioner of labor for the State of New York; his father, the late John DeLury, as president of the New York sanitation employees union. John DeLury was a colorful and outspoken New Yorker who was admired and respected by friends and adversaries alike. As a union leader for forty-three years, he succeeded in achieving greatly improved working conditions and a better livelihood for the people he represented. In 1990, President Bush appointed his son, Bernie DeLury, national director of the United States Federal Mediation and Conciliation Service.

Frank Durkan is a top civil rights attorney in the firm of O'Dwyer and Bernstein in New York City. He is an expert in extradition law and he has a large negligence practice. Frank Durkan has ruffled a few feathers in his day and irked more than one government. He does not hesitate to state his views.

United States Supreme Court Justice William J. Brennan Jr. has had an illustrious career. His decisions have affected vir-

101

tually every aspect of American law. Justice Brennan has been a consistent advocate in advancing the rights and human dignity of all individuals.

There have been countless Irish men and women who have made a difference. We have barely touched the surface. In fact, every person in this book has made a difference, each in his or her own way. The following stories show some of the scope of that difference.

Nellie Mooney McClung
Suffragette, Social Reformer and Novelist

Nellie Mooney McClung was born in Chatsworth, Ontario on October 20, 1873 to John Mooney and Margaret Fullerton McCurdy. Her father came from Nenagh, County Tipperary, arriving in Bytown, Ontario with his two brothers, William and Thomas, and cousin Robert Clark in 1830. John was eighteen at the time and the trip across the Atlantic took ten weeks. Misfortune befell John Mooney when his first wife, Nellie Scott, died suddenly. His second marriage to his cousin, Jane Shouldice, lasted just one year, when she also passed away. He then married Margaret Fullerton McCurdy, whose people came from Dundee, Scotland. This last marriage was to last until John died in 1892.

When the news of the death of John's second wife reached Nenagh, there was great concern. With John's two brothers also dead, John was now left alone in the wilds of Canada. One of the Mooney servants in Nenagh volunteered to go out to Canada to look after him. This lady, Judy Connor, was fifty years old at the time and she looked after John Mooney until she died, even after he remarried. After working in logging and farming for several years, John Mooney managed to get a homestead in what was later to become Sullivan Township in Ontario in 1850.

John Mooney's daughter, Nellie McClung, grew up to be a tireless campaigner in the successful drives for female suffrage in Manitoba and Alberta. She became a nationally known feminist, social reformer, temperance advocate, suffragist, lecturer, member of the Alberta Legislature and a novelist. Sixteen books and numerous articles made her one of Canada's best known authors. She was the mother of five children. As a feminist and a reformer, Nellie McClung was in the thick of the intellectual ferment of her time.

Nellie's public life really started when she got her first teaching job at the Manitou Public School in Manitoba in 1892. Nellie got her first taste of the injustice women were subjected to when she became involved with the temperance movement. She watched as a group of local women, the Women's Christian

Temperance Union, went to vote to have the sale of liquor prohibited. When they got to the polling booth, they found their names had been taken off the voters' list.

Soon after that, Nellie became involved with the Political Equality League, which was formed to have the existing laws changed to allow women the same rights as men. Nellie went to see the Premier of Manitoba, Sir Rodmond Roblin, and talked him into going with her to see the sweat shop factories where women were working under deplorable conditions. They visited the dank, smelly basements which had very poor lighting, no toilets and very little ventilation. After visiting several of these, the Premier expressed his shock and promised to look into the labor laws.

Taking advantage of the Premier's "shocked" state, Nellie told him that women wanted the vote. At the time women were not recognized as persons under the law. They were not allowed to hold office and most professions were closed to them. The Premier expressed surprise at Nellie's demands saying, "What in the world do women need the vote for? My mother never wanted to vote; nice women don't want to vote," he added, suggesting that any woman who did want to vote could not be nice.

Realizing that she was getting nowhere with the diplomatic and proper ladylike approach, Nellie and her cohorts decided it was time for drastic action. The group, later to become known as the "Famous Five," decided it was time to use a different strategy. They got together, wrote a satirical play, *The Women's Parliament*, hired a theater and on January 27, 1914 they presented their case. Nellie had attended the Provincial Legislature for weeks prior to the play's opening, making notes of the various motions and bills which were being presented to the Legislature. The play faithfully followed legislative protocol and the highlight was a private member's bill where male legislators were pleading their case to be allowed the vote, to be allowed to be guardians of their children and to be given the right to keep their own earnings -- all rights prohibited to women under the laws of that time. Nellie, playing the part of the Premier, shot down the "men's" plea, to hoots from the females in the audience.

Nellie's mother-in-law inspired her to take up writing. Her first story, which she submitted to *Colliers Magazine*, was

104

turned down as being too juvenile. The story was about the Watson family in 1902. She sent the same story to another publisher and this one liked it and wrote back saying she should do a book on the Watsons. Out of this came her very successful *Sowing Seeds in Danny*, which was published in 1906. It became a best seller in Canada and was well received in the United States, selling about one hundred thousand copies.

A slew of other books followed, including *Painted Fires, Second Chance, Leaves from Lantern Lane, The Stream Runs Fast* and *Clearing in the West*. She also wrote *Next of Kin* about World War I. Her son John served in some of the toughest battles in that war.

In 1921, Nellie ran as a Liberal Party candidate in the Alberta provincial election and was elected as a member of the Legislative Assembly. Nellie's party got only five seats. She was not a good party member, kicking up a ruckus whenever she thought the party was getting away from its ideals. She fought against a bill submitted in the Legislature which would have required that a married woman give up her job to a single girl. Nellie lost her seat in the 1926 election. She did realize a significant victory when the Privy Council declared on October 18, 1929 that women were indeed persons with all the same rights under the law. This reversed a ruling by the Supreme Court on April 24, 1928 that women were not persons.

Her many years of struggle for women's causes finally brought recognition. In 1938, Nellie was appointed by the prime minister to be a Canadian delegate to the League of Nations. She was a member of the Fifth Committee which dealt with social legislation. Later, she was appointed to the Board of Governors of the Canadian Broadcasting Corporation, Canada's national television and radio service.

After a lifetime of campaigning for women's rights and seeing legislation enacted which gave women the right to vote, to own property and to hold the highest office in the land, Nellie McClung retired to Victoria to live out the rest of her days. She died there in 1950 at 77 years of age. Nellie had five grandchildren. Two surviving grandchildren are John Wesley McClung, a judge living in Edmonton and Nellie McClung, who lives in Vancouver.

The second Nellie McClung has several books of poetry to her credit. Nellie laughingly tells us that she spent twenty years writing her masterpiece, *Pomegranate*, and made four dollars on it. Her interest now is in helping the starving children of the world. She says, "The only way to solve the world's problems is to let women run things -- but only for twenty-five years. After that they would start fighting among themselves, just like the men."

Nellie McClung shown with her granddaughter, also named Nellie McClung. The photograph was taken in Edmonton, Alberta in 1931. Granddaughter Nellie lives in Vancouver, British Columbia and like her grandmother is a writer.

Father Edward J. Flanagan
Founder of Boys Town

It was 1917 and World War I was taking a heavy toll in the trenches of Europe. Far away from the battle front, ten miles west of Omaha, Nebraska, a young Irish-born priest was struggling to establish a home for young boys -- mostly unfortunate children who were left homeless and neglected when their parents walked out, or lacked the means to care for them. The priest's name was Father Edward J. Flanagan and the home was called Father Flanagan's Home for Boys, later to become the world famous Boys Town.

In a few short years, Boys Town grew into a renowned school where unfortunate and delinquent boys were cared for and educated, where in the words of Rabbi Edgar F. Magnin of Los Angeles, "The love for wandering waifs, the driftwood of an ugly, cruel society; the little cains wandering over the earth with no place to lay their heads -- except Boys Town."

Boyhood Days

Father Flanagan was born on a farm near Ballymoe, County Roscommon on Tuesday, July 13, 1886. They called him Eddie. He was a frail and sickly child who enjoyed the outdoors, strolling the rolling green fields of the farm, called Leabeg, which his father managed for an absentee landlord. The Flanagan family lived in a modest farm house.

Nearby was the town of Ballymoe where the Flanagans went to mass on Sundays and afterwards stopped to talk with other parishioners. The national school Eddie and his brothers and sisters attended was nearby at Drumatemple. Each day after returning home from school, Eddie would spend his free time in the fields helping his father with the sheep and cattle. They called him the bookworm of the family because, as he herded the animals, he would always have with him some novel. Among his favorite authors were Scott and Dickens.

When he reached the age of fourteen, Eddie Flanagan went off to attend Summerhill College in Sligo. Life at Summerhill, a secondary boarding school for boys, was a rigid existence. Every deviation from the rules, even when unintentional, meant chastisement. Here he experienced his first taste of institutional life. Eddie, being an earnest and determined student, managed to keep clear of trouble. His grades at Summerhill placed him at the top of his class. During his free time he played handball, took walks around Sligo and occasionally went to a concert.

Heading for America

At eighteen, Eddie graduated with honors from Summerhill. Earlier that year his brother, Patrick, was ordained a priest and he accepted a distant post to a parish in Omaha, Nebraska. Eddie had decided to go on for the priesthood and was planning to attend the same seminary his brother had attended in Dublin. However, his plans changed when his sister, Nellie, home on a visit from New York, enticed his parents to let him return to New York with her. In 1904, he sailed on the S.S. *Celtic* from Queenstown to New York. In New York his uncles, the Larkins, arranged to have him meet Archbishop Farley. Farley recommended that he enroll at Mount St. Mary's at Emmitsburg, Maryland for his bachelor's degree and then enter Dunwoodie Seminary. Eddie attended St. Mary's and two years later, in 1906, he graduated at the age of twenty, the youngest graduate in his class.

He returned to live with his sister on East 20th Street in New York and soon after enrolled at Dunwoodie Seminary. In 1908, Eddie Flanagan became seriously ill with double pneumonia. At first, the doctors thought he might not recover. After three months, he began to show improvement but his lungs were weak. He was told by his superiors at the seminary to take a rest from his studies for a year and move to a dry climate to strengthen his lungs. He decided he would go out to Omaha to his brother, Father Patrick, where he rested until his health improved.

Rome and Innsbruck

Eddie Flanagan, still determined to continue his studies for the priesthood, enrolled at the Gregorian Pontifical University in Rome on October 4, 1907. Again his health broke down and he was forced to give up his studies. He returned to Omaha early in 1908 and within a year his health began to visibly improve. He took a job as a bookkeeper with the Cudahy Meatpacking Company in Omaha. He still wanted to be a priest and in 1909 he began to reconsider his plans for the future. When he was in Rome, he had heard students talk about the University of Innsbruck in the Austrian Tyrol, so he applied there and was accepted.

His First Assignment

His wish to be a priest finally came true when he was ordained at Innsbruck on July 26, 1912. On his return from Austria, he said his first mass in America at St. Ann's on East 12th Street in New York. Then he left for Omaha, where he awaited a posting from the bishop. He was sent to a town called O'Neill, about two hundred miles northwest of Omaha, as a curate.

O'Neill had been founded in the middle of the nineteenth century by an Irish rebel and adventurer, John O'Neill, as a settlement for a group known as the "Irish Colonization Society." A lawless frontier town in its early days, it had become a respectable cattle raising area when Father Eddie arrived there in 1912. His assignment at O'Neill was short. He was transferred back to Omaha where he was appointed assistant pastor of St. Patrick's Church. He began to involve himself in the social problems of the community. Each year thousands of itinerant harvesters would converge on Omaha when the harvesting was finished and remain there over the winter months awaiting the spring. Most years, when crops were good, they earned enough to see them through the winter.

The year 1913, when Father Flanagan was assigned to St. Patrick's, was a terrible year for the farmers. Searing heat had devastated the crops. By early autumn, Omaha was filling up with penniless itinerant workers who had not worked since the previous year. They were hungry and without shelter. Father Flanagan, seeing them as he made his parish rounds, decided that he would do something about their plight. With the help and generosity of friends and with the little money they had raised, he

110

found an unused hotel and turned it into a shelter for itinerant
workers.

First Home for Neglected Youths

Soon his compassion inspired him to reach out and help
disadvantaged youths -- the homeless and neglected young boys
from broken homes, many in trouble with the authorities over
petty crimes. Father Flanagan started his first home for boys in
1917 with only five boys, three homeless orphans and two assigned to his care by the Omaha juvenile court. A few days before,
he had rented a two-storey red brick building at Dodge and
Twenty-fifth streets, depositing ninety dollars borrowed from a
friend for the first month's rent. His only help was three nuns
lent to him from the Archbishop.

Within two months, Father Flanagan had fifty boys to
feed, clothe, school and look after. Support came from a small
group of friends making regular donations and help from volunteers. Father Flanagan persevered, the financial situation stabi-
lized and requests for admittance grew. Soon, Father Flanagan
was looking for larger quarters to house his ever-growing family of
boys. At South 13th Street near the stockyards, he found a spa-
cious structure ten times the size of the house on Dodge Street.
It had been a German-American Center before the war.

Many of the programs which would later become identified
with Boys Town were started here. An athletic program got the
boys involved in many types of sport. There was a music program
for the talented and farm and chicken-raising programs for boys
who came off farms. This was a school designed to fit the
particular needs of the boys. Father Flanagan, recognizing how
important it was that the public know how well the boys were
doing, started a magazine which was written and edited by himself
and the boys. The "Mothers Guild" was formed to help with the
duties around the home.

Boys Town Comes into Its Own

By 1921, Father Flanagan's Home for Boys had sheltered
1,250 boys and soon the old German-American house had become
overcrowded. More land was needed to grow their own food and

keep their own animals. Father Flanagan's concept of a home for neglected boys, rather than reform school, was gaining acceptance and financial support was increasing. With help from friends, Father Flanagan acquired a forty-acre farm on the outskirts of Omaha at Florence. He planned to build there but decided not to because of opposition from many within the community who were opposed to a "resort for young criminals" in their neighborhood. Instead, Father Flanagan located Overlook Farm away from any built-up community.

Soon a campaign was launched to raise two hundred thousand dollars to erect a new Home on the farm. In March of 1922, less than a year after the move to Overlook Farm, ground was broken for a new five-storey building. In the fall of 1930, the new headquarters was completed; Boys Town had come into its own. Its government of mayor and commissioners were boys elected to serve its two hundred and fifty residents.   The United States government gave Boys Town official municipality recognition in 1934 when it established a post office there.

Some of the boys Father Flanagan inherited were very talented; others had an aptitude for mischief. Probably the story of the two boys who came to the home following their attempt to invade Mexico is the strangest. The boys got the idea that they were going to capture the notorious bandit, Pancho Villa. The pair, fourteen and fifteen, organized twenty-five of their comrades from their town on the banks of the Rio Grande and armed them with food, guns and ammunition stolen from families and neighbors. They stole a motorboat, which they renamed the *Buzzard*, loaded it with the stolen supplies and guns and, under the cover of darkness, set out to hunt down Villa. Before long, they were spotted by the United States Customs and after a chase, were taken into custody.   Father Flanagan, hearing about the incident, wrote that he would be willing to take the pair of boys into his home. The authorities promptly replied that they were indeed glad to send him the two would-be *generalissimos*. During the time they were in Boys Town, these boys were never in trouble and remained good citizens after they left Boys Town.

In Father Flanagan's Boys Town, physical punishment was forbidden. He regarded whipping, or even a slapping, as an ad-

112

mission of failure by the adult -- an attempt to enforce obedience through fear of pain. That could never be enough to build character. Father Flanagan preached a philosophy of love in caring for children and in doing so created a new social awareness of the plight of neglected children. For his work at Boys Town, he received worldwide recognition.

Father Flanagan's work at Boys Town was immortalized in the 1938 movie, *Boys Town*, which starred Spencer Tracy and Mickey Rooney. A second movie, *Men of Boys Town*, paid tribute to Boys Town alumni who served their country in World War II.

Father Flanagan died of a heart attack May 15, 1948 while visiting Germany. At the time he died, Boys Town had grown to be a multimillion-dollar operation.

Dr. Patrick McGeer
An Unreasonable Irishman?

That great Irishman George Bernard Shaw wrote, "The reasonable man adapts himself to the world; the unreasonable man persists in trying to adapt the world to himself. Therefore all progress depends on the unreasonable man." Dr Pat McGeer's full and exhilarating life is succinctly summed up by Shaw's perception.

Pat McGeer represented Canada with the University of British Columbia Thunderbirds basketball team in London in the 1948 Olympic Games. He has a Ph.D. in chemistry and he is a medical doctor. He worked on the development of Delrin and Teflon while a chemist at du Pont. He created British Columbia's Knowledge Network and Open Learning Institute for Distance Learning, as well as serving as a politician for nearly twenty-five years. Today, he is still spouting radical ideas about the banking system, methane gas and very, very long bridges.

An Unlikely Politician

A straight talking, clear thinking person like Pat McGeer is the last person one would associate with politics in British Columbia, a place where politics has been a kind of undeclared war for as long as anyone can remember. Of course his Uncle Gerry -- the same kind of no-nonsense maverick as Pat -- was also a politician in British Columbia.

When Pat was a faculty member at the University of British Columbia a lot of people, fed up with the party which had been in power for years, kept asking him to run for public office. The legislature met for only two months a year, so it was something he thought he could do and still carry on with his scientific work. He was first elected in December of 1962 as a Liberal member. The Liberals were not the government. McGeer remained a Liberal for many years, until the free enterprise parties began to split, allowing a socialist party to take over power in British Columbia. The spending excesses and lack of responsibility of the socialists caused the free enterprisers to come together again under the

114

Social Credit banner. Pat McGeer and the rest of the Liberal Party amalgamated with Social Credit and in the 1975 election, defeated the socialists. Pat McGeer was made a Cabinet Minister.

Pat McGeer has the same intensity as his Uncle Gerry and he gets quite animated about the ruination of the free enterprise system by irresponsible politicians who keep getting the country into debt. He also rants a bit about the banks, just as his uncle Gerry McGeer did before him. Uncle Gerry used to thunder against the banks, with Graham Towers, then head of the Bank of Canada, as his principal target.

Gerry complained all his lifetime against the banks, their interest rates and the way they abused the population. There is room for another Gerry McGeer today, Pat McGeer believes, because of the way the banks are giving money away to real estate developers and other fly-by-nighters and putting the little guys out of business.

Pat recalls with great glee the time the government decided to take a look at the banking industry in Canada and set up a committee to study the banks. It was called the Banking Committee of the House of Commons. Gerry McGeer was the first one to testify. He thundered away for a full day, railing against the banks, interest rate policies, their treatment of the poor and the workers, their large offices and banker's hours. The socialists on the Committee loved every minute of it and they decided to invite Gerry back the next day for another crack at the banks. However, the committee chairman decided that he wouldn't allow Gerry any more time saying, "It's one thing to turn a hose on and something else to turn it off."

Pat McGeer is a charismatic character, highly esteemed and wildly popular with the majority of voters. His move to the Social Credit Party brought a whole flood of votes to the party and it handily won the election, roundly defeating the opposition. While McGeer was popular with the voters, he was rather a pain in the posterior to some ordinary politicians who just wanted to keep getting elected and did not want to rock the boat. Foolishly, the Premier made Pat McGeer a Cabinet Member -- not a very shrewd political move, but it would have been foolhardy to leave him out of the Cabinet.

Stick It in Your Ear, McGeer!

Pat McGeer was given the chore of overseeing the Insurance Corporation of British Columbia, a Crown Corporation set up by the previous socialist government responsible for insuring motorists and truckers in the province. It was the kind of job, McGeer felt, that was more of a punishment than a reward. The corporation was deep in the red when he took it over.

McGeer decided that to make this beast behave, he had to increase the premiums, a political no-no. As was to be expected, there was a great howl accompanied by protest marches, bumper stickers and calls for his resignation. When met by angry motorists protesting the higher rates, McGeer told them, "If people can't afford the insurance they should sell their car." This statement was not diplomatic and it caused the government a lot of headaches. One of the bumper stickers protesting McGeer's actions read, "Stick It in Your Ear, McGeer."

The Open Learning Institute

The Open Learning Institute was put in place by Pat McGeer during his term in government. The idea was to allow post-secondary education and the obtaining of a degree for people who could not attend university or college because of their location or because they could not afford to attend. British Columbia is a huge province, bigger than Washington, Oregon and California combined, making it next to impossible for many to attend post-secondary schools. People who were older and might feel out of place, or who lived in Horsefly or other such remote regions, could now get a university degree. McGeer had his detractors, as the university people wanted to keep degree granting a closed shop. They wanted to control this new Open Learning Institute through their system, which would have required more staff and money.

Despite bitter opposition, the Open Learning Institute is now flourishing, having more individuals registered than any university in British Columbia. It offers programs and has graduated many people. The Institute was also the first in North America to grant university degrees. Pat also originated the Knowledge Network, a television educational channel which works in conjunction with the Open Learning Institute. McGeer pushed through the Knowledge Network without asking or telling the government. He just took the funds out of his Ministry budget and put it in place. Knowing his Knowledge Network would be opposed by the academics and the bureaucrats, Pat just went ahead and created it. We feel sure old George Bernard Shaw would have approved.

A Bridge Much Too Far!

While he was a cabinet minister in the Government of British Columbia, Patrick McGeer came up with the proposal that the government should build a bridge which would link the Vancouver area of British Columbia with Vancouver Island, where the Provincial Legislature is located. The ferry costs about twenty-five dollars for one car and one driver each way. At the time of McGeer's proposal there was a strike taking place against the B.C. Ferry Corporation, which operates the ferry service. Since the ferries are the only link between the mainland and Vancouver Island they are more or less a continuation of the highway system.

"The bridge will be built," Pat McGeer says. Knowing his determination, we are sure it will. It would be like an enlarged version of the bridges that cross Okanagan Lake in British Columbia or Lake Washington in Seattle. The Gulf of Georgia, which the bridge would cross, is like a salt water lake in that it is almost totally ringed by islands. Therefore, it is a protected waterway and not like an ocean. The distance from the Vancouver area to Vancouver Island is twelve miles.

"It's technically very straightforward," says Pat with a straight face. "You would need to build an artificial island and a tunnel to connect to the artificial island. The tunnel would allow ships to pass overhead and then you would have just a twenty minute crossing from the mainland to Vancouver Island. It now takes an hour-and-a-half to get across on the ferry. The benefits are huge," Pat says. "The bridge would pay for itself in no time."

McGeer's idea for a bridge was vigorously opposed by the B.C. Ferry Corporation and by the Highways Department, but so was just about every new idea Pat McGeer proposed while in government. Fearing that the vested interests in the government would suppress his report on the feasibility of the bridge, Pat donated it to the public library, making it a public document available to anybody who wants to see it. Pat also has a copy in his office. It was the only thing he took with him when he quit politics.

Uncle Gerry McGeer

While Pat McGeer had a fairly turbulent time while in politics, there were the odd times when some humor crept in, like the time when he was leader of the Liberal Party, campaigning in Trail, a mining town in southeastern British Columbia. The publisher of the local paper, a fairly influential man in the town, said to him, "I could never stand you McGeers." Pat's Uncle Gerry had also been a politician and was mayor of Vancouver at one time.

"I said to this man," says Pat, "Uncle Gerry was controversial I know, but he has been dead for a long time."

The publisher answered, "It wasn't Gerry McGeer at all, it was your grandfather I couldn't stand!"

While still on the campaign trail, Pat ran into a "non-believer" in the town of Oliver in British Columbia who was also mad at him. Pat was asked, "Was Gerry McGeer your uncle?" Pat rather hesitantly acknowledged the dreadful truth. "Well," says this man in a rather truculent voice, "His dog bit me once." Another lost vote for the Liberals!

Uncle Gerry, the cause of much delight and some discomfiture for Pat on the campaign trail, was a combination maverick and visionary (a wee bit like Pat!). Gerry McGeer was disturbed about the poverty he saw all around him and was always trying to develop cures for the ills of the poor. One of his many proposals was that public housing should be built for them. Uncle Gerry also focused on the monetary system as it existed then, alleging that its failure caused the Great Depression. Like Pat after him, Gerry McGeer was wildly popular with the electorate and he became Mayor of Vancouver in 1935, in the depths of the Depression. Gerry McGeer took the fact that large numbers of people were out of work as a personal affront and he decided to do something about it. He made speeches telling the people that what Vancouver needed was a new city hall. Everybody looked at him strangely; there was no money for food, let alone a city hall. However, he was successful in getting the go ahead from the provincial government, but it had no money to give him for his new city hall. He went ahead anyway, scrounging money wherever he could. Then he came up with the idea of selling Baby Bonds. He hawked them all around the business sectors, the merchants and the professions, strong arming and shaming them until he had enough money. He built his city hall, which is still being used today. Gerry was happy, the people got work and his stock continued to rise.

He was later elected to federal office, serving two terms and in 1945 he was appointed to the Senate. Gerry McGeer died in 1946.

Coming to Canada

Pat McGeer's grandfather, Jim McGeer, left County Wicklow to work at the *Manchester Guardian* newspaper in Manchester, England. The family had a farm in Wicklow and as was the custom, the eldest son inherited the farm. Jim moved to Manchester and while working at the *Guardian,* he met a County Cork girl, Emily Cook, who also worked at the *Guardian.* They married, had two children and then they immigrated to Canada, settling in Winnipeg where Uncle Gerry McGeer was born. From Winnipeg they moved to Langley in British Columbia, a suburb of Vancouver and later they moved into Vancouver, where Pat's father, named Jim like his father, was born. Pat's father grew up to become a lawyer and was later made a judge. All the McGeers who came over from Winnipeg, except Aunt Timmie, who is getting on for ninety-six, have passed away.

Pat McGeer married his wife, Edie Graef, while at du Pont. Edie had her Ph.D. by the time she was twenty-two. Pat McGeer was known at du Pont as the guy who stole Edie Graef -- one of du Pont's most prized scientists. Pat and Edie have three offspring, all of whom have Ph.Ds. Rick, the eldest, is a computer scientist at the University of California at Berkeley. Brian Theodore (Tad) is an aeronautical engineer. He owns a company which is developing small robot aircraft. These robot planes will be used for flights out over the oceans to record and transmit me-

119

teorological information. Daughter Victoria is a philosopher and is on the faculty of Vanderbilt University.

The Fight Against Alzheimer's Disease

Dr. Pat McGeer and his wife Edie are both specialists in the chemistry of the human brain, each having some thirty-five years of experience working in that area of medicine. Both are chemists and both have good exposure to clinical medicine. Pat was able to continue with his scientific work and also spend time with politics because he had married, as he puts it, "someone who was smarter than me."

Since their partnership, they have published over three hundred scientific papers and have written a book on the brain, *Molecular Neurobiology of the Brain.* "The day I left politics," says Dr. Pat McGeer, "was the most exciting scientific day for my wife and myself. That was the first time we saw, in human brain tissue, the evidence of an inflammatory response taking place in a victim of Alzheimer's disease. Over the years, we began to document more and more the assembly of these immune proteins in cases of Alzheimer's."

Explaining the whys and wherefores to a layman, Dr. McGeer went on: "Alzheimer's has very specific lesions which are characteristic of the disease. These were described by Dr. Alzheimer in his discussion of the disease. Alzheimer's is a disease of specific areas of the brain, affecting particularly the area which carries the short term memory. Previously, people did not recognize it for what it was; they called it 'senile dementia.' It was not known that Alzheimer's is an active malevolent disease which doubles in its incidence every five years after age sixty-five. We now know that by the time people are in their eighties, a very substantial proportion are coming down with this disorder. It is not just an aging problem as previously thought. We now believe a prevention exists and the project we are working on will arrest the disease. We cannot reverse Alzheimer's, but we can arrest it and by intervening very early in the disease process, we can prevent it from developing."

Dr. McGeer, his wife Edie and their partner, Dr. Joe Rogers of Sun City, Arizona, have experimented with "off patent" drugs, well known for their effectiveness in limiting auto-destruction in other peripheral diseases, such as rheumatoid arthritis. Clinical tests carried out by Dr. Rogers with these drug combinations have proven very effective in arresting the progression of Alzheimer's, leading the team to believe that this is the first ever successful treatment for this disease.

Larger clinical trials will be required to prove the efficacy of the treatment. In addition, Dr. McGeer believes there are a variety of possibilities based on inhibiting auto-destruction by the immune system that have yet to be tried in Alzheimer's disease, without learning anything more than is already known about the fundamental process. And as the research grows, new information will become available which will lead to better agents in the future. "People who believe they are vulnerable to Alzheimer's have a great deal to be relieved about," says Dr. McGeer.

Because Dr. McGeer and his colleagues are working on "off patent" drugs, they have been unable to interest established drug companies in funding their research. "Drug companies," Dr. McGeer says, "are interested in developing new drugs and only work in areas where they will have an exclusive patent."

To fund the continuing research, Dr. McGeer and his colleagues have set up Gerex Biotech Inc. The company is now working on additional clinical tests and other requirements to meet Food and Drug Agency (FDA) standards. Dr. McGeer and his wife have had to step outside their roles as scientists and become entrepreneurs to get the clinical tests funded so their product can become universally available. The product, when and if approved, is expected to be in tablet form.

Pat McGeer is as excited about his battle against Alzheimer's as he usually gets about all the ventures he undertakes and his voice takes on a new resonance as he exclaims, "My God, it's possible to do it. This work we are doing is going to make it possible for one-third of the people to be able to reach the biological wall -- one hundred years -- in good mental shape."

Pat McGeer was one of a select group of Canadians asked to submit suggestions for a paper on how to fix Canada's economic ills. He wrote that he would provide First World economic leadership by creating a high technology industrial sector competitive with those of the United States and Japan. Industrial research, he believes, is the essential forerunner of such development. He cites the difference between Canada and Japan, noting that unlike Canada, Japan has almost no natural resources. Japan has proven that industrial scientists are a much more valuable asset to a nation than resources. He says that Canada has too few people inventing and developing goods in relation to the number of people available to manufacture and sell them. He concluded with the following: "I believe that Canadians would be willing to carry this tradition onward by making the small sacrifices for the decade it would take to put Canadian science on its feet. A national political leader has an unequaled opportunity to explain such a program to the public and thereby gain their support. The stakes are too high to ignore the challenge."

Methane -- Fuel for the Future

Dr. McGeer edited the book *Methane -- Fuel for the Future* with Enoch Durbin of Princeton University. Biomass conversion for energy and fuels is another one of Dr. McGeer's sensible proposals. He finds it unacceptable that a few small countries in the Middle East should be able to control the commercial life of most of the world, especially when just a very few privileged individuals in those oil rich countries reap all the benefits from a freak of nature.

Dr. Patrick McGeer and his wife and lifelong colleague, Dr. Edith McGeer, in their University of British Columbia research laboratory.

Patrick Reid
Canada's Goodwill Ambassador

Patrick Reid now and then takes a nostalgic trip to the dear old Donegal farm where he spent his childhood. The farm, which was his grandfather's, is now run by cousins. It was at his grandfather's farm that he learned to ride and from there he went off to war, serving in the North Irish Horse regiment in World War II. During active service in Italy, in support of the First Canadian Division, Patrick Reid was twice wounded in action. He won the Military Cross during the fighting in Northern Italy.

The Irish Horse is one of those venerable regiments. The very name conjures up visions of the Bengal Lancers and the Charge of the Light Brigade. Patrick Reid tells us that in the early years of the Irish Horse, one had to bring his own battle steed and a recommendation from his clergyman to join this regiment. Giving way to modern warfare, the Irish Horse became an armored regiment.

Patrick Reid was born in Belfast, Northern Ireland, where his Dad was a member of the Royal Ulster Constabulary (RUC). Members of the RUC were moved around regularly so Patrick spent his formative years on his grandfather's farm.

His grandfather was a horseman all his life and was still riding well into his nineties. He used to get on his horse by walking him up a bit of a hill and gently climbing into the saddle. One day, he misjudged an obstacle and fell off his horse and broke his collarbone. The doctor told him that he would never ride again. On hearing this terrible news, his grandfather decided there was nothing left to live for, so he just faded away. He was ninety-three.

When the war in Europe ended, Patrick volunteered for service in the Far East. To get in on the invasion of Japan, he transferred to the Provost Corps (Military Police). With the end of the war, there was chaos everywhere. The Indian Army was being sent home and all the veterans were being demobilized. Things in Southeast Asia were getting hectic, so Patrick, at the tender age of twenty, was placed in charge of over one hundred men, all of them more or less green recruits, to police Singapore.

Once he had more or less gotten Singapore under control, things started to get hectic in Malaya, so Patrick was posted to Kuala Lumpur and made Assistant Provost Marshall for Malaya Command. He remained in Malaya until 1948, then he joined the King's Hussars.

Operation Mainbrace

In the era leading up to the Cold War, Patrick Reid was seconded as a staff officer to Allied Forces Northern Europe -- this was at the start of the formation of the North Atlantic Treaty Organization (NATO). As part of its show of strength, NATO organized a massive war games effort, the biggest combined operations since the war. The exercise was given the name Operation Mainbrace.

Patrick's job was to wander around unobtrusively through Northern Scandinavia to see what the Soviets might be able to do in wartime. The Germans, who had been expecting an invasion in 1945 from the Murmansk area, had installed an extensive defense system against such an attack. Patrick was to gather the intelligence and help write an exercise for the NATO commanders. This consisted of working out a program of air support for land forces in the event of a confrontation with Russia.

Operation Mainbrace ended in chaos. Most nations in Europe participated with ships, aircraft carriers and aircraft. Apart from the language confusion, as the planes did their sorties, a "ruddy great storm" blew up and the planes could not find the right carriers, or any carriers, to land. Patrick found himself blamed for the shambles and even for the storm which had caused the problems.

After Norway, Patrick was sent to the Canadian Army Staff College in Kingston, Ontario. The Army had great plans for him and wanted to sharpen up his military skills. On getting a taste of Canadian life, Patrick wanted out of the forces, deciding there was a better life to be had outside the Army. His first efforts ran into the usual red tape. They told him that he had to serve five years after being at a staff college, which somewhat stunned him. However, Patrick was a bit of a barracks-room lawyer, so he researched the Army Council Instruction Manual and, to his surprise and delight, found that for some unknown reason, Kingston was the only Army Staff College which was not listed as requiring the five year stint, so he became a civilian.

An Immigrant in Canada

After leaving the Army, Patrick Reid made his way to Ottawa where he ran into Budge Crawley. Budge made motion pictures and television commercials and to Pat's great surprise, Budge hired him. Patrick believes that he, and a young lady by the name of Betty Zimmerman, made the first television commercials ever made in Canada. "They were bloody awful," Patrick recalls. "We made commercials for O'Keefe Ale and for Joe Feller's, a men's outfitter, that are best not remembered."

It was a fairly poor mouth operation in those days. There was only one glass of beer for the commercial and as the takes went on and on the beer got depleted and flatter and flatter. To give the beer the kind of head beer advertisers like to see, they had to keep topping up the glass with soap flakes. "Try drinking that after the third or fourth take," Pat recalled with a grimace.

Bud Crawley made films for industry and various government agencies. Patrick Reid, a man with an impressive presence, was given the job of crossing the continent, lauding Canada as a great tourist destination. He was also sent back to Ireland on occasion.

Mickey O'Brien and Politics

On one of his trips to British Columbia, Patrick met Michael J. (Mickey) O'Brien. Mickey's company, O'Brien Advertising, made its money from big commercial accounts such as B. C. Telephone Company. Mickey also handled the advertising for the Conservatives. In much the same way that Timothy Eaton (owner of the T. Eaton department store chain) would give anybody from Ballymena work, Mickey O'Brien would give an Irishman first preference when a job came up.

In 1956, Patrick went into the advertising business. Being your average Irishman, new in the country, Patrick knew little about Canadian politics. There were Conservatives, Liberals and CCF. Patrick suddenly found himself doing the promotion for the

Conservatives. This was the first Diefenbaker campaign, and the party did reasonably well. Patrick was getting quite enthused, although he still knew very little about Canadian politics.

Patrick was the man who gave out the ads to the media. He would get calls from various parts of the hinterland with a voice saying, "We've got a back page which would be just great for you," and he would say in his best professional promotional voice, "Run it." After the 1958 election was over, Mickey O'Brien invited Patrick into his office and greeted him with the news that he had over-spent the budget by $50,000 and that he would have to work off the debt by doing volunteer political campaigning.

Not long after, a provincial election was called and Patrick Reid was talked into running as a Conservative candidate for the Vancouver Center Riding. This was a dual riding, which meant that the riding would elect two members because of its population base. His running mate was Larry Echhardt. This was during the period when W.A.C. (Wacky) Bennett owned British Columbia politics. His party had been in power for about twenty years and he had eliminated everyone who ran against him.

Conservatives in British Columbia were a scarce breed, but Patrick Reid was a most popular fellow. He had over 600 volunteers working for him and everybody involved was all fired up about his prospects of winning. They had a great campaign. It was all high spirits and *esprit de corps*, with Patrick hawking his baby daughter around with a big sign hung on her, "Vote For My Daddy." Alas, when the votes were counted, Patrick lost. He did not lose his deposit, Patrick remembers, "But it was close. I knew something was wrong when I didn't get as many votes as I had volunteers." On election day it became clear that disaster was looming. Wacky Bennett, in his usual hell and brimstone voice, was telling everyone, "If you vote for a Conservative you will be splitting the vote." Patrick came in third or fourth, but what it did was get politics out of his and Mickey O'Brien's blood forever. He never did earn back Mickey's fifty thousand dollars.

Adventures in the Nature of Trade Shows

Forced now to earn an honest living, Patrick became interested in the trade show business. He was hired to sell sashless windows and folding doors throughout North America. On a trip to Newfoundland to select a distributor, Patrick encountered two brothers decked out in bowler hats and spats and as alike as two peas in a pod. During the discussion about the distributorship, the brothers took turns leaving the room. One would go off somewhere and as soon as he reappeared, the other one would leave. Patrick had assumed they were attending to business, but it turned out, as they later told him, they were having a nip of "screech," a very strong Newfoundland drink. They were suspicious of Patrick, an outsider and a "comeover," but by lunch time they were all bosom pals and all well lubricated.

Patrick went to exhibitions in the United States for his sash and door company. While he was in the United States, he discovered there was a competition, run by the Canadian government, for "Assistant Director of the Canadian Government Exhibition Commission." Patrick applied and got the job. That was the start of his extensive trade-show career, which culminated with the amazing success of Expo '86 held in Vancouver in the summer of 1986, which saw twenty-two million visitors descending on Vancouver.

In the Spring of 1962, Patrick ended up in Ottawa heading up a commission responsible for all Canadian federal government exhibitions, trade shows, cultural shows and promotions worldwide. Within a year Patrick was faced with some awesome decisions. The Canadian centennial was starting to gear up and Expo '67 was slated for Montreal. There were things happening in Poland, in the Soviet Union and many other places. Patrick's job was to give Canada the best exposure possible in all places. He had a budget of ten million dollars.

This job gave Patrick Reid a unique understanding of Canada from coast to coast and how the country was regarded by the various nations of the world. It instilled in him a desire to keep Canada great and to do whatever he could to see that the country prospered. His job also made him passably bilingual, as he had to operate in French from time to time.

There was a plethora of world exhibitions taking place. Every country was being represented by a Commissioner General, so Patrick Reid was boosted to Commissioner General for these events. By the time he had finished his stint with the world fairs, he had become Commissioner General seven times, which meant going off somewhere for six months at a time, representing Canada abroad.

Canada celebrated its centennial as a country in 1967 and Patrick Reid was heavily involved in this event. In the middle of the centennial celebrations, he got word that there was to be a world exhibition in Osaka, Japan in 1970. The competition for the position of Commissioner General, who would chair Canada's entry in the fair, was fairly strong. Judy LeMarsh, Secretary of State and two ex-ambassadors were in the running. The Minister of Public Works at the time was Arthur Lang and he wanted his department to take control of the Canadian entry in Osaka. He had considerable links with Japan and he wanted to strengthen them. Some backroom shenanigans then went on and Patrick Reid's department was transferred from the Department of Trade and Commerce to Public Works. Patrick did not like this one little bit and he went to his friend, Jean Luc Pepin, the Minister of Trade and Commerce. The outcome was that Patrick Reid was made the Commissioner General for the Osaka event.

Osaka, for Canada, was an incredible success and it was all due to the legwork done by Patrick Reid and his advance team. More people went through the Canadian pavilion than the whole population of Canada (about twenty-seven million). Explaining its success, Patrick Reid said, "We took a delegation to Japan six months ahead of the World Fair and traveled all around the country, all through the forty-three Prefectures. We had the RCMP in their dress uniforms, Canadian singers and a little Canadian schoolbus in psychedelic colors.

"We would set up shop in the schools, on a Saturday usually, and have about one thousand Japanese school children attend. At first it seemed a formidable task to get those well disciplined kids to break down and accept these crazy Canadians. Our first *faux pas* was to have an occidental, who spoke fluent and flawless Japanese, talk to the kids. They just would not believe the person standing in front of them was actually doing the speaking. They kept looking behind for the microphone, or the wires. They were so convinced this was some kind of trick, their response was dead silence. Their attitude seemed to be, "how is this happening?"

To overcome this obstacle, Patrick Reid produced a French-Canadian who spoke very fractured and funny Japanese. As soon as the kids heard his atrocious Japanese, they knew it was for real and the ice was broken. Discovering that the Japanese were taught, as part of their English lessons, "Michael Row the Boat Ashore," Patrick had a Canadian singer start them singing, "Row, Row, Row Your Boat." "Soon," says Patrick, "Everyone was joining in and having a great time, to the disgust of the very strict teachers who feared their discipline was breaking down."

At the start of the tour of Japan a survey had been commissioned asking the Japanese public, "If you did not live in Japan, what country would you most like to live in?" Switzerland came first in the survey and Korea was at the bottom. Canada was not even mentioned. Knowing that Canada would have fierce competition from the Soviet Union, the United States and sixty other countries, Patrick Reid toured Japan to get his message out. By the time the fair opened, Canada had captured the media all around Japan, which nobody else had done. It became a must for Japanese visitors to tour the Canadian pavilion. They had heard so much about Canada, the Canadian pavilion became the most popular pavilion in the whole show. Since then, Canadian pavilions have been most successful in all world fairs, as a result of the format for promoting Canada started by Patrick Reid.

At the end of the exhibition in Japan, a follow-up survey was conducted asking the Japanese which country they would like to go to if they were not going to stay in Japan. Right at the top of the list was Canada.

After Expo '70 in Osaka, Patrick Reid was earmarked to head Canada's participation in the world exhibition which was to be held in Philadelphia in 1976 to celebrate the bicentennial of the United States of America. He was to undertake the 1976 Expo and then represent Canada in a diplomatic role. Richard Nixon, who was president at the time, decided at the last minute not to put everything in Philadelphia (he was looking to get re-elected), but to spread the celebrations all over the United States. That killed the 1976 world fair for Philadelphia.

Patrick Reid went on to become Director General of Public Affairs in Ottawa, spreading the good word about Canada to the world. He established and ran a well-funded Bureau of Public Affairs. From 1972 to 1978, he was the Canadian delegate to the International Bureau of Exhibitions in Paris. He was also elected President of the International Bureau of Exhibitions. This office controlled the frequency and nature of world exhibitions. After completing his term at Public Affairs in 1978, Patrick was posted to London as the Minister in charge of Canada House, while retaining the job as President of the International Exhibition Bureau. He was the first non-European to hold the post and his was the first international nomination jointly sponsored by the United States and the Soviet Union.

During his London sojourn, Grace McCarthy, a livewire who was the Minister of Tourism for British Columbia, paid a visit to London. Patrick was told that she was not very happy as Canada House was not doing enough for British Columbia tourism. To try to mollify Grace, Patrick decided to take her to lunch at the Cavalry Club, a fairly old-fashioned place where women were not allowed to enter by the main staircase. Patrick spirited her up the back elevator and into the dining room.

During lunch it turned out that what Grace really wanted was to do something for Vancouver for 1986. "What about a world exhibition in Vancouver for 1986?" she asked. "I think I went white," said Patrick, "because just a little while previously we had tacitly agreed that Japan could have a world exhibition in 1986." He tried to skate around the issue, as he could see himself getting into a terrible conflict of interest, as he was in charge of the International Bureau of Exhibitions.

He advised Grace to go back home and persuade the Premier of British Columbia and the Prime Minister of Canada (Pierre Elliot Trudeau) that they wanted to have this world exhibition. Patrick expected Trudeau to say that British Columbia would have to raise the money for it. The federal government would not be in the mood to back another world exhibition after the huge cost overruns at Montreal's Expo '67 and the Olympics, which were still being paid for by the taxpayers. Grace said, "I'll do it!"

Within two weeks she had managed to get the government of British Columbia to back her idea. It so happened that the Japanese, for once in their lives, were asleep at the switch. With a little help from their friends, the Canadians turned up with a first class presentation for a world exposition for 1986. After a lot of palaver with the authorizing bodies and some scathing looks from the Japanese delegate, British Columbia was given the green light. However, the Japanese were determined to get back into the game and with some wheeling and dealing, got a world fair in 1985.

Patrick Reid felt that running the Vancouver Expo '86 would be a great way to close out his public service career. He was in his late fifties at the time and he had been on the go since his teens, in most of the active areas of the world. He had been promised an ambassadorial post, so it was a tough choice between the ambassador's post and Expo. In the end, Expo won out and Patrick was made Ambassador and Commissioner General for Expo '86.

Despite the fact that the Government of Canada was not prepared to fund Expo (it later paid for the Canada Place Convention Center and cruise ship dock), Expo '86 was the best specialized world exhibition ever held. It attracted over twenty-two million visitors and fifty-seven countries had pavilions on the site. From opening day in April to the closing in October, hardly a drop of rain fell to spoil Patrick Reid's glorious show. The whole world seemed to pass through Vancouver that summer. At the closing ceremonies on the last day of the fair, Patrick Reid concluded his closing speech with an old Irish blessing:

> May the road rise up to meet you,
> May the wind be always at your back,
> May the sun shine warm upon your face,
> And the rains fall soft upon your fields,
> And until we meet again,
> May God hold you in the palm of His hand.

This was a most stirring and fitting climax to a sensational fair.

After surviving Expo, Patrick was looking for his ambassadorial reward in Europe, but it was not to be. There was a change of Prime Ministers and it was political payoff time. The post was given to a party member. He went to San Francisco as Consul General instead. Shortly after, he became an officer in the Order of Canada.

Designing the Canadian Flag

While still involved in his trade show activities, Patrick Reid got a call from Prime Minister Lester Pearson's office asking for help in completing the design of a new Canadian flag. At that time, Canada's flag was a variation of England's Union Jack and there was a feeling that Canada should have its own distinctive flag.

Patrick Reid was called upon because someone in the Prime Minister's office recalled that old axiom, "If you want something done get a busy man to do it," and Pat Reid was a busy man. Also, there was bound to be all kinds of controversy over the new flag and Patrick, used to controversy, was given the job. The instructions on completing the new flag were fairly terse: "Do something, we must have a flag in some kind of form by February." This was in January. When stuck for an idea, Patrick called on his wife and they worked out the basic criteria.

His wife said that the flag should be the same on both sides. Patrick, who knew little about design, heartily agreed. They were now at first base. The second criteria was that it had to be simple enough that a child could draw it. The third criteria was that it had to be heraldically correct. With the parameters established, they called in Jacques St. Cyr, a designer on Patrick's staff. He came up with a thirteen-point maple leaf. Judge Mathieson (who was then a Member of Parliament and representing Prime Minister Pearson) and Patrick held the design up to study it. Patrick was bothered by the thirteen points. He said it was too busy. He suggested that eleven points would be just right and everyone agreed.

The flag was now ready for its first airing. This was to be at the Prime Minister's house and Ken Donavan, an Ottawa Valley Irishman employed in Patrick's department, volunteered his daughter Molly to sew up the hems of the flag. When this was done, Ken Donavan was given the job of raising Canada's new flag on the flagpole outside the Prime Minister's residence. Ken carried the new flag in his battered old van. When he got to the Prime Minister's house, the Mounties would not let him enter. After a few telephone calls, he was finally allowed to put the flag in place for the Prime Minister to view the first thing next morning.

However, there was a little gremlin problem. Patrick Reid, dog tired after the long debate on the flag, had given the wrong color code and the new orange Canadian flag was waving bravely in the Ottawa breeze instead of the bright red one it was supposed to be. It took a few days to get the flag remade in the proper color. So for the history buffs, we can say that Canada's national flag was put together with the help of a couple of Irishmen and an Irish colleen.

The Rick Hansen Tour

Amanda, Patrick Reid's only daughter, is married to Rick Hansen, the disabled wheelchair athlete who stunned everybody by first declaring, and then completing, a trip around the world in a wheelchair.

Some time in 1984, during the build-up to Expo '86, Rick Hansen and some of his entourage came into Patrick Reid's office in Vancouver. Rick wanted Expo to sponsor him on his proposed World Tour to promote Expo '86. "I thought he was out of his mind, quite frankly," remembers Patrick. "He had this dream and he wanted us to pay for it."

Amanda Reid, a physiotherapist at the G. F. Strong Rehabilitation Center in Vancouver, which specializes in sports injuries, met Rick Hansen after he had fallen out of his wheelchair while participating in a marathon race. He ended up at G. F. Strong and asked for a pretty physiotherapist. Amanda fitted the bill and over the course of his treatment, she got to know about the world tour he was proposing to her Dad. In an effort to bring them together, she invited Rick to the house. The doorbell rang, Patrick opened the door and "here was this guy in a wheelchair at the top of the steps." There were five or six big steps down to ground level. Patrick said, "How the hell did you get up here?"

"I got up here the same way I'm going to go around the world," Rick responded to Patrick.

Patrick became involved, but he was not prepared to provide financing as far as Expo '86 was concerned. With a little help from Patrick's friends, Rick Hansen's tour took off from Vancouver, with their van packed high with gear. The first overpass they came to, the gear on the top of the van hit the overpass and everything was strewn all over the highway. Patrick wondered, "How is this lad ever going to get to the Mexican border?"

Patrick continued his story, "They had passed through Washington State, going into Oregon when Amanda comes home from work and says to her mother and me, 'I have to go down and see what these people are doing because Rick has sores.'

"We said fine, after all, she was a grown woman. Amanda went down and patched him up as best she could and came back. Then she says, "I think I had better go with him; they have problems.' Amanda took a leave of absence and two weeks later she joined the tour."

Rick Hansen has said that Amanda was important to the eventual success of the venture and Patrick Reid says he believes the tour would never have been completed without her along. "We'd get phone calls," says Patrick, "from all sorts of unbelievable places, collect of course. For me it was the most expensive world tour I have never undertaken! One time she phoned from some place in France, outside Paris. She said, 'We're here and we're not quite sure where we're going and even if we are going to be fed.'

"However, one way or another they survived. Having my only daughter along was tough enough to bear, and then my son, Michael, joined the tour in New Zealand. He had just finished university. He became cook, bottle washer and what have you and eventually he took charge of security. This experience was to prove valuable to Michael. He now has his own security business in Vancouver.

"On one glorious occasion, when they were in Tokyo, Michael phoned us in Vancouver to ask where his hotel was located, in Tokyo -- a collect call! He was out and about in Tokyo and he forgot where his hotel was located. Fortunately, we knew."

In Japan, for the most part, it is difficult for the disabled to get out and about, so they remain hidden away. The reverse was true in China. However, when the news of Rick Hansen's wheelchair tour got out, the disabled in China and even in Japan joined them.

Amanda's hardiness stood her in good stead. She survived the two-year trip without any serious ill effects, unless falling in love with Rick Hansen could be classed in that category. They married after the world tour and have given Patrick Reid two granddaughters.

The trip raised nearly twenty million dollars for research on spinal disorders. Before the tour was over, there were beneficial spin-offs from the publicity. A four-wheeled wheel chair for use in the snow was developed with sensors that would alert the wheelchair user if they were getting frost bitten -- the users have no feelings in their limbs. The research end is progressing. One of the discoveries is that if a person gets medical treatment in the early stages of being disabled, the permanent damage can be minimized.

Amanda and Rick Hansen now have their own business and Rick does a lot of motivational speaking.

Running Vancouver Port Corporation

At sixty-eight, with a lifetime of achievement behind him, Patrick is running the Vancouver Port Corporation and again fighting the good fight against red tape and naysayers as he battles to get his container port on stream at Roberts Bank Superport outside Vancouver.

The Vancouver Port Corporation has twenty-eight terminals in the Greater Vancouver area, handling billions of dollars of cargo each year. An enormous amount of Vancouver Port business is with the Orient and Patrick Reid spends more time in China these days than anywhere else. He gets positively high when he talks about the opportunities in China.

His current obsession is to help keep Canada's transportation system competitive in today's very rapidly changing world. Patrick calls it the Maple Leaf Route and he is selling the idea that it is more efficient to move cargo through Vancouver to any point in North America and on to Europe. He is trying to sell the Japanese, the Chinese and other Asian exporters and importers that Canada has a viable transportation system and can

136

deliver from their points of origin to markets in North America and Europe.

Being the ultimate trade promoter for Canada, there seems little doubt that he will be successful. Patrick is part diplomacy sprinkled with a great dollop of blarney and an even greater share of experience and ability. This is the kind of man Ireland could have used to good advantage.

Patrick's Sense of Humor

"At one of those official functions I attended during my time as Trade Commissioner for Canada, I got into a discussion with a group of Danes, Norwegians, Swedes and Icelanders over who got to North America first. I tried to convince them that it was the Irish who had arrived in Canada around 935 A.D.

"Asked what I had to support this statement, I had to reply that I had no hard evidence, but I just knew it was so.

"The President of Iceland was one of those I was trying to convince. When she got up to speak to the crowd attending the function, she very sweetly acknowledged my point, telling those gathered there, 'I think I'll concede that the Irish were first in North America. When our people arrived off the shores of North America, we had, of course, some Irish slaves with us that we had picked up on the way over. We chucked them ashore first to see what would happen to them. When they survived, the rest of us came ashore. So Patrick is right -- the Irish were there first.' "

Patrick Reid in his capacity as Chairman of the Vancouver Port Authority presents Russian President Boris Yeltsin with an Indian Peace Stick during the Clinton-Yeltsin Summit held in Vancouver in 1993. (Below) Patrick pictured as a youngster in Donegal with his father and sister in the pony and trap.

Captain Patrick Reid in full regimental regalia. Patrick served during World War II and was decorated during the Italian Campaign. After the end of the European war, he served in the Military Police in Singapore and Malaya. He quit the army to move to Canada. He is still an honorary Captain in the Canadian Navy.

Bernard E. DeLury
Master Conciliator

"**I** wish my father could have been there, God rest his soul, Bernie DeLury mused. He was talking about his installation as the twelfth National Director of the Federal Mediation and Conciliation Service (FMCS) on March 30, 1990. With his wife, Jane, holding the family Bible and surrounded by family, friends and associates, the new FMCS National Director placed his left hand on the Bible, raised his right hand and repeated the oath of office administered by his older brother, the Honorable John DeLury, Judge of the Supreme Court of the State of New York. Also among those present at the swearing-in ceremony was Ireland's Ambassador to the United States, Padraic McKernan.

The agency Bernie DeLury was nominated by President Bush to administer was created in 1947 as an independent agency of the United States federal government to mediate and resolve matters involving labor-management disputes in the United States. Its work is entirely reliant on the services of its mediators who serve as third party neutrals in assisting management and labor in developing solutions whenever problems arise.

Growing Up in Brooklyn

Bernie was born in Brooklyn, New York on April 1, 1938 to John Joseph Aloysius DeLury and Margaret Theresa Donnelly. As Bernie tells the story, "My brother and I were born at the Brooklyn Hospital, next door to the Raymond Street jail. We didn't cost a lot of money to be born because our folks didn't have a lot of money in those depression days. We lived on Cumberland Street. I think part of Cumberland Street is still there but most of it has been replaced by housing projects."

The DeLurys moved from there to St. Alban's in Queen's County where Bernie went to St. Pascal Baylon Grade School for eight years with the Sisters of St. Joseph. He then attended St. John's Preparatory School run by the Vincentians in Brooklyn for two and a half years and finished his final year at Delahanty High School in Jamaica, Queens.

After completing high school, Bernie went on to St. John's University in Queens, receiving a Bachelor of Arts degree in Social Science. He pursued a post-graduate degree taking night courses at C.W. Post College, which is part of Long Island University at Green Vale, Long Island, where he earned a Master of Arts in Sociology.

Bernie joined the New York State National Guard Army Reserve in 1956 when he was eighteen and served seven years until his discharge in 1963 -- with the rank of Corporal. Bernie married Jane Frances Sheldon (whose mother was from County Longford) in 1959. His first job after he got married was as a wire lather, more easily recognizable as an iron worker. According to Bernie, "I got a union permit to work from Local 46 of the old Wood, Wire and Metallic Lathers' Union. I always liked construction work. I was good with my hands. At the same time, I was going to university at night.

"Jane's father was a member of Local 46; he spent fifty-five years on reinforcing steel. My first permit job was a summer job as a laborer in 1957 on the subway. In 1959 I received a permit to work on the construction of the Indian Point Power House. It was the first nuclear power house built in the country. I worked there from 1959 until 1962 putting steel in place -- steel walls, steel beams, steel decks and steel columns."

Bernie left construction work after a bad accident in 1965. It happened at the Belmont Race Track -- the vertical stage of the construction collapsed. "I went down forty-five feet with twelve tons of steel and walked away," Bernie remembers. "I was terribly lucky! My partner lost the tip of his ear. One of the fellows working on the ground had his leg crushed. Fortunately for him the leg was a wooden one! Believe it or not, none of us knew he had a wooden leg until the accident happened. We were taken to the hospital for x-rays and tetanus shots and then sent home." Six months later, however, Bernie had to go into St. Vincent's with some serious problems as a result of the accident.

The Road to Albany

Bernie DeLury, only twenty-seven at the time of his accident, began to think that maybe there was something else he should be doing with his life. He went to work for the New York State Labor Department as a safety inspector. Shortly thereafter he went political and worked for Nelson Rockefeller's campaign for state governor. When Rockefeller was elected, he appointed Bernie his Deputy Commissioner of Labor for the State of New York, where he served for six years.

During his term as commissioner, the New York State Assembly passed workplace safety legislation -- the New York Occupational Safety and Health Act. His Department conducted the first hearings on safety violations and drafted the regulations. It was also during Bernie's term as commissioner that Congress passed legislation establishing manpower training programs. While this law was passed at the Federal level, it was implemented at the State level. Funding came out of Washington to enable the States to train their people to administer the program. During that time, there was also the drive to promote equal opportunity in the workplace. As Bernie DeLury remembers, he "worked hard prevailing upon the National Alliance of Businessmen and its members to make equal opportunity a priority for all employees. It was also a crazy time when there were protests over the Vietnam War. And to make matters worse, my father went to jail for calling an illegal strike while I was commissioner."

His Father, John DeLury

Bernie greatly admired his father who passed away in 1980. "My dad wasn't a very tall man -- only about five and a half feet tall. He was stocky with a ruddy complexion and very quick witted."

John DeLury came from a family of thirteen children. He was a public employee with the New York Department of Water and Sewer. He dropped out of high school in the tenth grade in order to help support his family, taking a job as a messenger on Wall Street. For the next several years he worked at a variety of jobs before he decided on upgrading his schooling. "My mother often mentioned what it was like in those times," Bernie relates. "You had to shop around to find work and often you had to grease the boss's palm to get the job. There was corruption! My mother always knew when my dad got work -- he would come home dirty and change his clothes in the hallway before entering. When he didn't get work he would walk in without changing."

John DeLury figured that he had to make a move if he was going to improve his lot in life, so he enrolled in extension courses in labor relations and public speaking at St. John's College. In the midst of the Depression in 1935 he landed a job as a dump laborer with the New York City Bureau of Street Cleaning, later to become known as the Department of Sanitation, making about fifteen dollars a week. According to Bernie, "He worked at the various incinerators around the city. My mother had a picture of my dad working at a garbage incinerator wearing a belt with a chain locked to a spike. This was to prevent him from falling into the incinerator pit in case the fumes overcame him. That was an example of the City of New York workers' safety in the 1930s."

John DeLury soon started thinking about a union for the men working at the incinerator sites. With six fellow-workers, they formed the Uniformed Sanitation Men's Association and affiliated with the American Federation of State, County and Municipal Employees Association (AFSCME). Says Bernie, "It was a difficult time for the unions. The problems were many, such as getting some grievance machinery in place of the system of favoritism and pay-off for a day off. There were incidents of interference and intimidation. My father was a scrapper and he finally built the union into a cohesive 11,000 member organization. He pulled out of AFSCME in 1950 when he got a charter from the Teamsters to form Local 831." John DeLury not only founded the union, he also served as its president for forty-four continuous years, until his retirement in 1978.

John DeLury spent his entire adult life leading the struggle for a better life for his union's members and turning their aspirations for better working conditions and better benefits into realities. The test of his leadership and resolve came in 1968 when he challenged Mayor Lindsay of New York by calling an illegal strike for improved working conditions for his men at the Sanitation Department. The strike lasted eight days and garbage accumulated on the city streets. Mayor Lindsay charged that DeLury and his union were holding the city in bondage. The strike continued in violation of New York State law prohibiting public employee

143

strikes.   The city went into the courts and sought an injunction order to stop the strike. The union fought it with their County Mayo-born attorney, Paul O'Dwyer. The union lost and John DeLury was arrested for failing to obey the order.

Says Bernie, "My dad was sentenced to jail for thirty days and the union was fined $10,000 a day. The men still stayed out. Governor Rockefeller knew that the only way to end the strike was with a negotiated settlement, so he released my father from jail, under guard, to negotiate with the city representatives.

"Of course, Mayor Lindsay was quite upset with the Governor's decision, but eventually a settlement was reached. The union won many improvements in their working conditions. My dad was returned to jail to serve out his sentence and the union members returned to work. I believe my dad was the second New York union leader to go to jail for violating the State's anti-strike law.   Kerry-born Mike Quill, head of the Transport Workers' Union, was the other -- he was jailed in the sixties for calling out the transit employees.

"My dad was a colorful, outspoken union leader with a keen intelligence and a gift for negotiating. He was loved and re-spected by the members throughout his long career as president of the union. Between 1935, when he founded the union, and his retirement in 1978 he was opposed for reelection only twice. He never lost, which showed the respect and loyalty his members held for him."

Five years after his death, DeLury Plaza was dedicated at Fulton and Gold streets to commemorate a man who had dedi-cated much of his life fighting to improve the lot of his union members -- New York's refuse collectors. A replica of the horse-drawn water sprinkler wagons used to wet down the city's streets in the late eighteen-hundreds and an antique horse-drawn refuse cart used for hauling away ashes from the coal-fired heating sys-tems of the same period adorn the Plaza.

Mister DeLury Goes to Washington

When Richard Nixon was reelected President in 1972, he appointed Peter Brennan as his Secretary of Labor. Bernie DeLury knew Peter; he was also a construction worker and head of the

New York Building Trades. "Peter asked me if I would like to become Assistant Secretary of Labor for the Employment Standards Administration (ESA) and I said yes," Bernie relates. "I was confirmed by the Senate on April 10, 1973 and sworn in on May 10. I served in the post for three and a half years."

A lot of things happened during Bernie's stint as Assistant Secretary for ESA. Congress passed the Vocational Rehabilitation Act preventing discrimination against handicapped persons. Enforcement of this law was assigned to ESA where they wrote the regulations establishing guidelines for reasonable accommodation of handicapped workers in the workplace. There was great emphasis on equal opportunity at that time due to the passage of the Rehabilitation Act.

The Vietnam Veterans' Era Readjustment Act was passed at the same time and ESA was assigned enforcement responsibility. Then Nixon resigned under threat of impeachment and Gerald Ford became President. President Ford offered Peter Brennan the Ambassadorship to Ireland. He turned it down. He wasn't a wealthy man and he felt he would have had to supplement the ambassador's salary of $35,000 and $10,000 entertaining allowance out of his own pocket. Bernie describes his reaction, "I went to him and said, 'Peter, for God's sake you owe it to every Irishman and every Irish-American to take the job. You would be the first Irish-American Catholic in that job.' He thought about it long and hard and suffered over it, but his family was here and his wife may have been sick at the time -- she died not too long after that."

When Peter Brennan resigned in 1975, Bernie DeLury handed in his resignation to the incoming Secretary, John Dunlop. Dunlop handed it back to Bernie saying, "Do you think I'm crazy? I'm not going to let you go. Who else wants to do this bloody stuff"? John Dunlop resigned eleven months later following a dispute with President Ford over situs picketing legislation. President Ford had promised to sign the legislation which Secretary Dunlop had worked so hard to get through Congress. It was getting near election time and Ford was prevailed upon to veto the Bill. Dunlop was replaced as Secretary of Labor by Bill Usery. Bernie handed in his resignation again. Usery transferred him to the position of Assistant Secretary for Labor-Management Services Administration (LMSA) and Bernie served there until the Ford Administration was replaced by the Carter Administration. During Bernie's term, Congress passed the Employee Retirement Income Security Act protecting the retirement benefits of American workers. The administration and enforcement of this law was shared between LMSA and the Internal Revenue Service.

Farewell to Washington

The Carter Democratic Administration entered the Washington scene in early 1977. Bernie DeLury, a Republican appointee, was out of a government job. He returned to the private sector and joined SeaLand Services, Inc., the world's largest steamship company, as Director of Labor Relations. He was made Vice-President of Personnel in 1982 and Vice-President of Labor Relations 1989.

Washington Beckons Again

Thirteen years later, Bernie DeLury caught Potomac fever for the second time. Bush became President in 1989 and Bernie DeLury was nominated for the position of Director of the Federal Mediation and Conciliation Service. It was nearly a year later before the Senate finally confirmed his appointment. He was confirmed by the Senate at 8:00 p.m. on March 1, 1990 and at midnight the Amalgamated Transit Union called a nationwide strike against the Greyhound Corporation.

Bernie DeLury remembers, "I arrived at the office the next morning only to discover that President Bush hadn't signed my papers which would have placed me on the government payroll. He finally signed them on the 5th, which meant working three days without pay. That didn't concern me as much as getting the parties back to the bargaining table.

"I immediately set to work to contact the President of the Amalgamated Transit Union, Jim LaSalla, and Fred Currie of the Greyhound Corporation and invited them to meet with me. It became a very protracted and difficult process. That strike lasted three years before a settlement was finally reached. It was one of the most bitter strikes in United States labor history. Greyhound went into bankruptcy and restructured its organization. They did away with many routes. There were nine thousand employees when the strike started; employment had dropped to thirty-five hundred by the time the strike was settled."

Bernie talks about his job running the FMCS. "I am the twelfth Director since the agency was established in 1947. The FMCS has an honorable tradition and history. Its mission is to try to prevent strikes from happening and when they do happen to try to curtail them and also to promote good labor-management relations in the United States. We have over two hundred experienced mediators available throughout the country and we rely heavily on them.

"I get involved as National Director only when it is useful to do so. Sometimes the parties want the boss or sometimes the situation gets critical and we invite the parties involved to come to Washington, like we did with the *Pittsburgh Press* and *New York Daily News* strikes.

"I really enjoy mediation. I don't care whether your background is in management, labor, or academia, once you become a mediator you have taken on the roll of a neutral. You really become a peace keeper and an advocate for the process we call collective bargaining. You do your best to preserve and defend it and make it work for both sides -- for the benefit and profitability of management and likewise for the benefit and profitability of the employees."

Bernie DeLury points out that mediation can be a difficult task especially in times like the present, when it is difficult for both management and labor. "In October of 1990 there was a major work stoppage at the *New York Daily News* called by the Allied Printing Trades Council over the use of replacement workers and management rights. In November, I escalated mediation efforts by inviting representatives of the newspaper and the unions involved to Washington to resume negotiation efforts. Fortunately, subsequent events led to the newspaper being purchased by a new owner and a new agreement was reached which ended the dispute.

"The Caterpillar Company employees, represented by the United Auto Workers' Union, went on strike for seven months and we were involved in helping the parties end that strike. Fortunately, our mediation efforts were able to help resolve many collective bargaining disputes and prevent work stoppages.

"We assisted in a settlement at United Parcel Service, preventing the union for 160,000 employees from calling a strike. We also mediated settlements between American Telephone & Telegraph Company and 120,000 employees represented by the Communications Workers Union and the International Brotherhood of Electrical Workers."

Irish Roots

Both the DeLurys and the Donnellys are of Irish stock. Bernie's maternal grandfather, Bernard Donnelly, came from Dungannon, County Tyrone and his maternal grandmother, Mary Ellen O'Rouke, came from Kilfinnane, County Limerick. They settled in New York City and across the river in New Jersey, where his mother was born in 1902. His father's family, the DeLurys, came from County Cork

Bernie's father, John, was born in Irishtown, Brooklyn. Most of the immigrant Irish who didn't go to the West Side of Manhattan -- Hell's Kitchen -- had settled there and worked in the shipyards. "Many of my uncles lived there up until the time they died."

Bernie's parents left Brooklyn in 1940 and moved to the St. Alban's neighborhood of Queens close to Jamaica on Long Island. "They bought a little house there -- three bedrooms, a front porch and a garage at the back." Says Bernie, "The house cost them $4,000; it would have sold for $6,000 when it was built in 1928, that was before the depression."

The Family

Bernie and Jane have five children: Bernard, Kevin, John, Laura and Erin. Bernard is a lawyer at Bally's Casino in Atlantic City. He was an officer in the U.S. Navy and he is still in the reserves. He and his wife, Margaret, have one son, Bernard. Kevin works for the R.J. Reynolds Company in Indiana as a regional sales manager. He and his wife, Wendy, have two children, Kevin and Caitlan. Laura is a communications specialist and is working towards a teaching credential. John is a songwriter, singer, stage actor and part-time stage hand in Washington. Erin is a sophomore at Bishop O'Connell High School in Arlington, Virginia.

Bernie's only brother, John, is a New York State Supreme Court Judge. He is married to Alice Hannagan. They have one son, John Jr., a medical doctor.

Visiting Ireland

Both Bernie DeLury and his brother John have made nostalgic trips to Ireland. Bernie remembers his first visit there quite well. He was on his way back from attending a conference in Tunisia and stopped off in Ireland for a couple of nights. "I arrived in Dublin where I met with the United States Ambassador to Ireland. I rented a car and took off the next morning bright and early, driving on the left hand side of the road, to Limerick and Shannon Airport. I picked up about twenty hitchhikers along the way, got a good education and had a lovely time. I tried to locate some relatives in the short time I was there, but was unsuccessful. I looked for them in a place called O'Brien's Bridge down in County Limerick.

"There was this hitchhiker I picked up by the name of Joe Ryan, a young fellow, a nice guy and he told me he knew where there was a DeLury. He took me over to O'Brien's Bridge and we found this fellow who resembled my father's side of the family, but his name was DeLacy, not DeLury.

"They took me up a country road to watch the sun go down over the River Shannon. I looked down into the valley and saw a nice thatched cottage with smoke coming out of the chimney. Being a somewhat suspicious New Yorker, I was wondering to myself what in the hell am I doing out here in the middle of nowhere with these two Irish guys, both bigger than me. And I'm being very cautious and one of them said to me, 'Did you ever see a sight so beautiful in your life?' And I knew I was not standing in harm's way at all. Just two country guys, as poetic as any scholar you'd ever want to meet.

"I got on the plane next morning at Shannon. As it took off I was gazing out the window, enchanted by the patchwork of green fields below, when the stewardess came around serving tea and scones. She said to me, 'Is there anything wrong?' I had tears in my eyes and I don't know why. I was thinking that I had been there before and I was leaving home. It was an eerie feeling.

"I made two subsequent trips over to attend Longshoremen's conferences in Dublin. It was in the winter time and I was there about three or four days each trip. That was 1978 and 1980. I took my wife, Jane, with me in 1980. One of these days I'm going back again!"

Subsequent to this interview, Bernie DeLury resigned as Director of the FMCS on August 29, 1993 to accept the position of Labor Relations Vice President at AT&T in New Jersey. Accepting his resignation, President Clinton stated, "I appreciate your service to the Nation and your assistance during this recent period of transition."

Bernie DeLury being sworn in as the 12th director of the Federal Mediation and Conciliation Service by his brother, Judge John DeLury. Holding the Bible is Bernie's wife, Jane.

Bernie DeLury's father, the late John DeLury, distinguished unionist. He dedicated much of his life fighting to improve the lot of New York's uniformed sanitation employees.

Shellyn Gae McCaffrey
The Fire Within

Shellyn Gae McCaffrey, born in the south suburbs of Pittsburgh, Pennsylvania in 1957, is proud to be an American, but she is just as proud of her Irish ancestry. In ten short years, from 1979 to 1989, she went from a working scholarship in the office of Senator John Heinz of Pennsylvania to becoming deputy undersecretary for international affairs in the United States Department of Labor. She has worked with a passion and a belief in the American political system.

Being a key person ideally situated in international affairs for the Department of Labor when Polish workers led the revolution against Communism in 1989, she was able to provide support and programs promoting Solidarity's desire for a free economy and for a free and open political system. Shellyn McCaffrey continues this work today as a business consultant and facilitator for American business enterprises who wish to become established in Poland.

The Fire Within

Shellyn instinctively feels a remarkable empathy and understanding of the aspirations and motivations of oppressed people, whether in Eastern Europe or in other parts of the world. She says this knowledge comes directly from her father, Leo Joseph McCaffrey, the major influence in shaping who she is today.

"My father and I were very close and we shared a love for books, horses and baseball. The qualities which I think I gained most from him are an appreciation for humor, an idealism and impatient desire to achieve something in life having lasting meaning or impact and a drive to be an entrepreneur to gain flexibility and greater control over one's own life."

Her Irish Roots

Leo McCaffrey was born in Carrickmacross, County Monaghan. When he was a child, his family moved to Seacome,

England because of lack of jobs in Ireland. His older brother remained behind in Ireland where he farmed for the remainder of his life. Leo's father subsequently immigrated to Pittsburgh, Pennsylvania. Leo and his two sisters stayed behind in England with their mother until their father had earned enough money to pay for their passages.

Tragedy befell the family when Leo's mother died shortly after her husband departed for Pittsburgh. Then, soon after Leo and his two sisters joined their father in America, he too died. They were placed in the care of a childless aunt and uncle in Carnegie outside Pittsburgh. Leo became the man of the family, a situation apparently less than ideal because of his aunt's temperament. Leo's older sister married and moved to California. His younger sister didn't marry and she remained in the house, where the children were brought up, after the aunt died.

Leo McCaffrey started his work career in a hotel in the Pittsburgh area. He subsequently went to night school at Robert Morris college and studied real estate marketing. His career was interrupted when he was drafted into the service during World War II. He served in the Signal Corps in China, India and Burma as a master sergeant. He married Elizabeth Stegman, a German/Polish girl from Keysport, Pennsylvania. Upon his return to private life, he went into the real estate appraisal business. When he died suddenly at age 54, he was vice president of a savings and loan bank in the Pittsburgh area.

Shellyn's Dream

Shellyn and her father had a dream of going on a visit to Ireland. It was their secret. They would go to see her uncle in Ireland. She built this idea of going to Ireland to such a fantastic level that "somehow it had to be everything, it just had to be perfect for me to go." Unfortunately, after her father died, her uncle also died before she made it over to Ireland and that diminished considerably the attraction of going. Her father always had the longing to go back to Ireland and to take her with him.

When Leo McCaffrey died, Shellyn was only eleven years of age. Her mother died one year later when she was twelve. She was brought up by an aunt on her mother's side. Her father's

153

sister was her godmother. She was close to her, maintaining her Irish ties.

To Shellyn McCaffrey, Ireland is "a kind of feeling, a way of thinking" rather than a place in particular. In discussions concerning anything political with her Irish aunt, or anything about life, Shellyn feels a connection with her aunt and her memory of her father. She knows her aunt will reflect exactly her feelings, or she will feel, when she is doing something, that she knows her father would have done the exact same thing.

It is almost as if Shellyn is locked back in the time period when her father left Ireland, with all his early experiences and the stories handed down by his father. To Shellyn, "Ireland was more an idea than a place, an idea about life, a passion for life. Ireland was a fire inside me. I guess I get more satisfaction out of thinking I'm Irish when I'm involved in something like Eastern Europe, in a program. Something I'm accomplishing."

When Shellyn finally went to Ireland with friends on a tourist itinerary (she thought anything for a first taste), she couldn't fully appreciate it. She said if she had it to do again, she would have rather gone and just wandered around. Shellyn remembers being so wrapped up in memories of her father that it was difficult to fully appreciate the trip. She said she would almost rather not to have gone at all than to have anything break the fantasy she had of a perfect trip. Shellyn explained, "It was the aura, the relationship we had. I think it was more having my father show me Ireland for the first time than it was any thing in particular.

"I realize in hindsight that probably I should not have gone on a tourist trip because I felt like I was in Disneyland. There was another whole side of Ireland that I glimpsed from the car -- the fields and the small towns, and that is what I imagined I would have seen. Instead, I guess I saw mostly tourists. I did not feel any closer to the concept of Irishness by going to Ireland. I almost feel as if I am more Irish being removed from it and carrying around in my mind what Irishness is. I have this idea that the Irish is the most passionate part of me, being someone who would rail against something for principle and be willing to die for it -- wanting to accomplish something great."

154

A Foot in the Door

Shellyn McCaffrey attended Catholic schools and went on to Pennsylvania State University where she earned a Bachelor of Science degree with High Honors. She was the Commencement Speaker.

While working for Senator John Heinz of Pennsylvania, Shellyn met a Republican National Committee member who was a strong supporter of George Bush. As a result of this association, Shellyn worked for George Bush in 1978 and 1979 in the southern United States. When he dropped out of the race, friends invited her to work for Ronald Reagan and she accepted.

Ronald Reagan won the election and Shellyn's work in the campaign won her a place on the White House Staff. The reality of that experience dispelled some of the myths that are part of campaign work. Shellyn explained: "A campaign is a great place to get experience because you can rise very quickly. You get a lot of responsibility as a young person. But a myth we were all told is that if your candidate wins there will be jobs for everybody in the White House. It wasn't really that way. And the way I got into the White House, I think, was by tenacity, being in the right place, willing to do anything and visiting the same people over and over -- perseverance and a willingness to work hard.

"While doing temporary work in the White House, I got assigned to the director of the President's Economic Cabinet Council. He was doing economic policy for President Reagan. He was so busy it was easy for him to absorb another person. For two years I was listed as a temporary worker, which meant that every month or so I had to be renewed. The first two weeks of the month were great, the last two weeks were horrible because I was scared that I was going to be let go."

Shellyn McCaffrey gained acceptance and a permanent appointment in the White House through hard work and tenacity. She went to law school at night at American University and earned her law degree at the Washington College of Law. As a staff member of the Office of Policy Development from 1981 to 1985, she helped to developed policy positions on financial institutions, telecommunications, deposit insurance reform, housing, federal credit policy, pensions and unitary taxation. "Policy making for

155

the President is kind of a wheel," she remembers. "We were the hub, the people who pulled together the papers, developed the options and prepared the agendas for the Cabinet meetings on economic issues."

From 1985 through 1988 Shellyn McCaffrey, as Deputy Executive Secretary of the Economic Policy Council, assisted the President in developing and implementing domestic and international economic policy. Accomplishments included the Superconductivity Initiative and Legislation in 1987, and in 1989, development of the President's Forty-Three Point Competitiveness Initiative and Omnibus Legislation, the Commercial Space Initiative, and the Tenets of a New US-Japan Science and Technology Agreement.

Shellyn did not have direct access to President Reagan, but her impressions in being close to him were "that he was so much larger than life -- even in person and really, in my mind, he was just the greatest President. Even though I worked for George Bush earlier, Ronald Reagan was the greatest President that we'll have in my lifetime, and I'm even discounting that there could be somebody great I don't about yet. He had such a vision for the United States, such an aura. Just being in the same room and seeing him -- he was truly larger than life."

Shellyn thinks the reason she survived the pace in the White House was because of her youth and enthusiasm. In reading about the Clinton Administration, and the long working hours, she says it was always that way. It was normal for people to be in the White House from six in the morning until ten or eleven at night and to be there on weekends. "Part of it is competition, part of it is a feeling that you are part of something important and part of it is the excitement of the work. It becomes almost like an obsession, a sickness, which is partly why I went to law school to find another interest."

From Commerce to Labor

Shellyn McCaffrey was appointed Associate Deputy Secretary in 1988, deputy to the number two person in the Department of Commerce. The Secretary, Malcolm Baldridge, had just died and the new Secretary, William Verity, had a very specific agenda. Part of this agenda was science and technology oriented, which was Shellyn's experience area in the White House. She was brought over as someone who could quickly work to achieve the priority agenda items for the one-year Verity appointment. She was there for one year, which was the end of the Reagan Administration.

Shellyn was among the very small group of people who had worked for George Bush before 1980. "So I knew I was somewhat favored. And I very much wanted to do something internationally oriented rather than continue in science and technology. The Bush people wanted me to go to the Labor Department to head the International Bureau. I didn't know anything about this job and it was not my first choice. I was quite upset at the time. This was a great lesson to me not to prejudge things, because it turned out to be a perfect job.

"Everything is becoming international these days. No matter what department you are involved in, you touch international matters. At the Labor Department most things are oriented towards protecting the American workers -- a big regulatory department! But the International Labor Bureau is unique with its focus on international activities that affect American workers, trade, international labor standards, and workers' rights. You have a lot of flexibility. You are able to shape things and are not hampered by having to develop regulations or having to enforce laws.

"Soon after I arrived there, the president announced his desire to negotiate the free trade agreement with Mexico and Canada and at the same time Communism fell. Both of these things had a impact on American workers and workers in foreign countries. This gave me an unlimited horizon to work towards making the American workforce more competitive. This also gave me an opportunity to help workers in foreign countries who so desperately longed to turn to the American capitalist democracy model.

"I was fortunate to work for two Secretaries of Labor, Elizabeth Dole and Lynn Martin, who gave me a great deal of flexibility to shape programs and develop ideas. It was the ability to be creative and the flexibility that I loved so much. Basically, I am an entrepreneurial person and that is why I am now trying my hand at my own small business.

"The negotiations on the free trade agreement were led by the United States trade representative, but the Labor Department was responsible for the labor aspects of the trade agreement and the parts of the agreement that affected American workers. We attempted to defend American workers' jobs and not do anything that would harm them. We were in charge of labor standards, again to make sure that Mexico would provide protection for workers in the areas of safety, health, environment and child labor, and to accomplish agreements with Mexico that would come up to American levels within a certain period of time.

"It was probably the most responsibility the Labor Department has ever had in the area of trade and international agreements. For this reason, I felt this was a key time for the Labor Department to be out there on the cutting edge of trade agreements in order to boost the competitiveness of American workers."

Her Other Ireland

In 1989, the Polish workers led the revolution against Communism, an issue that immediately captured Shellyn's imagination and continues still today.

Shellyn explained why her commitment was connected with her Irishness: "I often thought, in an Irish way which was unexplainable to people who worked for me or with me, why I cared so passionately about trying to help these workers to reform with democracy. The best explanation is that it has definitely something to do with Ireland. I have always seen Ireland as kind of a cause and maybe this is a fault of many Americans. They see the Irish situation in simplistic terms -- the Irish are somehow great patriots and some day they will break through with creativity and tenacity and will break free. I even think when I went to Ireland this was an expectation. Maybe if I had any disappointment it was that I did not see that fervor, that passion, that somehow I expected to see manifest itself.

"I just prefer to think of Ireland like that, as this wild horse breaking to be free. That is why when Poland burst out of

158

Communism, I transferred exactly what I thought of Ireland to what was happening in Poland. Since then I have drawn all these parallels of a passionate people, very bull headed, almost to a fault, and an almost one hundred per cent Catholic country. I don't know if there are any people in my mind that are closer in nature and spirit, other than the Poles and the Irish, who have both overcome going to the brink, but sometimes liking being the underdog, reveling with a sort of melancholy capacity to deal with being oppressed.

"Like the Irish, the Poles were underdogs. They fought in the American Revolution with Lafayette and Washington. They were not able to win their own revolution so they fought in other peoples' revolutions, just as the Irish did. For years and years the Poles went up against tanks. I mean they went up against high technology on the backs of horses, with swords and were totally underdogs. It is admirable in the sense of principle winning out. This is what I expected to feel in Ireland.

"After Poland came Hungary and Czechoslovakia and we had programs to help workers in these countries. The lion's share of the programs and money available however was spent on Poland," says Shellyn. "There was something about being on the cutting edge -- I have heard people refer to it as a Klondike. This is how it would have been in this country a hundred years ago. To be involved in something, that when you were doing it you thought you could make a difference in life. It is difficult to really make a difference but with these people in Poland I knew I was, and I felt I was part of history. So the Poles, uniquely among all the other cultures in Eastern Europe, I could not do enough for them."

Looking to the Future

Shellyn McCaffrey feels that if politics are in her future, down the road she would like to be a mayor of a town where she could have an impact and see something through. She says the idea of being part of Congress where so little gets done and so much talk goes on is not attractive to her at all, "like sausage making." One can have a bigger effect at the local area. Right now she is running her own business and finding time to know

159

her brothers again. Leo McCaffrey, named after her father, owns an Irish bar named "Shawn - Ryan," the names of his two sons. He is a very "laid back" fellow. The younger brother, Terrence Patrick, is in the import-export business, an "eager sort of fellow, ardent and industrious with great optimism about opportunities in life." As for herself, Shellyn believes that after twelve years in government, the private sector now offers her the opportunity to pursue her entrepreneurial interests.

Shellyn McCaffrey with her favorite friends. Below, Shellyn's dad, Leo McCaffrey, as a young boy in Ireland.

Frank Durkan
Champion of Individual Rights

Frank Durkan is one of the most respected citizens in New York's Irish community. A prominent attorney, he has an excellent reputation as a champion of civil rights causes and for supporting Irish cultural endeavors. Through the Mayo Foundation for the Handicapped and the Irish Institute of New York, two organizations where he serves as trustee, funds are raised to promote culture and charities in Ireland. It is often said of Frank that he is one of the unsung heroes of the New York Irish-American community, chiefly because he has been over-shadowed over the years by his illustrious uncle, Paul O'Dwyer.

Arriving in New York

On September 8, 1947, Frank Durkan arrived in New York aboard the liner *Mauritania*. It was a blazing hot day and like most everyone else on board, he got his first sight of the "Lady of the Harbor" from the port side of the ship. But the sight that amazed him most was the hundreds of cars speeding along the Brooklyn shoreline to and from Coney Island and the Rockaways. Having just arrived from petrol-scarce Ireland, he remembers wondering, "How long can this keep up? There cannot possibly be enough fuel in this city to sustain such extravagance."

The Mayor of New York at that time was his uncle, William O'Dwyer. Like Frank, William O'Dwyer had grown up in Bohola, County Mayo, attended Lismirrane National School and later on St. Nathy's College in Ballaghadreen, County Roscommon. In no time at all Frank found himself installed in Gracie Mansion, the mayor's official residence on the upper Eastside of Manhattan. Frank had never known such luxury: fresh fruit on every side-board, his own room with private bath attached, a television which permitted him to watch the boxing matches from St. Nicholas Arena, a butler/chef to cook his meals and a waitress to serve them.

This idyllic situation did not last for long. His Uncle Paul inquired, upon arriving back from his Irish vacation one week later, "Where's the kid?" Upon hearing the words "Gracie Mansion," Paul, a very practical man, issued a crisp and firm order. "Get him out of there!" The bewildered immigrant was bundled off to much less glamorous quarters on East 97th Street and Lexington Avenue, where he took up his duties as a janitor in a five-storey apartment house. Paul was not about to let the glamor and trappings of high society go to the young man's head.

Frank had thoroughly enjoyed the ocean voyage which was made all the more exciting by the fact that the Kerry and Cavan football teams were on board, along with the elite of Ireland's Gaelic Athletic Association. They were heading for New York's Polo Grounds to face off in the 1947 All-Ireland Final. It was the first time that two county teams had played for the All-Ireland championship outside of Ireland and there was great excitement among New York's Irish.

Frank was not prepared for New York's heat wave that September of 1947. "The one thing that I really remember most of all about New York was the heat. It was brutal! During the day, I couldn't stay awake and at night, I couldn't get to sleep." Three months later, in December, Frank experienced the other extreme when a terrible snow blizzard crippled the city for days. Despite the extremes in temperature, the city prospered that year. A postwar building boom was adding additional skyscrapers to the city's skyline. Levittown, a new concept in community living, was being built on Long Island and *Finian's Rainbow* played to full houses on Broadway.

In September 1947, Frank enrolled at Columbia College and from there he graduated with a B.A. degree in 1951. While he attended college, he continued to support himself working at a variety of jobs. He worked as a clerk in Morley's Liquor Store on Third Avenue and as an office clerk for the White Rock Beverage Company in Brooklyn.

After graduating, Frank entered New York Law School where he earned a Bachelor of Laws degree in 1953. While he was attending law school, he worked as a law clerk for his uncle's law firm -- O'Dwyer and Bernstien. He was admitted to the New York State Bar in 1955 and then joined the firm of O'Dwyer and Bernstien as an attorney.

Civil Rights Advocate

Frank Durkan has been engaged in active practice as an attorney in New York since 1955 and has done extensive trial work in the criminal and negligence fields. In addition to his practice, Frank has been active with his Uncle Paul in civil rights matters.

He has been active in Irish-American social organizations, is a member of the Mayo Men's Professional and Businessmen's Association of New York, a former President of the Irish Institute of New York and a Trustee of the Mayo Foundation for the Handicapped.

He is an active member of the Brehan Law Society, a group of Irish-American lawyers who have come together for the purpose of providing aid and assistance to young men and women who have experienced legal difficulties because of their identification with the ongoing conflict in Northern Ireland. The Brehan Law Society team successfully defeated the British government in its attempt to extradite Irish Republican Army (IRA) member Desmond Macklin from New York. This case was the first of a series of cases which so frustrated the United States and British governments that they resorted to changing the treaty involving extradition between the two countries.

In 1972 and 1973, Frank traveled with Paul O'Dwyer to Fort Worth, Texas where they gained international attention defending five New York men who were jailed in Texas on suspicion of alleged gun running to Northern Ireland. This case, known as the "Fort Worth Five," resulted in a Congressional investigation and subsequent curtailment of grand jury abuse by Federal authorities.

Frank Durkan represented the "Baltimore Four" in Baltimore, Maryland, another group of Irish-Americans who were alleged to have supplied firearms for the IRA in Northern Ireland. He also represented a number of individuals in the New York Courts on similar matters. In 1981, he was a member of the defense team which successfully defended five Irish-Americans on gun running charges in a case known as the "Brooklyn Five." One of the defendants was Michael Flannery, a well-known and highly-respected Irish-American.

164

In 1990, he was instrumental in organizing the defense team which represented the "Florida Four," a group of Irish-Americans charged with attempting to purchase a "stinger" missile in Fort Lauderdale, Florida. He is part of the defense team for the "Tucson Fourteen" who are presently awaiting trial in the Federal Court in Tucson, Arizona. He has appeared in the Federal Courts in New Hampshire, Boston, Atlanta, New Orleans, Philadelphia and Hartford on behalf of Irish-Americans similarly charged. In keeping with policy laid down by Paul O'Dwyer in such cases, the firm of O'Dwyer and Bernstien has served without fee.

The Political Offense Exception

In the area of extradition law, Frank Durkan has become somewhat of an expert, mainly because of the success he has had in persuading the courts to deny extradition requests, using the "political offense exception" clause contained in all extradition treaties. One case in particular, *United States v. Mackin*, brought Frank international headlines and, according to Frank, "was an education to the New York Bar on the intricacies of extradition." His success in using the "political offense exception" defense frustrated the Reagan Administration. They claimed this clause provided a loophole which allowed terrorists an escape hatch to enter the country. Subsequently, the Senate approved changes considerably restricting the "political refugee" definition as it applies to the United States Extradition Treaty with England.

The Mayo Foundation for the Handicapped

Frank Durkan is a trustee of the Mayo Foundation for the Handicapped which he co-founded with his uncle, Paul O'Dwyer, several years ago. Their involvement started when they decided to donate the O'Dwyer family home in Bohola and its three and a half acres to a charitable cause. According to Frank, "The title was in my grandparents' names, Patrick and Brigid O'Dwyer, and was passed on to my mother. When she and my father both retired from school teaching and moved to Dublin, my Uncle Paul decided that rather than let the house decay, he would buy the property from my mother and put up a new house. Originally, he wanted to give the property to the Gaelic Athletic Association but the land wasn't suitable for playing football. He then offered it to another charity but it didn't work out. Finally, he was introduced to Leonard Cheshire, the founder of the Cheshire Homes for the Handicapped in England.

"Cheshire was one of the most decorated British World War II heroes. He was a bomber pilot who flew over Germany and France during the closing years of the war, engaging in very dangerous bombing missions. He was also a British observer when the atomic bomb was dropped on Hiroshima. One day in England after the war, Cheshire ran into an old buddy who told him about several old friends who were physically and financially in bad shape. Cheshire, an independently wealthy man, decided to do something about their plight, offering one of his houses for their use. Apparently, Cheshire felt great guilt over the destruction he had caused by being a bomber pilot during the war, so he decided that he would use his personal wealth and income to help alleviate the distress of crippled people. He set up the first of a number of Cheshire homes throughout England, Scotland and in the United States.

"It was a Dr. O'Beirne from Galway who told Paul the Cheshire people were looking for locations to expand into Ireland in the early 1970s. A meeting was arranged and Paul offered them the old homestead. When they looked at it they said, 'Good Lord, it would cost £25,000 to put this place into any shape.' In those days, £25,000 was quite a lot of money. Paul wrote them a check for £25,000. Later, they were back asking for another £25,000. It didn't stop there either. By the time the place was finished, the tab had gone up to £200,000. The beauty of it all was, when they got up into those high figures, the Irish government came forward and matched the amount donated. The Cheshire Home in Bohola today accommodates some twenty-eight residents, mostly adults with severe handicaps.

"The whole concept of a Cheshire Home is built on community support. In other words, a Cheshire Home in and of itself cannot survive. There is no government support other than to provide medical services to the handicapped patients. The Bohola Cheshire Home is sustained through funds raised by the Mayo

Society of Dublin and from contributions in the United States and Ireland. The Cheshire Home Society in Dublin is actually an adjunct of the Mayo Society. Each year, in November, they run the Cheshire Home Charity Ball in Dublin, which is one of the biggest fund raisers in the country."

The Irish Institute of New York

Frank Durkan is a trustee of the Irish Institute of New York, an organization which provides financial support for cultural endeavors in Ireland and the United States. Originally organized to acquire and operate a building at 326 West 48th Street, the building was the home for many of New York's Irish-American clubs and organizations from 1960 to 1982.

The Irish Institute makes grants to various artistic endeavors under its philanthropic policy. In 1966, it contributed $150,000 to the John F. Kennedy Memorial Arboretum in Wexford. In recent years, the Institute gave the Irish American Cultural Institute $100,000 to endow an Irish Research Fund and another $93,000 towards the funding of research into the history of the Irish in New York City. It has supported many worthwhile community groups in Ireland and has contributed to the restoration of several historic sites, including Strokestown Park House, County Roscommon where Ireland's Famine museum is located.

His Irish Roots

Both of Frank's parents were school teachers. His father, Bernard, was also a great footballer. He captained the Mayo county team for many years and played in the All-Ireland Finals of 1916 and 1921, but never got a medal. His mother, Mary O'Dwyer, is a sister to Paul O'Dwyer and the late Bill O'Dwyer, former mayor of New York and United States Ambassador to Mexico. Frank's brother, William, practices law in Dublin and his older brother, Aidan, is retired from the Anhauser-Busch brewing company and lives in New York.

His Uncle the Mayor of New York

It is with a touch of nostalgia that Frank talks about his famous uncle, Bill O'Dwyer. "He was the mayor when I arrived.

He had served as mayor of New York from 1945 to 1950. He was an enthralling storyteller with a tremendous personality. He could hold a room in the palm of his hand, seemingly without effort. Had he stayed a lawyer, he would have been one of the great trial lawyers of the country. Before he became mayor, he was a district attorney and later a judge. During World War II, he served in the army and became a general. After the war he was put in charge of Italian refugee relief. In 1950, President Truman appointed him as Ambassador to Mexico."

Frank's other uncle, Paul O'Dwyer, is a well known Democratic Party leader in New York. He has served as president of the Manhattan City Council. In 1968, he was an ardent supporter of Eugene McCarthy's challenge for the Democratic nomination and was mentioned as a possible vice-presidential candidate on the McCarthy ticket.

Boyhood Days in Bohola

Frank remembers Boholo's famed storyteller, Tony McNicholas. Says Frank, "He was the number one storyteller in the west of Ireland. He had a great gift for being able to hold one spellbound while he spoke with that air of great conviction. He was probably one of the most popular men in the area when I was growing up as a child.

"He was known to everyone around as Tony Charley. He acquired the nickname Charley because in the village of Lismirrane there were sixteen McNicholas families and many with the same first name. My grandfather, Patrick O'Dwyer, was the village's first interloper. He arrived there from Tullylease, County Cork in 1888 to teach at the local school. He married Brigid McNicholas and became a permanent resident." Frank remembers hearing of his grandfather arriving in Tuam, County Galway by train from Cork and then walking the thirty-five miles from the train station to Bohola.

Says Frank, "I was privileged also to have Dudley Solan of Kiltimagh as my National School principal. A man of ready wit and great personal charm, he was a keen student of Irish history and enthralled his students with vivid accounts of some of the great confrontations between the Irish and the English down through the centuries. He may have embellished a little here and there, for I have never read in any book his personal descriptions of such events as the Battle of Benburb or the death of Brian Boru swinging his sword the weight of a horse-cart in one final act of defiance. But his imagery was magnificent. You could practically feel your blood pulsating with pride as the master took you on the headlong dash with Sarsfield to blow up the English siege-train at Ballyneety!"

There were no pleasures or comforts while attending St. Nathy's, according to Frank, but as far as an academic education was concerned, St. Nathy's ranked among the best in the country. Frank went on to say, "When I enrolled at Columbia, I found that I was well ahead of my colleagues from American high schools in subjects such as mathematics, languages, geography and history. I believe that the basics I acquired in St. Nathy's have served me better than anything I have learned in any other school."

Life in the "Big Apple"

In the beginning, Frank found life in New York somewhat difficult. The change of pace from a small rural area like Bohola to the fast pace of a large metropolitan city like New York was a culture shock. But after his initial homesickness, Frank settled down and ultimately grew to love the city and the nation that he has adopted.

The practice of law has been a scintillating challenge for him. In the courts, he has come into contact with people from all walks of life and from various ethnic backgrounds. In his negligence practice, he has almost exclusively represented plaintiffs seeking compensation for injuries. He has found, to his surprise, that middle and upper class Irish generally are less sympathetic to the plaintiffs than those of other races. People of Italian extraction likewise tend to be conservative. The people he likes best on a negligence jury are those of Jewish and Afro-American descent. He rationalizes that possibly because of more recent injustices suffered by them through discrimination, they are apt to be more sympathetic to the plight of an injured person.

Frank spoke of a case he tried in Bronx County before a six-person jury. "My client was a very charming seaman of Irish-

American descent who, following successful abdominal surgery in a local hospital, emerged totally blind. The substantial jury award in favor of the plaintiff was by a vote of five to one. The dissenting juror was the only Irish person on the jury and spoke with a distinct West of Ireland brogue.

"Similarly, in a case in Brooklyn some years ago, when the jury of twelve individuals issued a verdict in the plaintiff's favor by a vote of ten to two, the two dissenting jurors were the only Irish persons on the panel. The plaintiff was a retarded boy who had been knocked down by a truck."

Frank Durkan, prominent New York attorney and his wife, Monica, during the 1993 Easter Week Commemorations in New York City.

His Views on the Northern Ireland Situation

Frank is concerned about the apparent apathy of the forty million Irish-Americans towards the conflict in Northern Ireland. Their influence in Washington has been negligible because the vast majority of Irish-Americans seem to have accepted the propaganda emanating from the United States State Department and the British Information Service that the sole cause of the troubles in Northern Ireland is the "terrorism" of the IRA. Frank says, "For some strange reason they have not been impressed one way or another by the ruthlessness of the security forces, the human rights violations, or the travesty of a system which passes for "justice" in the Diplock Courts of Northern Ireland."

He goes on to say, "If only we could speak out against the Northern Ireland tragedy and Britain's responsibility for it with half the conviction displayed by our Jewish and African-American brethren, I am convinced Washington would have acted long ago to bring about a peaceful solution. A young Irishman spent almost nine years in a New York jail charged with no crime, but held on an extradition warrant filed by the British Government. Every attempt to release him on bail was vigorously opposed by our Government, while people charged with heinous crimes walk the streets." Frank asks, "Would any other ethnic group tolerate such treatment?" And he goes on to say, "I don't think so. It is an old axiom that once the wrinkles leave the belly, people tend to forget. And I must reluctantly conclude that as many Irish-Americans have scaled the economic ladder they have considered the other man's wound less and less."

Irish-Americans and Ireland

However, Frank is delighted with the growing number of Irish-Americans who look to Ireland with great affection. He points out that even those who have never visited that country often refer to it as "home." Appeals for help to aid a widow or orphan or to raise funds for an injured workman are invariably responded to with great generosity. There is hardly a church in rural Ireland that has not had the benefit of "money from America," often donated by persons who have never seen the place or even

171

hope to see it. Of late, Irish-Americans who hitherto vacationed in Europe, are flocking to Ireland. Irish-Americans have a sense or feeling of "belonging" upon visiting Ireland and this has proven to be a great boon to the economy of Ireland.

Frank points to the fact that "pressure by Irish-American politicians in Congress has resulted in favorable treatment to would-be immigrants -- witness the Donnelly and Morrison visa programs which have increased dramatically the number of immigrants permitted to enter the States from Ireland. There is a new awakening among many congressional representatives concerning the ongoing Northern Ireland conflict, thanks to the efforts of the Americans for a New Irish Agenda and the Congressional Ad Hoc Committee on Irish Affairs. Representatives Joe Kennedy, Tom Manton, Peter King and others have launched a spirited campaign in Washington to obtain official United States government intervention with a view to bringing peace and justice to Northern Ireland. If Washington can get the Israelis and the Palestinians to shake hands on the front lawn of the White House, why can it not strive to do likewise to solve the Northern Ireland conflict?"

The Gaelic-speaking Lawyer

A story Frank likes to tell involves his representation of the "Fort Worth Five" in Texas in 1972. "My co-counsel were Doris Peterson from the Center for Constitutional Rights and a Jesuit priest from Chicago, the late Bill Cunningham, who was also a brilliant constitutional lawyer. The atmosphere was hostile. The five Irish-Americans from New York, Kenneth Tierney, Danny Crawford, Tom Laffey, Matty Reilly and Pascal Morahan, had all refused point blank to testify before the Grand Jury about an alleged plot to ship guns from Mexico through Texas to the IRA in Northern Ireland.

"The judge was furious. The prosecutors were apoplectic and the media were everywhere. Five brave Irish nurses from a local hospital were outside picketing the Courthouse, condemning the Grand Jury investigation.

"The defense desperately needed a one-day adjournment in order to prepare a particularly important motion. We knew we couldn't get the adjournment, but Father Cunningham's fertile

New York mayor William (Bill) O'Dwyer (center) escorting Ireland's Minister of External Affairs, Sean McBride, into New York's City Hall in 1949. William O'Dwyer was born in Bahola, County Mayo. After he immigrated to the United States. he studied law and went on to become district attorney, mayor and ambassador to Mexico. Sean McBride was a founder of Amnesty International

mind was not to be denied. I had complained to him earlier that morning that I had lost a filling from a tooth. Now he stood before the glaring judge and announced in stentorian tones that an adjournment was essential 'because co-counsel Durkan is suffering from a severe toothache and needs attention.'

"The judge was not impressed. 'There are still two lawyers available,' he said, 'you can carry on without Durkan.'

"The Reverend Bill never batted an eye. 'Your Honor,' he said, 'Mr. Durkan is the only Gaelic speaker on the defense team. Without him we cannot communicate with our clients.'

"The baffled judge looked at the prosecutors. The prosecutors looked at the five men. The five men looked uneasily at the floor (for none of them, except Laffey, could speak a word of Gaelic) and finally, the judge in exasperation said, 'request granted.'

"Doris, Bill and the five men went looking for liquid refreshment! I went looking for a dentist."

Frank's Family

Frank is married to the former Monica Goggin, a native of Dublin. Monica worked as a flight attendant for Pan American World Airlines before taking up her new career as a teacher in the Westchester County School District. They live in Rye, New York with Mary Louise and Aisling, Frank's two daughters from a prior marriage. Both girls have graduated from college, Mary Louise from Emerson and Aisling from Northeastern University in Boston. Mary Louise plans to go to law school and Aisling, who majored in languages, would like to obtain a position with the United Nations.

Justice William J. Brennan, Jr.
United States Supreme Court Justice

...there is virtually no aspect of American law today
that does not bear his gentle imprint....
-- *The Evening Sun* -- July 23, 1990

When he retired on July 20, 1990, William J. Brennan, Jr. had served for thirty-four years on the United States Supreme Court. Admirers and critics acknowledge that his influence was wide-ranging and profound.

Justice Brennan was the architect of numerous landmark rulings. The conservative *National Review* wrote in 1984, "No individual in this country, on or off the court, has had a more profound and sustained impact upon public policy in the United States for the past twenty-seven years..." than Justice Brennan. In a 1987 article in *The National Law Journal*, Norman Dorsen, president of the American Civil Liberties Union wrote, "We would be living under a very different Constitution if Justice Brennan were not on the Supreme Court."

Justice Brennan was a powerful judicial activist and his contribution to jurisprudence on the United States' highest bench will, no doubt, place him among the company of the Court's great men, Oliver Wendell Holmes and Louis Brandeis.

In its editorial of July 23, 1990, the *Baltimore Evening Sun*, commenting on Brennan's retirement, wrote, "...Brennan's contribution to American jurisprudence in 34 years on the nation's highest bench will require volumes to properly illuminate. Even after the word had been given an opprobrious connotation, 'liberal' was a philosophy which Brennan espoused openly and proudly, and there is virtually no aspect of American law today that does not bear his gentle imprint. His consistently liberal position is found in great cases demanding fair procedure in criminal trials. He wrote the supremely important decision establishing the right to equal representation in state legislatures. In the area of human rights, Brennan's name is found in countless decisions, more lately in eloquent dissent against the erosion of those rights than in upholding them...."

His Irish Parents

Justice Brennan was born in Newark, New Jersey in 1906, the second of eight children. His father, William Joseph Brennan, had emigrated to New Jersey from Frenchpark, County Roscommon in 1893. Later he met and married Agnes McDermott, who came from Castlerea, a relatively large County Roscommon town just seven miles south of Frenchpark.

After arriving in America, the elder Brennan worked in a factory in Trenton. He later went to work as a coal heaver at the Ballantine Brewery in Newark. The work there was backbreaking and working conditions were dreadful. Dissatisfied with the treatment the brewery employees were receiving, William Brennan set about organizing a union. It was not an easy task for him as there were no laws then that protected working men in their efforts to organize. He succeeded in his endeavor and went on to became prominent in the labor movement in Newark. By 1916, he had become a member of the Essex County Trades and Labor Council.

Being a difficult time for organized labor, the elder Brennan, hoping to improve the working man's lot and get support for collective bargaining, successfully sponsored a drive to have Newark's form of city government -- mayor and aldermen -- replaced with five commissioners, each of whom was assigned to supervise a department. He entered the race for commissioner in the 1917 city election, coming in third out of a field of eighty-six candidates, and took over the supervision of Public Safety. With jurisdiction over the police and fire departments, he clamped down on strike breaking by the police as had happened in the 1916 transit workers' strike. Brennan served continuously as commissioner until his death in 1930.

Boyhood Days in Newark

Justice William Brennan's boyhood in Newark was that of the typical American youth. He attended parochial and public schools, graduating from Newark's Barringer High School. Outside of school he worked to earn himself some pocket money by delivering milk in a horse-drawn wagon and working at a filling station pumping gasoline.

After High School, Justice Brennan went to the University of Pennsylvania, graduating *cum laude* from its Wharton School of Business in 1928 with a degree in economics. He decided to study law and entered Harvard University that same year. Tragedy befell the family when his father died in 1930. Left with little income to pay for his tuition, he obtained a scholarship which helped him finish law school.

Brennan received his law degree from Harvard Law School in 1931. He was admitted to the New Jersey bar in 1932 after joining the Newark law firm of Pitney, Hardin and Skinner. For the next ten years he practiced law in Newark.

In 1942, he entered the army as a major in the legal division of the Ordinance Department. He specialized in manpower and personnel work during his Army career, and was separated with the rank of Colonel in 1945. He was given the Legion of Merit award. He returned to Newark where he rejoined his law firm as a name partner.

Judiciary Appointment

In 1949, William Brennan ascended the bench as a trial judge in the New Jersey Superior Court. Two years later he was elevated to a judgeship in the appellate division of the same court and in 1952, Governor Driscoll of New Jersey appointed him an Associate Justice of the New Jersey Supreme Court. While serving on that court, he was given recognition for his role in the nation-wide drive to clear up court congestion and delays in litigation and was chairman of the New Jersey Supreme Court's Committee on Calendar Control and Pre-Trial Conference Procedure.

On October 16, 1956, President Eisenhower picked Brennan for a recess appointment to the Supreme Court to replace Associate Justice Minton, who had resigned. The Judiciary Committee unanimously approved his nomination, with the only opposition coming from a group opposed to putting a Catholic on the Court and from Senator Joseph McCarthy. Although not on the Judiciary Committee, Senator McCarthy requested permission to question the nominee, particularly about remarks he had made to the Charitable Irish Society of Boston on St. Patrick's Day in 1954. McCarthy aparently was irked about the remark Brennan had made "about certain things going on in the country that were reminiscent of the Salem witch-hunts."

Landmark Decisions

One of the most important landmark decisions Justice Brennan wrote related to First Amendment rights curtailing the ability of public officials to silence newspapers through the threat of libel suits.

This case -- *New York Times* v. *Sullivan* -- arose when, in 1960, Police Commissioner Sullivan of Montgomery, Alabama sued the *Times* for publishing an advertisement, signed by a group of prominent people, accusing Southern authorities, among other things, of conducting a "wave of terror" against black students demonstrating for their civil rights. Although his name was not mentioned in the ad, Commissioner Sullivan claimed that he would be responsible for many of the actions mentioned there. A jury awarded him a half million dollars in damages.

Reversing the lower court's verdict, Justice Brennan established, for the first time in United States history, that "the constitutional protections for speech and press limit a state's power to award damages in a libel action brought by a public official against critics of his official conduct."   Brennan had based his opinion on the papers of the principal author of the First Amendment, James Madison, who wrote, "The censorial power is in the people over the Government, and not in the Government over the people."

Justice Brennan was a persistent guardian of civil rights protection for blacks. His dramatic opinion drafted for the Court in *Cooper* v. *Aaron* (1958), was signed by every other member of the court in a show of unity that was unprecedented.   What led to the decision was the action of Arkansas's Governor Faubus in 1957 in sending in the Arkansas National Guard to block desegration of the Little Rock public schools. His action prompted President Eisenhower to send in federal troops, paving the way for the students to enter the schools. However, the President's action brought hostility from the white community and the school board decided the following February, with lower court approval, to delay implementation of the integration plan for thirty months.

*United States Supreme Court Justice William J. Brennan, Jr. His
parents emigrated from County Roscommon; his father, William J.
Brennan, was from Frenchpark and his mother, Agnes McDermott,
was from Castlerea. Appointed by President Dwight Eisenhower,
Justice Brennan served on the Supreme Court from 1956 until 1990.*

The Supreme Court heard arguments in the case in August and subsequently issued an opinion constructed by Justice Brennan, which read: " The controlling legal principals are plain. The command of the 14th Amendment is that no 'State' shall deny to any person within its jurisdiction the equal protection laws. ... Article VI of the Constitution makes the Constitution the 'supreme Law of the Land.' "

Cherishes His Memories

Justice Brennan has wonderful memories of his parents and his boyhood days in Newark. He loves to talk about Ireland and recalls many of the stories told to him of his father's boyhood experiences in the historic town of Frenchpark before the turn of the century. Justice Brennan cherishes his County Roscommon roots and became a founding member of the County Roscommon Society of Washington, D.C. in 1988.

Justice Brennan married Marjorie Leonard in 1928. They had three children: William Joseph Brennan III, a lawyer in Princeton; Hugh Leonard Brennan, with the United States Department of Commerce and Nancy Brennan Widman, director of Baltimore's City Life Museum. Marjorie Leonard Brennan died in December of 1982. The following year Justice Brennan married Mary Fowler who had been his secretary for twenty-six years.

While many sons of Erin have achieved prominence in many walks of life over the centuries, few have towered, as Brennan has, in advancing civil rights and human dignity for all individuals.

Movers and Shakers
in Banking and Commerce

The Irish impact in industry and commerce has been less conspicuous than in other fields, probably because the industrial revolution was slow to reach Ireland. Notwithstanding, there have been many sons of Ireland who succeeded in making fortunes in banking and the business world.

Alexander Brown emigrated from Belfast to Baltimore in the early 1800s. He founded the mercantile and banking house Alexander Brown & Sons, the first investment banking firm in America. Brown was a major shareholder in the Bank of the United States and was a key figure in promoting America's first railroad, the Baltimore & Ohio. Michael Cudahy, who established the Cudahy Meatpacking Company and pioneered the use of cold storage, emigrated with his family from Ireland in 1849. William Grace emigrated from County Offaly in 1851 and went on to found the W. R. Grace & Company, one of the world's foremost shipping companies and chemical producers.

John Tone, born in Dublin on Oct. 11, 1719, immigrated to America in his early twenties, along with his brothers, Joseph and William. John Tone's descendants, Jehiel and Isaac Irwin Tone, founded the Tone Brothers Spice Company, Inc. in Iowa in 1873. They were processors and wholesalers of coffee, tea, spices and extracts. Tone Brothers originated many marketing ideas including selling pepper, cinnamon and ready roasted coffee in cans. The longest continuously operating spice company in America, it was the first such company to expand west of the Mississippi. John Tone was a first cousin of Peter Tone, the father of Wolfe Tone, one of the leaders executed following the ill-fated 1798 Irish Rebellion.

One of John's descendants was Franchot Tone, who starred in many movies including the original *Mutiny on the Bounty* and *Lives of the Bengal Lancers*. Another descendent is Jay Tone Jr., the last of the Tones to be involved with running the Tone Brothers Spice Company before it was sold to Mid Continental Industries in 1969. Jay lives in Iowa.

Andrew Mellon of Pittsburgh, whose immigrant father founded the Mellon Bank, made possible the National Gallery in Washington, D. C. through a huge endowment. Joe Kennedy, the grandson of emigrants from County Wexford, built a family fortune in banking and motion picture production and was a millionaire many times over by the time he was thirty-five. Timothy Eaton, from Ballymena, County Antrim, founded the T. Eaton Company which became Canada's largest retail enterprise. His great-grandson, Fredric S. Eaton, is a director of the Ireland Fund of Canada. Eugene O'Keefe immigrated to Canada from his native County Cork around the time of the Great Famine and founded the O'Keefe Brewing Company in Toronto. A devout Catholic, Eugene O'Keefe made large contributions to the Church and he financed the building of St. Augustine's Seminary.

Since World War II, North America has been blessed by a new generation of Irish immigrants -- entrepreneurs, who are displaying their executive skills in the boardrooms of corporate America and Canada. Among them is Dublin-born Dr. Anthony J. (Tony) O'Reilly, chairman and chief executive officer of the giant H. J. Heinz Corporation, the global food processing company that manufactures its products in fifteen countries. Dr. O'Reilly also has a controlling interest in Independent Newspapers, the largest publishing group in Ireland, with chains of newspapers in Australia and an advertising agency in Mexico. Dr. O'Reilly is the founder of the American Ireland Fund, the largest private organization in the world raising funds for projects in Ireland.

There is Meath-born Matt Barrett who is chief executive officer and chairman of the Bank of Montreal, Canada's oldest and one of the fastest growing and most diversified banks in North America. Another success story is that of Dublin-born Rowland Fleming, the president and chief executive officer of the National Trust, who started his banking career as a credit officer with the Bank of Nova Scotia in London, England. The Barrett and Fleming stories that follow are two modern Irish successes.

County Mayo-born Tom Flatley is president of the Flatley Company, the largest sole-proprietor company in the United States with holdings that include hotels, commercial office buildings and apartment complexes worth over a billion dollars.

Left: Timothy Eaton, who emigrated from Ballymena, County Antrim and founded the T. Eaton Company coast-to-coast chain of department stores in Canada. Right: Fredric S. (Fred) Eaton, great-grandson of Timothy. Fred is a director of the Ireland Fund of Canada. He received the Fund's Award in 1990 for his work for Irish benefits.

"It is my heritage, and in respect and honor of my great-grandparents who came from Ireland." This was one of the reasons given by John Connelly (above) when, on April 2, 1993 he announced that he was pledging one million dollars to the American Ireland Fund with a further nine million dollars to follow in a bequest program.

184

Above left, Dr. Tony O'Reilly, founder of the American Ireland Fund and sister funds in Canada, Australia, New Zealand and France photographed with Brian Dolan of Toronto, a director of the Ireland Fund of Canada, and Brian's wife, Patsy.
Brian Dolan is a prime mover behind the development of the Toronto Irish Center, a multimillion-dollar Irish heritage center.

Belfast-born Tom Savage rose to become chief executive officer of ITT of Canada. He molded ITT Canada's many diverse operations into a cohesive administrative unit in a few short years. The Tom Savage story that follows offers a blueprint for success.

Others who left Ireland and who have achieved conspicuous success in their adopted countries are Tipperary-born John Dunne who is chairman and chief executive officer of Atlantic and Pacific Supermarkets and Dublin-born Geoffrey Farrer the president of Barclay's Bank of Canada. Dundalk-born George Moore is chairman and chief executive officer of Targus Information Corporation. His subsidiary company, Erne Heritage Holdings, owns the Belleek China Company. Dublin-born Patrick Maher is president and chief executive officer of Washington Gas and Light Company while Belfast-born Robert Kearney is president and chief executive officer of Bell Canada.

Throughout North America, Americans of Irish ancestry fill executive officer positions in scores of multinational corporations. John McGillicuddy, the grandson of a County Kerry immigrant, runs Chemical Banking Corporation; John Curley is chairman and chief executive officer of the Garnett Company -- a world-wide media operation; John Dooner, whose people came from County Roscommon, is president and chief operating officer of McCann Erickson, the world's largest advertising agency operating in seventy-three countries including Ireland. Thomas Ferguson, whose parents came from Counties Leitrim and Clare, is president and general manager of the *Washington Post* and Michael Quinlan, whose grandparents came from Counties Limerick and Wexford, heads up the giant McDonald's Corporation with 12,000 fast food restaurants in fifty-four countries.

These are a new breed of Irishmen, with imagination, competitiveness and determination, who are capturing a good share of the upper echelons of corporate America and the stories that follow tell how some of them did it. If Lord Macaulay were to return today, he would no doubt say, "There are Irish of great ability, energy, and ambition... ," but instead of finding them on the battlefields of Europe he would find them distinguishing themselves as entrepreneurs in the global market place.

186

Matthew W. Barrett
Banker
A Modern Irish Success Story

"I think I'm going to like this country," Matt Barrett mused to himself as he made eye contact with the lovely Irene, an employee of Bank of Montreal. Matt was sitting in the bank's office waiting for the manager to make an appearance so he could present his papers. He had just arrived in Canada the evening before and had booked into a hotel, so Irene was the first young lady he had seen up close in Canada. Later on, he married her and they are now the proud parents of Tara, Kelly, Andrea and Jason.

The premonition that he was going to like Canada was realized beyond his wildest dreams. He now heads up the one hundred and ten billion dollar financial behemoth Bank of Montreal -- Canada's oldest bank and one of the fastest growing and most diversified in North America.

Matt Barrett's rise to the pinnacle of world banking has been meteoric. Still in his forties, one has to wonder what worlds are left for him to conquer. The marvel is not that he has reached heights undreamed of by most young men, especially young Irishmen, but that he is still a most approachable chief executive. Perhaps it is this amazing ability to be at ease with just about any other human being that has made his rise to the top seem so effortless. As senior executives go, this man is certainly a new breed -- a great blending of sophisticated business acumen and Irish charm.

His Irish Roots

Matt Barrett's maternal grandparents come from Castleisland just outside Tralee, in County Kerry. The family was living in London before he was born. Feeling that it would be almost a "mortal sin" to have a child born in England, Matt's mother went home to Tralee, where Matt was born on September 20, 1944. Matt's dad was the famous Jack Barrett of the Jack Barrett Orchestra -- a contemporary of such 1940s and 1950s greats as Geraldo, Mick Delahunty and Johnnie Butler, bands of the Big Band era. Jack Barrett also had his own *ceilidh* band, the Boyne Quartet, which performed at clubs and concerts.

Matt Barrett
Chairman, President and Chief Executive Officer
Bank of Montreal

The family home was in Kells in County Meath where Matt received a typical Irish education from the Christian Brothers. He finished school at eighteen and from there his story takes on a kind of aura.

The Early Years

With nothing to do in Ireland, Matt Barrett headed off to London with the hope of becoming a journalist. However, common sense told him that first he had to get work that would pay the rent. He also soon realized that he was not really cut out to be a writer, but was a whiz at balancing checkbooks. Fortunately, he did have an entree into check balancing. His dad had worked at the Bank of Montreal branch in London during the war. That was enough of an opening for Matt to squeeze in.

About a year after Matt started, his dad, who had returned to Ireland, was taken ill and died -- a tragic time for the Barrett family. Jack Barrett was just forty-five years of age. Matt returned home to help his mother and stayed for a year to settle his dad's affairs. Leaving his mother and sister at home, Matt returned to London and the bank.

Evidence that Matt was a man who was going to make his mark came in a letter he wrote home to his mother, "You're not going to believe this, but after just two years, I have already been made a teller." Being made a teller was just the first step. Matt soon came to the notice of the bank examiners. These not too welcome head office "spies" toured the various branches looking for trouble; they also evaluated new employees as future prospects. Soon after, Matt was invited to join the bank's home base in Canada. "This sounded like a lot of fun," thought Matt. "Lots of good clean air and miles of open spaces." He figured the job would be good for a couple of years and more than thirty years later, he runs the bank and he still thinks it's a great place.

Matt Barrett's Bank

The Bank of Montreal was founded in 1817 and acted as Canada's Central Bank until the founding of the Bank of Canada in 1935. The Bank of Montreal funded the building of the Lachine Canal in Quebec in the 1820s, the first Canadian railway, the

Champlain and St. Lawrence in the 1830s, and the Grand Trunk Railway from Quebec to Sarnia, Ontario in the 1850s.

Over the years, the Bank of Montreal has grown to be Canada's third largest bank and has diversified its operations with the acquisition of the Harris Bankcorp of Chicago and the purchase of Nesbitt Thomson, one of Canada's major investment houses. Today, Bank of Montreal has operations all over the world with an asset base of one hundred and ten billion dollars and over 34,000 employees. In all of North America, there are only fifteen banks in its class.

Matt Barrett was made chief executive officer in 1989 at age 45. Under Matt's guidance, the bank has registered record years for revenue increases and asset accumulation and has operations in all the major money centers of the world, including London, Frankfurt, Hong Kong, New York, Chicago and Tokyo. The bank has made solid penetration into the rich midwestern United States through Harris Bank Corp., and through investment dealers, it is involved in the stocks and bond business in a big way.

Matt Barrett's strategy for his bank is to have it evolve into four operating pillars. One would deal with the consumer, small business and mid-market businesses in Canada. A second pillar would deal with a similar clientele in the United States Midwest. The third would carry on corporate and institutional business on a global basis and the fourth would deal with investment banking and the securities business. The objective for the United States operations is to have that sector provide half of the bank's revenues. The Bank of Montreal also has branches throughout Asia, Europe and South America.

How Matt Barrett Rose to the Top
Usually, it takes all kinds of business degrees to reach top management positions in today's financial institutions. "I had no university education when I entered the bank'" says Matt. "However, the Bank of Montreal is a world-class financial institution and has a very sophisticated range of training and education programs for its people, and I took advantage of them all." Asked why the bank would pick Matt Barrett to go to Canada

when they usually breed, clone or incubate their own men, Matt says, "I really don't know, but to me the most marvelous thing was the fantastic opportunities I saw when I came to Canada. To answer your question, I guess they must have been impressed with me. I was a good performer at the London branch. The Bank in London had just one branch in the West End and the head office so there was not a lot of opportunity to progress. They asked me if I had ever considered the opportunities in Canada and I answered that I had not, but I would be happy to consider them.

"I really came over on a training program -- a management training program. I did a lot of studying, going to university at night. I bought all the books that had anything to do with banking and finance. Actually, I was quite frightened at the time as the Bank was only hiring university graduates for management positions. And here I was thinking how am I going to be able to compete? I bought all the same books they were reading.

"I wouldn't have a tutor, but I knew that I was on trial and I did find a way. I received a lot of assistance from the people in the bank as I went through the system. It took me a little time to get over the shock of realizing the size of Bank of Montreal. All I had been used to was the one small branch in London and the office there, while in Canada there were almost 1,500 branches across the country and abroad.

"The realization of the opportunities in Canada and in the Bank was the most marvelous feeling. After Europe, it was like being given the key to the treasury. This was, and is, a land of great opportunity and you could progress as fast as your abilities could take you. There were not the artificial limitations you find in the United Kingdom, especially if you are not one of the establishment or don't have the right accent. This dawned on me as such a lucky break that it fueled an ambition that had never been in me before.

"I had never considered myself an ambitious young man. But when I came to Canada, I realized that I could get a really good job here. I worked very hard at getting on at the Bank and getting to know this marvelous country. Then I hit upon a scheme, which probably changed my career path in a most positive way and which, I believed, would advance my career. I thought to myself, why don't I volunteer for all the worst performing branches. I went down to Head Office and asked for the worst branch of Bank of Montreal -- the most screwed up one. They told me they had just what I was looking for, right in Montreal. So I asked for that branch to clean up. They thought I was crazy. The thought that I might make matters worse never entered my head. Anyway, they took a chance and let me go to it.

"I fixed up that branch and feeling like the old western sheriff, I went down to Head Office again and asked for the next foul-up that needed fixing. They gave me another one and then another one and I was quite successful and this came to the attention of Head Office.

"Now they came to me and asked how I was fixing the branches. I had to confess that there was no secret formula and that I had no idea how I was doing it. Really, I wasn't fixing them at all. What I was doing was getting the people in the branch who were causing the problems to fix them. I figured as they were causing the problems, they knew best how to fix them, and they did."

The young Matt Barrett was, at age 24, displaying the real key to his successful career. He had an ability with people. The Bank, however, recognized it and promoted him into Human Resources at Head Office where he worked in personnel, employment and the like. From all his voracious reading, Matt Barrett became aware very early on that major changes were occurring in the technological field. He saw where this technology had a major part to play in the future of the banking system. He started recruiting and hiring technology people for the bank.

It also dawned on him that he had better get himself clued in on the technology too. So he hit the books again, burning the midnight oil and he became excited about what he was learning. He decided that the wave of the future involved industrial engineering and computer systems, the new disciplines emerging in banking and in business.

Matt Barrett was not only a go-getter for Bank of Montreal, he also had the good fortune to be on the leading edge when the old manual systems used for generations in the banking business were giving way to the new computerized ones. The Bank developed one of the first on-line real time banking systems in the world and started recruiting heavily for scientists, programmers and software people. Bank of Montreal was a leader in this field and Matt Barrett was a leader among leaders.

"We developed that system, but it wasn't without its rocky days," Matt recalls. "In retrospect, we were pioneering and although we didn't invent the phrase 'the computer is down,' we truly understood it and often used it. But it worked and the system is still alive and running today -- the same system we devised in those far off days." Apart from the introduction of new systems, Bank of Montreal was also undergoing enormous changes. Banking worldwide was changing, moving from an old era of stability and lack of change to an era of dramatic changes.

Knowing that Matt had a penchant for searching out problems to solve, when he asked to transfer over to the technological side the bank agreed. He spent the next two years learning industrial engineering, management systems and project management and picked up more than a passing familiarity with each aspect. He ran the human resources department and facilities planning. By the time he had spent four years in that area, he was running all the staff functions within the technology division. Matt was then made a vice-president of Bank of Montreal to oversee all the management services functions of the bank within Domestic Banking Canada.

Matt Barrett's career with Bank of Montreal is an extraordinary demonstration of one man's ability to adapt, improvise and foresee. Matt came from a small town in Ireland and is now the head of a major financial organization of North America with its myriad financial institutions, investment houses and moneyed financial families that carry on billions of dollars' worth of business on a day-to-day basis. Learning the intricacies of such business in one's own country is tough enough, but getting a handle on it in a foreign environment within such a short time gives a small understanding of the mental stature of this man. Matt, of course, had prepared himself well for the chores ahead of him -- he had volunteered for just about every job in the bank and had proven that he could handle and master each one with aplomb and competence.

Matt Barrett worked in all departments and at all levels of domestic banking and international banking and with all kinds of people. By the time he reached the top echelon at the age of forty years, he was the complete "renaissance man" as a banker. He had become senior vice-president, executive vice-president, deputy group executive and so on. He had managed international and domestic banking and the networks and became the deputy chief of treasury globally.

He always pursued a high risk, high reward course. "Playing it safe and comfortable," Matt says, "never gets one to the top." Every time the bank was at the leading edge of something new, or there was a major problem in the bank's operations anywhere in the world, the reputation of Matt Barrett was such that the advice would be "You go to Matt."

Matt has kept his bank running in high gear by working on the belief that most people know their jobs. "If you give them a clear direction, a clear vision of what has to be accomplished, give them the tools to do the job, motivate them and reward them for doing it, then you will find," Matt says, "that people will solve the problems themselves." Those principles have stayed with Matt Barrett throughout his career.

Things Irish

Matt Barrett is involved with the Ireland Fund of Canada, an organization supporting cultural and economic programs in Ireland.

Asked how he is able to explain his exalted position on his frequent trips home to Ireland, Matt says, "When you go home what you do is keep a low profile. When they ask me what I do, I say I work in a bank and when they get a little more inquisitive, I say I work in the head office. No way am I going to tell them I run an outfit the size of Bank of Montreal. If you tell them the truth, you're liable to get, 'Who does he think he is?' I like to have a quiet Guinness with them and just melt into the great feeling of being at home among my own."

Rowland W. Fleming
A Blueprint for Success

When he arrived at the Bank of Nova Scotia branch office in London, England, Rowland Fleming was given the job as credit officer responsible for small loans. Being observant and perhaps somewhat ambitious, Rowland noticed that anybody who was a somebody in financial circles in London was reading the *Financial Times* every morning as he traveled to work or after he arrived. This was the "pink" paper, and being pink it was at once obvious that those men reading it were people of worth and substance. He started reading the *Financial Times*.

After reading the *Times* for a while, Rowland Fleming focused on a section of the paper with advertisements which would read, for example, "Mexico -- $300 million." This type of announcement would appear "as a matter of record only," listing where the securities had been placed and naming the banks involved in the financing. Rowland noted that he had seldom, if ever, seen the Bank of Nova Scotia listed as one of the lenders. He asked his manager what these advertisements were all about. He was told they were "tombstones." The banks named had put together loans and were announcing them as a matter of record and as an investment. His manager explained that there was an agent bank which helped put the package together. Rowland asked why the Bank of Nova Scotia was not listed, and the answer he got was, "I suppose because we were never asked to participate." When Rowland asked if they would like to participate, his manager replied, "I guess we would. I suppose they'll call us when they need us." Roland went back to his desk and from then on started clipping those "tombstone" advertisements, mainly because he did not have a very busy job and it gave him something to do.

Using that initiative and acting on his own, Rowland started calling the agent banks which were arranging these financings. His conversations with these people enabled him to pick up much of the financial jargon that was common in the business. He would call CitiBank or Wells Fargo, or whichever bank headed up the particular syndicate and ask to speak to the person responsible for putting the deal together -- generally an American. Rowland would say, "I saw your 'tombstone' in the *Financial Times*," trying to sound as if he knew all about this type of finance. "How come you didn't ask us to participate?" Often, back would come the answer, "Oh, would you be interested in participating? I just happen to be packaging a deal and I'll send the details over."

To cut a long story short, those phone calls generated a flood of telex messages marked for his attention, outlining proposals and offerings for the bank   to join a syndicate. "I would analyze them and write them up for review and approval," Rowland said. Soon there was no shortage of offerings and the job got so big the bank promoted him and assigned him help. Rowland Fleming had made his paper clipping project pay off in a big way.

His initiative generated billions of dollars for the bank in major loans to less developed countries, ship and tanker financing for the North Sea and the Gulf, as well as for drilling platforms and the oil recovery and gathering systems. As a result, the bank also participated in financing projects for countries such as Mexico, Brazil, Argentina, Indonesia, Yugoslavia and many other countries around the world.

Boyhood Days in Ireland

Rowland Fleming was born in the Rotunda Hospital in Dublin on August 27, 1943. The family lived in Dublin until Rowland was about ten and, after a short sojourn in England, moved to Ardamine, a little place near Gorey in Wexford. His father's health was poor and he needed a complete rest and change of climate. Ardamine was the perfect spot for him. His father had left school at fourteen and after serving an apprenticeship, started out on his own and built a successful cabinetry and joinery business.

His mother, Dorothy Fleming, graduated from Trinity College, Dublin in 1932. She earned a degree in Commerce and the Arts. This was an amazing accomplishment for an Irish woman in 1932.

Rowland attended a one-room school at Ardamine. Because he was born into a Protestant family, when it came time for secondary education, the normal practice was to go to boarding school. Protestants represented about five per cent of Southern Ireland's population. However, his parents could not afford the fees, so Rowland made a virtue out of necessity and chose to go to the Christian Brothers School in Gorey. He rode his bicycle to school -- five miles each way each day and many's the time his endurance was tested when the bicycle broke down. He was the only Protestant among two hundred or so boys. "I had the most wonderful time," he recalls fondly. Also, he had, for a youngster in Ireland, the most wonderful choice. He could choose to go to mass or skip it and there was the odd occasion when he decided to skip it!

For Rowland this sojourn amid Catholics provided the opportunity for him to learn a lot about himself, the differences between religions, and the importance of tolerance. The debates on the various religious beliefs and the willingness to listen to other views and creeds instilled in him an appreciation for all creeds. During the seven years he spent at the Christian Brothers School, there was only one incident involving his religious difference. The boy was reported by the other boys and expelled.

In 1962, when it came time to go out into the world and find a job ("a good pensionable job" was the order of the day at the time), Rowland had the choice of emigrating, working for the Guinness Brewery, or working in a bank. He chose to work with the Bank of Ireland; he was hired as a junior clerk, earning less than it took to live on. Four years later, the Irish banks went on strike and Rowland, who decided that he did not like the idea of being unionized or told when he could work and when he couldn't, went to work in 1967 as a teller for the Bank of Nova Scotia in Dublin.

By his own admission, he was not a great success at this particular job (he didn't always balance!) and found he enjoyed other parts of his junior post a little more. His inquisitive nature and desire to get ahead saw him learn and do most jobs in the branch before he was asked to move with his young wife and one-year-old son to the bank's office in London, England.

The Road to Success

The Bank of Nova Scotia (later to be known as Scotia Bank) office in London to which Rowland was transferred in 1971 was located next to that venerable Old Lady of Threadneedle Street -- the Bank of England. At Scotia Bank, Rowland became involved in the Eurobond market, lending money to major corporations, the so-called LDC's (less developed countries) and in financing projects all over the world. He was all of thirty years old.

By mid-1974, Rowland had developed a name as an innovative banker who produced big revenues for his employer. He knew the Eurodollar market and knew the players. At this time he was approached by a major merchant bank with a great job offer at twice that of his employer, Scotia Bank, who offered him the opportunity of moving to Canada to work in its home operations. Rowland decided to go to Canada. His sixth sense must have been working overtime, for the merchant bank went belly up later.

In Canada, Rowland was given the job of assessing the creditworthiness of the loans being generated by the bank's offices in the United States as a credit analyst. It was on his recommendations that the loans would be approved or turned down by senior management of the bank. Many of the loans were to Fortune 500 companies. Rowland read copiously to get himself familiar with the multitude of American companies and, as always, he asked a lot of questions.

Apart from business courses at London University and at a Canadian University which Scotia Bank had arranged for him, Rowland is a self-taught banker and businessman. There were really no courses for the market savvy needed in the work he was doing -- it was strictly on-the-job training. "I was self-taught all the way," he says in a kind of semi-confessional way. "I never even picked up my leaving certificate from school." He was ill at the time of the exams.

Rowland Fleming credits a lot of his success to working for supportive people during his growth years. Of course, without the right material to work with, it would not really matter what kind of support was out there. His salary when he came to Canada was $13,000 a year to keep a wife and two children. In London, he had been an assistant manager, then senior assistant manager in charge of all the bank's Eurodollar deals. The Canada move was, at best, a lateral one, not a promotion, but it served to broaden his experience and knowledge. He saw opportunity where other people might have seen walls.

United States Assignment

After a year of scrutinizing the business in Toronto, Rowland was asked if he would like to work in the New York office. For him, New York was a kind of terror planet; all he knew about it was what he had seen on television. It was not his idea of the best posting in the world. His job in the New York office was the opposite of what he had been doing -- he would be developing business for the bank, the wholesale side of banking, with the Fortune 500 group of companies.

Rowland became a Wall Street banker, living in New Jersey and commuting every day. He was given part of New York and all of New England as his hunting ground and he went "cold calling." However, he knew that this part of the banking business was for him when, as part of the handing over ceremony, he was introduced by the banker who was leaving at a large Boston-based multinational company. Rowland had landed a hundred-million-dollar transaction, while his predecessor had been knocking on that door for ten years without success.

After much canvassing in the Boston area which generated a lot of business, Rowland suggested that the bank reopen the Boston office, which had been closed in 1942. The bank said yes, if he would run it and some eighteen months later, he was on the move again with his family. The plan was to have the Boston branch in the black within five years; he had it profitable within one year. This success did not go unnoticed.

After a most enjoyable year for Rowland and his family in Boston, he was summoned to Toronto. The call was from a boss with whom he had a flaming row a short time before. Thinking he was going to get his pink slip, Rowland tells him, "If you're going to fire me, do it over the phone. Don't waste my time dragging me all the way up to Toronto." However, he made the trip, and he was told there was a job opening to run the United States activities for the bank and he was asked if he would accept it.

He took the position and returned late in 1979 to work out of Toronto. "I was given the title of assistant general manager of United States operations. Then I was promoted to general manager and subsequently to senior vice-president for the United States, with all the operations in the United States reporting to me."

Aside from the long term relationships with Fortune 500 companies, the United States operations involved, in part, dealing with the leveraged buyouts which were so prevalent during the 1980s, the so-called junk bond era. Large financing for energy and real estate companies was also high on the agenda and, while most deals worked well for the bank, Rowland often became directly involved in those that went sour. Texas became almost a second home, as he worked overtime on managing a number of multibillion dollar bankruptcies, including the Hunts and the wealthy Davis family of Fort Worth. The Davis's bankruptcy was unusual, with murder trials and death threats in the background, and billion dollar lawsuits reaching the Supreme Court of the United States before the case was finally wound up.

The bank divided up the United States operations and Rowland Fleming became the senior vice-president for Western Canada and the Western United States.

On one lovely sunny October day in 1986, Rowland Fleming received a call from the vice-chairman of the bank. He said, "Congratulations. You have just been appointed executive vice-president for all of Canada!" This was a major promotion for Rowland Fleming -- overseeing all the branches, all the retail operations, all the commercial operations. His response was that he did not know anything about that side of the business.

He had never worked in retail banking and questioned whether he was the right man. The job involved 18,000 people and 1,100 branches and covered everything that moved in Canada, retail and commercial. Rowland reported to the deputy chairman of Scotia Bank-- the job was one of the top eight in the whole organization. The bank has assets of over $80 billion and 33,000 people on staff. Rowland Fleming had progressed in a

200

fairly short time from being a teller in the Bank of Ireland in Dublin to being one of the top executives in Scotia Bank. His new boss was also the bank's president. He had the reputation of being a very difficult man to work for. Rowland Fleming was warned by friends inside and outside the bank that his life expectancy in that position was two years at best -- that had been the fate of all his eight or so predecessors in the job.

Two years down the road, he was still in the job and doing well, but there were very clear signs that the welcome mat was being rolled up -- all the warning signals were there. It was becoming clear that he was not going to survive in the job. "I did manage to stay another year, but the last six months were perhaps the most calamitous and difficult in my career," Rowland remembers. On January 3, 1990, Rowland Fleming "quit" Scotia Bank; he was unemployed for the first time in his working life.

The bank, being a publicly traded company, had no choice but to issue a press release on Rowland Fleming's so-called resignation. The next day, the front pages of the business sections of Canada's national newspapers, the *Globe and Mail* and the *Financial Post*, all blazoned headlines such as "Senior Executive Fleming Quits Scotia Bank." The story was picked up by the *Economist* and the *Wall Street Journal*. Rowland remembers the press had all kinds of nice things to say about him, but he still did not have a job.

He took some time off for a much needed rest and then started looking for work. The search took him six months. Then a "headhunter" asked if he would be interested in putting his name in the hat to run a property, casualty and insurance company -- a business he knew little, if anything, about.

From Banking to Insurance

He got the job of running the Dominion of Canada General Insurance Company, one of the country's largest insurance companies. It is interesting to note that Rowland was following in the footsteps of Sir John A. Macdonald -- the first president of that company in 1887.

Macdonald was president of Dominion at the same time as he was prime minister of Canada. The coat of arms of the

Dominion Insurance Company is the same as the coat of arms of Canada. The photographs of all the previous presidents of the Dominion Insurance of Canada are on the walls of the company's boardroom. Now a County Wexford interloper shares the same gallery as Sir John A. Macdonald and many other famous Canadians.

Rowland had been running the insurance company for about eighteen months, when he got a call from the chairman of National Trust Company inviting him to head it up. Five days later, following a meeting with its board of directors, Rowland was appointed deputy chairman, president and chief executive officer of the company.

National Trust is one of Canada's premier financial institutions that has been around for about one hundred and fifty years. It has over 190 branches coast-to-coast and has some $16 billion in assets and manages some $33 billion more of other people's money. The market seems to like the idea of Rowland Fleming running National Trust -- the stock has increased in value substantially since he took over the reins.

Aside from his latest challenge in a fascinating career, Rowland devotes a lot of time to outside business and charitable organizations. As a director of eight or so public companies (including a newspaper!) and of the Canadian Chamber of Commerce, he manages to use his experience in a variety of ways. He enjoys being on the boards of the Toronto YMCA (one of the largest in North America), the Stratford Theatre Festival, and of Junior Achievement. These activities, along with some fund raising for the United Way, allow him to give something back to the community. Ireland does not get forgotten in all of this, since Rowland is also active as a director of the Ireland Fund of Canada.

County Wexford Connections

Both of Rowland Fleming's parents, now in their eighties, live in Ireland in Ardamine. He has two brothers, Hedley and Victor, who each run successful trailer parks in Courtown Harbour in County Wexford, within five miles of the childhood home. Rowland makes the annual pilgrimage back home with his wife, Kate. His two children are at college in Canada. Rowland tells us that he has a good full life in Canada, where, with the support of his family, he has achieved more than he ever dreamed possible.

However, despite his success and position as one of the leading businessmen in Canada, he is ever mindful of his origins and of the values he took from his parents and those early years in that small town in County Wexford. His philosophy is simple: "Enjoy what you do, do the best you can and never forget where you came from."

Rowland Fleming and his lovely wife, Kate, enjoy a quiet meal far from the hustle and bustle of the banking business.

Ted McConnell
Toronto's Irishman of the Year 1992

Ted McConnell is fiercely Irish and like most Irish, his Irishness is not really definable. The Irish are able to understand one another without a lot of explaining and in ways which others never comprehend. Ted gives an unconscious example of this unique ability in relating a small incident at Shannon Airport. On a business trip to Dublin, the Boeing 747 made its compulsory stop at Shannon. As the plane came to a stop, Ted was looking out of the window when his eyes focused on a worker away out in the middle of a field. This worker was just leaning on his shovel, watching the plane. "I couldn't see his face," Ted says. "But I could see by the body language the wistfulness of the man and I instinctively knew what he was thinking. After about an hour of discharging passengers, we boarded again to resume the flight. I looked out the window and there was your man, still leaning on his shovel and his body still giving off the melancholy the stay-at-home feels about the departing emigrant. That really gave me an emotional tug; Ireland does that to you," Ted said.

Ted the Business Man

Ted was a single man when he came to Canada. He had no great plans of making a career in North America. His primary objective was to get a job and it did not matter what kind, just something to tide him over for the year he expected to stay in the country.

Ted had graduated from the Faculty of Law in 1954 at Queens University in Belfast and had worked in England for the summer. Then he got to thinking about what he wanted to do, long term, with his life. He had plans to go back to Belfast to work with a solicitor but he thought he should see some of the world first.

On a very cold, miserable November night in the east end of London, Ted was on his way to visit a sick priest in the hospital. "There I was feeling cold and damp, standing in an open Tube station not very far from the present day Canary Wharf. In the midst of this misery, my eye caught this great big sign on the wall, a big poster with the Rockies and the blue sky, big trees and the Mounties sitting on their glorious horses. It was the kind of scene every kid dreams about. On the poster there was a big sign saying, 'Come to Canada.' That poster stuck in my mind and got the wanderlust going. I went along to the Australia House, the New Zealand House and Canada House. The Canadians seemed to want me, so I decided that I would go to Canada for a year, then go back to Belfast and settle down to the legal business.

"I had, up to that time, lived a very insular life and did not know anything about any place, except Belfast. My first stop was in Montreal. I had given little thought to where I was going as I did not intend to stay."

Ted worked as a fuel oil dispatcher in a department store and at a variety of other uninspiring kinds of employment. Then a friend of his suggested that with his qualifications he should investigate the trust companies, as they were always looking for qualified help. Having someone tell him that he was qualified for something gave Ted a big lift, so he started going through the yellow pages and did some telephoning. One of the trust companies did hire him.

Knowing nothing about that business, Ted nevertheless managed to give the impression that he knew what he was doing. To further this illusion, he joined the Junior Board of Trade in Montreal and entered one of its debating competitions. Ted won and to cap it off, he and his partner won the doubles event.

This great feat of verbosity did not go unnoticed and a little while later Ted received a call inviting him to moderate a political discussion on a radio program. What Ted knew about moderating at this stage in his career was zilch. What he knew about Canadian politics was even less. Undaunted, he took up the challenge and once again his eloquence proved to be a big hit.

The executive officer of the Guardian Trust Company heard the program and he sent a representative around to see Ted to arrange an interview. Ted was offered a job with significant improvements over his current employment. Ted was married by this time and a father. Although he liked the company he was working for, he took the job with Guardian. His new job was assistant

205

to the president, more or less. After two years of getting his feet wet in the executive suite, a friend at Guardian Trust told him that City Bank would like to talk to him. This was an American outfit that owned the Mercantile Bank in Canada and International Trust. Ted was hired as acting general manager of International Trust in Canada and was sent to Toronto to head up the operations there.

Ted's progress from vice-president to executive vice-president to president and chief executive officer was fairly rapid with International Trust. International Trust was not a traditional trust company because it essentially managed money for pension funds and institutions.

By 1975, Ted was starting to get the itch again. He had been thinking about going out on his own, despite the fact that he had a very good job. He had this entrepreneurial drive. With some trepidation, he set up his own business, E. J. McConnell & Associates Ltd. and he waited for the crowd to start calling. Ted had no assets under management when he started and his innate sense of honor would not allow him to go after clients of his former employer. Ted did have some money of his own and he did know people in the business world. After a while, Ted and his partner, Ted Raven, started to develop a clientele. Ted Raven left after a short time and Ted McConnell had to carry the ball himself.

It took a long time to develop E. J. McConnell. Ted had to prospect new ground. In time, some of the customers of his old employer came to him and Ted solicited business from many of the successful Irish people that he knew. The Irish community was enormously helpful. The first three or four pieces of business he secured were from corporations where the chief financial officers were Irish.

People like Tom Savage of ITT, Jack Donnelly, who ran the Sheet Metal Workers Union, Michael J. Reilly from County Westmeath, who ran the Laborers Union and Patrick Hughes of Northgate Mines all came on board. The business gradually built up from this humble beginning and Ted was eventually handling something in the order of $3 billion of clients' money.

The success of Ted's operation attracted the attention of England's Barclays Bank which bought into the company and changed the name to Barclays McConnell. A search is now on for a new head man, so Ted can quit the business and devote more time to his hobbies, golf and tennis, and to his work for the Irish community.

The Athletic Ted

Ted McConnell was a sportsman in his youth, boxing, hurling and even playing some Gaelic football. He says that one of the reasons he came to Canada was to be able to see the Friday night fights at a decent hour. As a hurler, Ted McConnell has a record which probably will never be broken. He captained the Belfast Under 14s Hurling Team in what, he believes, was the greatest shellacking ever suffered in that noble sport. His team lost with the score being nineteen goals and sixteen points to a goal and one point. For the uninitiated, that means the score was seventy-three points to four points.

Ted's other record is a bit more glorious. This time, again in hurling, he was captain of Queens in the Universities Championship. He does wax a bit nostalgic when he recounts this event. "Queens," he says in his best Belfast accent, "has been playing in the Fitzgibbon Cup since around 1870 and had never won the Cup, that is until I captained them in 1952." For the first time in its history, Queens won and Ted has the gold medal to prove it! The next year he captained the football team in the Sigurdson Cup, but it lost in the last minute.

The Queens team of 1952 had a reunion in 1992 and Ted took his children and his medal to the event. Now, his children know nothing about Gaelic football or hurling (hockey and baseball, yes), but when they saw their father standing up there with his gold medal, they were properly impressed.

Irish Culture and Traditions

Ted McConnell is a force in the International Fund for Ireland. This organization is funded by the governments of the United States, Canada, England and New Zealand. The Fund, where Ted is the Canadian Observer, was set up to help those areas most damaged by "the troubles" in the border counties. Newry is one of those areas. The restoration in some of the core areas has to be seen to be understood. Ted says the young people are starting to come back to the cities again and the Fund workers are trying to create an environment where kids can go out at night without fear. There was nothing for them to do. The work undertaken by the Fund is now starting to show results. Many interesting projects have been carried out by the Fund throughout Northern Ireland. Canada is committed to providing ten million dollars for this work.

The Ireland Fund of Canada is another organization in which Ted McConnell is involved. There are Ireland Funds in several countries. This is the pet project of the great Irish philanthropist, Dr. Tony O'Reilly, who heads up the giant Heinz food conglomerate. The Ireland Funds are privately funded, with corporations and individuals financing many worthwhile causes in Ireland.

One of the joys of this work for Ted McConnell was his visit to a school in Mississauga, a suburb of Toronto, where he was invited to see the program in action. The school had students from Limerick, Derry and from parts of Belfast. They attended this school together, they got to know each other and they have gone on trips together. "One gets a tremendous sense of the barriers coming down," Ted says, "with young people tending to recognize each other for what they really are and not by the labels which have been pinned on them. My big hope is that when they go back to wherever they live, they will carry that feeling with them. A lot of this kind of work is being fostered and sponsored by the International Fund for Ireland."

Ted is also involved with the Irish Chamber of Commerce. The Chamber was set up to foster good business relations between Ireland and Canada. A forum is provided where Irish business people can meet and get to know each other. This allows them to co-operate on projects which can be helpful to Ireland. The Chamber is connected to similar chambers across North America and there is a branch in Dublin.

Ted says that his feeling now is that, "The Irish in North America are beginning to talk up the old country and they are finally starting to come together. Almost everybody I know who has any drop of Irish blood in them has gone to Ireland. I think

Ted McConnell with his wife, Pauline, and Emmett Cardinal Carter, retired head of the Archdiocese of Toronto, when he was presented with the Canada Irishman of the Year Award in 1992. Ted has received many honors for his work on behalf of Ireland and the Irish community in Canada. His investiture into the Order of the British Empire took place at Buckingham Palace on November 17, 1992.

the Irish Tourist Board is doing a fantastic job and Irish people themselves are talking it up."

Asked how Northern Ireland people feel about the Southern Irish, Ted tells us, "That is one of the great problems in Northern Ireland. You take the Ulster Unionists -- they're not Irish, they're not English. So what are they? There is that very real identity crisis. But I am not in any way confused in my own mind about my Irishness. I was born in Ireland. I'm an Irishman and if anyone asks me what my nationality is, I'm Irish. It's that simple."

The McConnell Family

Ted's wife is Pauline Murphy, whose mother was from County Roscommon. Her father came from Fermanagh. Both of them have passed away. Ted and Pauline have five children; Eamonn, Stephen, Michael, David and Eileen.

Ted McConnell was presented with the Canada Irishman of the Year Award in 1992. He has received many honors for his work on behalf of Ireland and the Irish community. His investiture into the Order of the British Empire at Buckingham Palace took place November 17, 1992. He was awarded a Doctorate of Law from his Alma Mater, Queens University, Belfast, and was the first non-resident to become president of Queens Graduate Society in 1992.

Ted is a great lover of Irish traditional music and he had the great pleasure of having the Chieftains play at his house one night after a Toronto concert. His children have been exposed to traditional Irish music, which is hardly the genre of today. The great concern in Ted's house seems to be "will Dad get enough tickets for all of us" when the Chieftains come to town. The McConnell family are very proud of their Irish heritage.

Edward Anthony Sheeran
New York 1990 St. Patrick's Day Parade
Grand Marshall

Early in 1990, Edward Anthony Sheeran resigned from the Chase Manhattan Bank to enter the entrepreneurial ranks. He founded the Rockfield Corporation to engage in the development of hotels and resorts. The first major undertaking for Rockfield is the development of the eight hundred acre Lough Key Hotel and Golf Resort in Ed Sheeran's native County Roscommon. This resort, set in one of Ireland's most scenic areas, will, says Ed, attract one million tourists a year and give a much needed boost to Ireland's economy.

Ed Sheeran, a banker, marketer, administrator and businessman, continues to be very active in the promotion and development of things Irish in and around New York. His Irish charm and congeniality have helped him immensely in his business dealings and in raising funds for the many worthy Irish causes he espouses. Being located in the Bronx area of New York City as manager of the Kingsbridge branch of Chase Manhattan Bank, an area heavily populated by Irish, got him a lot of business and exposed him to the Irish community and all its cultural happenings. Ed is heavily involved with the Irish Dancing and Music Association, the Ancient Order of Hibernians, Bronx Division, and was personal banker to several Irish organizations in the Kingsbridge area of the Bronx.

Getting His Feet Wet

"If I had had any money, I would have been on the next plane back straight away," was Ed Sheeran's feelings after landing at his Uncle John Saunder's place in Washington Heights in Upper Manhattan in 1961. He was eighteen and what he knew about life in the Big Apple would fit in a matchbox. His first job was with United Parcel Service founded by Irish-American John Casey. It was for the Christmas season and consisted of loading trucks. It lasted one month.

211

With a month's work behind him, Ed managed to get a number of jobs, picking up experience until he was, he felt, ready to take on the big city. Having been in a bank two times in his whole life, Ed felt his financial know-how was ready for marketing. He got a job at the 149th Street and Third Avenue branch of the Chase Manhattan Bank.

Before he left that fine establishment in 1990, Ed had worked his way through the whole system, from assistant teller to branch manager to assistant treasurer of Chase. In the process, he managed the opening of several new locations for the bank. He organized marathon races with Chase as sponsor, attracting new business and establishing a tradition, "The Chase is on" marathon which still brings positive attention to the bank.

Realizing that just being Irish, while great, was not good enough to further his banking career, Ed enrolled in Fordham University where he earned a Bachelor of Science degree and, subsequently, a Masters in Business Administration at Faerliegh Dickenson University in Rutherford, New Jersey.

Chase Manhattan's Man in Australia

His enthusiasm and tireless work habits earned Ed a vice-presidency in 1982, with responsibility for nineteen Chase branches in Westchester County, New York. His remarkable achievements with Chase Manhattan did not go unnoticed and he was picked to open the bank's Australian operations, the first foreign bank to open in Australia.

Ed spent his first six months in Australia working fourteen to sixteen hour days, seven days a week. He traveled the length and breadth of Australia, often hitting three different cities in the one day. Starting from scratch, he put in place a staff of 119, who reported directly or indirectly to him.

Chase was in partnership with the Australian AMP Insurance Company and Ed's job was to make the Australian company, Chase-AMP, the premier foreign bank in Australia. Ed opened seven full service banks and ten banking facilities within building societies (savings and loan associations). After twenty months in Australia, Ed Sheeran came back to New York. In October 1986, he entered Sloane Kettering Hospital for major

212

surgery -- the removal of a tumor from his lung. He made a complete recovery.

Back in New York

The bank then made Ed Division Executive of Chase Manhattan's Queens network, overseeing the staff of 223 branches. His stature now was such that public relations and fund raising assignments rapidly came his way. Ed tackled these with the same verve he brought to his banking duties. He was appointed First Chairman of the United Way of Queens and he developed the United Partnership of Queens, a combined business-United Way venture set up to find solutions to community problems in the Borough of Queens. With the help of John Phelan, New York's top financial figure and chairman of the New York Stock Exchange, Ed raised over three hundred thousand dollars for this venture in just two years.

His next involvement was heading up Junior Achievement, followed by involvement with the Jamaica Development Corporation.

St. Patrick's Day Parade Grand Marshall

Over the years, Ed Sheeran has kept very much alive his involvement with Ireland; he has made some forty trips back home in the past thirty years. He has brought to the New York area such well known groups as The Chieftains, the Wolfe Tones, Frank Patterson, Makem and Clancy, the Dubliners, Forster and Allen, and Paddy Reilly. He is also a great John McCormack aficionado; he has all the great man's records and was the driving force behind a memorial concert at Carnegie Hall in his honor.

In February 1990, Ed was elected Grand Marshall of New York City's St. Patrick's Day Parade. He was the youngest individual ever to have this honor bestowed upon him.   Ed is a member of the Knights of St. Patrick, a fifty-member group of prominent Irish Americans who financially support the St. Patrick's Day Parade in New York -- the world's largest parade.

In June of 1992, Ed was called upon to head up a search committee for a Gaelic Athletic Association sports field in New York. Ed had long mourned the lack of an Irish center in the tri-

213

Ed Sheeran, Grand Marshall of the 1990 New York St. Patrick's Day Parade photographed with Helen Hayes, First Lady of the American Theater. Helen Hayes passed away on St. Patrick's Day 1993.

Ed Sheeran shown with Congressman Joe Kennedy, son of the late Robert Kennedy and nephew of the late President John F. Kennedy.

state area. Ed broadened his quest and founded the 58-acre complex in Briarcliff Manor, New York, to be known as The Tara Circle, Inc. As its Chairman, he seeks to establish an educational, cultural, entertainment and sports center -- an active living legacy for all Irish-Americans.

He serves the County of Westchester as member of the Board of Directors of the Hudson Valley National Bank. He is Vice Chairman of Yonkers Industrial Development Agency and Vice President of the Yonkers Development Agency.

For his untiring efforts in promoting the Irish presence in the New York area and in helping the less fortunate, Ed has been honored with numerous awards and recognition from many groups and organizations including: the County Roscommon Society, the Bedford Park Shamrock Club, the Bronx County Ancient Order of Hibernians, American Cancer Society, the Boy Scouts of America, Junior Achievement and the March of Dimes.

The Sheeran Clan

Ed Sheeran is married to the former Priscilla May Johnson of Irish-Swedish ancestry. They have three children: Erin, Edward Jr. and Douglas Conan.

Ed's brother, Patrick, lives in Bethesda, Maryland with his wife, Kathleen, and their two sons, Peter Joseph and Robert Emmet. Patrick is active in Irish affairs in the Washington, D. C. area. He is a charter member and past president of the Sheridan Circle, an Irish-American professional association which promotes exchange of business and cultural information between Ireland and the United States. He is also co-founder of the Roscommon Society of Washington, D.C. and an active member of Conradh na Gaeilge/Washington and the Washington Gaels Irish Football Club.

Patrick holds two master's degrees and a Doctorate in Public Administration from the University of Southern California in Los Angeles. He is the author of two books, *Women, Society, the State and Abortion: A Structuralist Analysis* and *Ethics in Public Administration: A Philosophical Approach* and several published articles on management in the public sector. He served as an officer in the U.S. Air Force and at the Department of Defense. He currently works for the U. S. Department of Health and Human Services and is an adjunct professor of Public Administration at the University of Southern California and George Mason University in Virginia.

The Sheeran family has had a long and noteworthy history in County Roscommon. The family had a thriving blacksmith business until the Famine of 1848 when many of them died and others were forced to immigrate to the United States. Some of them made their new homes in New Jersey, others in Denver and San Francisco.

Ed's second brother, Peter, lives in Dublin with his wife, Patricia, and their two children, Deirdre and Patrick. Peter is now retired as National Distribution Manager for a United States Oil Company based in Dublin. When in Ireland, Ed generally makes his brother's home in Dublin his base of operations. But he spends as much time as possible "down home" in Kilglass, County Roscommon.

Edward staunchly maintains that the lakes of Kilglass are as beautiful as any you will find in Kerry or other counties of Ireland. Ed's affection for his native Kilglass parish is aptly captured in the following poem by another native son, Henry Freyne, who emigrated to Passaic, New Jersey about 1850, and who, like Ed, became a banker and businessman.

> Farewell Kilglass 'tis my birthplace, I now must bid adieu
> To all my friends and neighbors and kind relations too.
> My turn now has come at last like some brave men before
> And tomorrow at the break of day, I'll leave Kilglass once more.
>
> It is not the parting from Kilglass that grieves me o'er and o'er
> Or yet the separation of the many friends I know.
> 'Tis the parting of each comrade boy when all our sport is o'er
> That makes me think of you Kilglass and love you evermore.

Peter Grace
Multinational Corporation Titan

When J. Peter Grace stepped down as chief executive officer of the New York-based W. R. Grace & Company in 1993, it was the first time in the 140-year history of the company that no Grace family member would be running the multibillion-dollar conglomerate. Peter Grace ran the company for forty-seven years, the longest reign ever by a chief executive officer of a major New York Stock Exchange listed company.

Describing Peter Grace's contribution to the company's growth, the 1992 W. R. Grace & Company annual report says that when Peter Grace inherited the mantle of leadership from his father in September of 1945, World War II had just ended. The ensuing forty-seven years saw one of the greatest transformations in corporate history. With an entrepreneurial flair that became his trademark, Peter Grace bought and sold more than 150 companies. He moved the Grace company away from its dependence on Latin America and into the more stable economies of Europe and the United States, building a solid foundation in specialty chemicals.

Grace is now the world's largest specialty chemicals company and holds a leadership position in specialized health care. The company is also active in packaging, water treatment, construction products and catalysts. Through Erike, a subsidiary of Grace's National Medical Care, the Grace Company operates a medical supplies plant in Clondalkin, County Dublin, employing 150 persons.

The Founding of W. R. Grace

Among the pioneer emigrants who set sail from Ireland in 1851 to join John Gallagher's sugar plantation colony in Peru were James Grace, sons William Russell and Michael Paul and daughter, Ellen. The Grace family had been land owners at Ballylinan, Queen's County. The famine of 1846-1848 had wrought great hardship on their tenants and on the family. In Peru, the Grace family's attempt to establish a fertilizer business

217

failed, as did John Gallagher's sugar plantation. Unable to find the kind of opportunity in fertilizers they sought in Peru, James Grace returned to Ireland with Michael Paul and Ellen.

Son William stayed on, having found work in a ship chandler's shop owned by John and Francis Bryce. William soon worked his way into a partnership with the Bryces. Ultimately, William Grace bought out the owners and launched W. R. Grace & Company and numerous subsidiaries. In time the Grace companies cornered trade between the United States and several South American countries. They engaged in railroad building in Peru, in sugar, rubber, nitrates and above all, shipping.

Moves to New York

Suffering from poor health, William Grace left Peru for New York in 1865, leaving his brother, Michael, back from Ireland, to look after Grace Brothers & Company. William started the New York division of the company, naming it W. R. Grace and Company. Using its Peruvian connections, the Grace company became agents in the United States for Peru's nitrate of soda used in the manufacture of fertilizers.

The first major recognition the company received was when a group, representing European bondholders of Peruvian bonds, approached Grace to have him work out an agreement on $250 million in bonds which were in danger of default. Peru's economy was in poor shape after its war with Chile in the 1880s and the investors wanted some protection. Grace succeeded in making a deal with the Peruvian government under which the bondholders got the rights to the state-owned railway for sixty-six years, rights to Peru's guano production (used in the manufacture of fertilizer) and several mines. Part of the agreement had the bondholders repair and expand the railway system and the Grace company got the contract to supply the materials needed for the railway construction. In its early years, the Grace company relied exclusively on South America for its business expansion.

William Grace was elected mayor of New York in 1880 on a Democratic ticket, sixteen years after he had moved there from Peru. He was the first Irish Catholic to hold that job. His religion, an issue in the campaign, was soon forgotten when he named a

Peter Grace, grandson of Irish-born William R. Grace, founder of the multinational corporation W. R. Grace and Company. Peter Grace had served forty-seven years as chief executive officer of the company bearing his name when he stepped down in 1992.

Presbyterian as president of the school board. He became a reformer of New York's corrupt politics dominated by Tammany Hall. Grace successfully ran again for mayor in 1884 and he retired from public office in 1886.

Son Joseph Takes Over

William passed away in 1904 and the running of the company operations was taken over by his brother, Michael. In 1909, William's son, Joseph, succeeded Michael as head of the company. When Joseph took charge of the company, he embarked on expanding the South American trade substantially and helped set up the first international air service to South America in partnership with Pan American Airways. The airline was called Pan-American Grace Airways (Panagra). Joseph remained head of the company until 1945 when he turned it over to his son, Joseph Peter Grace.

Joseph Peter Grace, grandson of William R. Grace, undertook an ambitious expansion of the company. He first explored the investment possibilities in petroleum, but found that it was too tightly controlled by the oil cartel. He then expanded into the chemical industries in the 1950s. Today, Grace company is the nation's fifth largest chemical producer. Grace has also branched out into retailing and restauranting. During Peter Grace's forty-seven years as chief executive officer, the company bought and sold control of the Miller Brewing Company, Grace National Bank, restaurants, sports manufacturers and a collection of companies too diverse and numerous to list.

Upon his election as president, Ronald Reagan appointed Peter Grace to chair a private sector commission to look at ways of cutting waste in the federal government. This commission, named the Grace Commission, did a full-fledged study of government management and made a number of cost saving recommendations which were adopted by the Reagan Administration.

220

Robert Moran
He built the battleship USS
Nebraska, rebuilt Seattle and gave us
Rosario Resort on Orcas Island

On June 6, 1939, Robert Moran was made President of the Pioneers Association of the State of Washington at a ceremony in Seattle. This was a fitting tribute to the man who served first as a council member and subsequently two terms as mayor of Seattle. Robert Moran was the mayor when fire destroyed the city in 1889. A primitive water supply system was unable to cope with the fire and Moran's business premises and most of the city burned. Moran had been trying to force the owners of the water company to either sell out to the city or upgrade its plant. After the fire, the city bought out the company. Moran then brought in the engineer who had constructed Chicago's water and sewer system and had him construct the present systems which still serve Seattle.

Robert Moran's shipbuilding enterprise was responsible in a large way for bringing Seattle into the twentieth century and it laid the foundation for the great city Seattle has become today. When Seattle was still a small town, Moran went after the contract to build the *Nebraska* -- the first of the "big gun" battleships. The big shipbuilding companies thought the application by Moran was a joke, but when the dust had settled, Robert Moran came home to Seattle with the contract.

When the *Nebraska* was launched, Admiral Kountz told the one thousand six hundred people assembled that the *Nebraska* was the finest ship ever built for the navy. Unfortunately, it was the first and only battleship ever built in Seattle. The *Nebraska* became part of the American fleet and did escort work for merchant ships during World War I. She was also employed bringing doughboys home from France at the end of the war.

The Moran Company acquired much of its shipbuilding expertise during the Klondike gold rush days. At one time, the company had 2,600 employees and produced most of the vessels

221

which serviced the gold seekers on the Yukon River trips to and from the gold fields. Within a six-month span, the Morans built fourteen sternwheel river steamers, each one hundred and seventy-five feet long, and six freight barges, including engines and boilers, all delivered in time for them to make one or two trips that season before the ice closed the river.

Robert Moran's shipbuilding feats brought him high esteem in the United States, but more important were the benefits to Seattle that the myriad skills of such a huge undertaking bring. Over the years, the operations produced hundreds of engineers and provided a great school for mechanics, draftsmen and technical experts. Of immense value, the Morans led the nation in steel shipbuilding during World War I.

From Humble Beginnings

When Robert Moran first arrived in Seattle in 1875, Washington was still a territory. He was a lad of seventeen with ten cents in his pocket and without kin or friends in what was then a small town of about one thousand five hundred people. He was befriended by Hash House owner Bill Gross, who first got him a job as a cook in a logging camp.

Robert Moran's skill as a cook left a lot to be desired. Hardened loggers with the constitution of a horse reacted with dismay to the culinary offerings he presented. The loggers flatly refused to eat the food he prepared for them and after three days he was run out of camp.

Robert returned to his mentor, Bill Gross, who then got him a job as a deckhand on an old side-wheeler. After spending some time on the boats, Robert managed to save $500 and with that stake he sent for his mother and four younger brothers and sisters, who joined him from New York.

Robert Moran had started his working life at fourteen, working for his father who operated a machine shop making belts for the Singer Sewing Machine Company. The skills Robert picked up at that time were to stand him in good stead on the boats and later, coupled with an enormous amount of home study in mathematics, engineering and drafting, enabled him to make it to chief engineer. After saving $1,600, Robert Moran went into business

222

for himself in 1882, at the age of twenty-five. He opened a marine repair shop on Yesler's Wharf. When that operation was burned out, he set up his shipbuilding plant nearby. The area is now part of downtown Seattle's more expensive real estate, home to the Seattle Kingdome and many waterfront businesses.

A False Alarm and Rosario

At the height of its growth and prosperity, Robert Moran sold his shipbuilding operations. Feeling under the weather and looking gaunt and skinny, he contacted his doctor and was told he had from six to eighteen months to live with an organic heart disease condition. He discovered, many years later, that he was stressed out and badly overworked, physically and mentally. He decided to retire to Orcas Island in the San Juan chain of islands off the Washington coast.

The salubrious atmosphere of Orcas rejuvenated Robert and instead of dying, as was expected, he got a new lease on life. Never one to sit around and do nothing, he went about building Rosario. This started off as a modest ambition, but before it was finished, it was a small town. Today, Rosario has been turned into a resort hotel, using the facilities Robert Moran built for his home. The complex has three pools, one indoor, a complete spa and fitness center, great dining and Robert Moran's magnificent organ, brought in at a cost of $16,000.

Many of the hundreds of photographs Robert Moran took during the early part of this century are displayed at Rosario. No effort was spared in the construction of the Moran mansion. The windows are of ship's glass, about three-quarters of an inch thick and the furniture and woodwork are built to last as long as men sail in ships. The present complex covers twenty-six acres. Originally, Moran had 7,800 acres on Orcas Island which included four fresh water lakes plus Constitution Mountain, the highest point on the island. He turned over most of the land to the State. This property is now known as the Robert Moran State Park. Moran built all the access roads and the bridges and trails in the park at his own expense.

After being given just a few months to live in 1904, Robert Moran spent the rest of his time, until 1943, building and lavish-

Betty Moran Burns, granddaughter of Robert Moran and below, Rosario Resort, where Betty grew up when the resort was a family home.

The Robert Moran family. (Seated) Robert Moran and his wife, Melissa (Paul). (Standing L. to R.) family members, John, Nellie, Mary, Malcolm. and Frank.

ing all his energies on Rosario. He installed a bowling alley in the mansion to entertain his guests. He built a world class yacht which he never sailed, he built his own dam to supply the place with electricity and he built a school for the children of the workers who spent years building Rosario.

Robert Moran was the last of his family to pass away. He died in 1943. His nine brothers and sisters had predeceased him. He was married to Melissa Paul, a Canadian girl, and they had three sons, John, Frank, and Malcolm and a daughter, Nellie. The couple also adopted Mary, the daughter of Robert's brother.

Robert Moran's great-grandfather, Edward Moran, was a marble mason from County Mayo where he worked in the Connemara marble quarries. He left Ireland some time in the eighteenth century and Betty Burns (Moran) remembers her grandfather Robert telling her that Edward worked on building the marble staircases in the old city hall in New York City.

Robert Moran was born in the East River end of Grand Street in New York City on January 26, 1857 and he worked for his dad for a while before taking Horace Greely's advice and heading west. His father had fought in the Civil War on the side of the North. Robert Moran lived to see Seattle emerge from the status of a hamlet into a major metropolis. He witnessed statehood for Washington and his Rosario Estate is now part of the National Historic Register.

Frank Gaudette
Microsoft's Financial Wizard

New York-born Irishman Francis John Gaudette brought Microsoft public, overseeing the company's initial public offering in 1986 at twenty-one dollars a share. He sat in the underwriter's office watching the tape and seeing the price skyrocket to more than twenty-seven dollars a share in its first day of transaction. Since the initial offering, Microsoft has continued at a dizzy pace on the stock market and in its sales and marketing operations.

Today, Microsoft is the world's largest software factory with annual sales of $3 billion and climbing and a market evaluation of some $175 billion. Frank Gaudette never really gloried in his success at Microsoft. Bill Gates was the genius who put the company together; Frank was the one who looked after the engines which made the company prosper: finance, manufacturing, human resources and the European Operations.

Frank Gaudette made Dublin the manufacturing headquarters for Microsoft in Europe and production at that facility accounts for 35% of worldwide sales. Dublin also has a division of Microsoft's Products Group and both facilities employ more than 800 employees.

When pressed in a February 1992 interview to explain his contribution to the phenomenal success of Microsoft Frank replied, "I allow myself more credit for the logistical part than the strategic part. You just don't make twenty-five per cent after-tax profit, or grow at fifty-eight per cent by luck. It takes some jerk like me to make it happen."

Frank Gaudette was a tough, intelligent, street-smart New Yorker who gloried in his Irish heritage. Although his surname is Nova Scotia French, three of his grandparents were Irish. One of his grandfathers, Francis McGorty, came from Belleek, a town famous for making china on the boundary between Counties Fermanagh and Donegal. His father was a New York City mailman and he had Frank parading as a drummer in New York's St. Patrick's Day Parade when he was a youngster. Growing up tough

227

The late Frank Gaudette was Microsoft's chief financial officer and executive vice president of operations when he died in April of 1993. To the people at Microsoft's European headquarters in Dublin, he was simply "Uncle Frank."

and smart in a rough neighborhood, Frank, as a sixteen-year-old, fought in the New York City Golden Gloves tournament. Later, he served a four year hitch as a United States Army Paratrooper, seeing active service during the Korean War.

After army service, Frank put himself through Southern Methodist University in Dallas, Texas, working the four-to-midnight shift at the Post Office to help pay his way. He graduated with a degree in accounting and went into the workforce, polishing up his skills and accumulating a mass of knowledge about every phase of business from taxes and auditing through the financial markets and bringing companies public.

In 1984, Microsoft, then in its infancy, caught his sharp eye and he applied for the job as vice-president of finance and administration with the company. His New York style gave the interviewers a few doubting moments, but his Irish wit, charm, intelligence and his workaholic temperament, which he called "the historical Irish work ethic," overcame any of his very few shortcomings. He was hired and he immediately proceeded to get his nose into every phase of Microsoft's many-faceted operations, from production line to warehouse and management.

Frank was in his early fifties, ancient by computer company standards where the average age of the Microsoft employees was twenty-nine. He was a father-mentor figure who retained his sense of mischief and caring. He would dress up as Rocky Balboa at Microsoft meetings, be shot from a cannon as the "Great Gaudetti," or beat the bejapers out of the younger players at racquetball.

One of his proudest moments was St. Patrick's Day in 1992 when Frank was Grand Marshall of Seattle's St. Patrick's Day Parade. It rained, of course, just like it does in Ireland. Frank had a voracious appetite for the "joy of life." He was a fitness addict who played racquetball at 6:00 a.m. so he could spend evenings with his family and he had a delicious sense of the ridiculous.

In one of his last interviews Frank said, "My biggest frustration is that there is so much to do at Microsoft. So much is happening and there's so much to do that is very positive and right, that it is hard to draw the line on where one can contribute.

There's a certain amount of frustration -- there are things that may not get done." Frank didn't get everything done, but what he did accomplish is the kind of monument that very few achieve in a lifetime.

Francis John Gaudette passed away on Friday, April 23, 1993, after an eight-month battle with cancer. Friends and co-workers at Microsoft held a memorial service on Microsoft's Redwood campus. Bill Gates, founder of Microsoft, had this to say about his departed friend: "He helped me grow up. Frank was a great man and a humble man. Sometimes, when we traveled for long hours, he talked about his early years. He was proud of his early years. He was proud of his father, the mailman. He was proud of working full time when he was in college. He loved his stories about being a paratrooper in Korea. I always had a hard time picturing Frank dropping into Korea.

"So many of his accomplishments will last on -- world class manufacturing, our financial strength. But even more than that, it's his values, his spirit, his joy. He had so many friends here. He had planned to continue working until he was sixty.

"I have to say I think of Frank as a philosopher. But he wasn't just a philosopher -- he was practical and he was fun. He added an incredible amount to all our lives."

Thomas H. Savage
ITT's Man in Canada

Thomas H. (Tom) Savage took a circuitous route to get to Canada and to the top position at ITT Canada Limited (a wholly owned subsidiary of ITT Corporation). His first choice was Australia, but when he went home to his wife, Nan Gilmore (since deceased) and told her he wanted to immigrate to Australia, she would not hear of it. The journey was four to six weeks by boat. "In those days we didn't think of commercial airline flying as we think of it today," Tom remembers. "I gave it another week's thought or two and because there was no way I could convince her, I came back a week later and asked her how about Canada, that's only a week away by boat. So that's how Canada was chosen. It's strange how some of your biggest decisions in life are taken."

The Green Years of Tom Savage

The first career choice for Tom Savage when he finished high school after World War II was as a cadet in the Indian Army. This wasn't surprising given that his father had served in India for fourteen years before World War I. His grandmother was born en route to India and had spent the first thirteen years of her life there and his great-grandmother had taught school in India for many years.

Tom was sixteen and a half when he took his military entrance examination and upon passing all the tests, headed for England to train as an Indian Army officer. However, his career was cut short when, in 1947, Prime Minister Churchill started negotiations with India for its independence. The cadets hung around and did some more officer training and advanced academic studies, but they ultimately became redundant. Tom had a choice of a career in the British Army or finishing basic service and returning to civilian life. He chose the latter with a view to going to university.

He returned to Belfast and while he was waiting for the university to reopen in September, he took a part-time job with the Northern Ireland Hospital Authority. The British National Health Scheme had just come into existence at the time. Probably because of his army training, he ended up supervising and managing people even though he was only a temporary employee. He was encouraged by his supervisor to take the Civil Service examination, the concept being if you're an established civil servant, you have it made.

After about four years of working for the bureaucracy, Tom Savage became somewhat disenchanted and realized that this was not the way he wanted to spend the rest of his life. Emigration was the option he considered, an option that was on the minds of many in Ireland in the 1950s era, and so he set sail for Canada. Tom remembers arriving in Montreal in 1952 on the first boat up the St. Lawrence after the ice broke up in mid-April.

He spent four days in Montreal looking around. He had two job offers, one with the Bank of Nova Scotia and the other with Fairbanks Morse Company. Montreal was bilingual and much more cosmopolitan than the Belfast he had left. Tom decided that he was not comfortable in Montreal. He remembers thinking that, "If I can get two job offers in Montreal, I can also get job offers in Toronto. Toronto was then a very provincial town, much closer to the Belfast I had left. So, I headed by train for Toronto."

Getting a Start

Shortly after arriving in Toronto, Tom got a job as assistant secretary and manager at the Lambton Golf Club, one of the more prestigious clubs in the city (he is now a senior member there). This gave Tom the time to look around and save some money so that he could bring his wife over from Ireland.

After becoming fairly settled, Tom recalls, "I was able to sit back and decide what direction I wanted my life to take in terms of an occupation. One area I had been looking at, curiously enough back in Ireland, was a discipline called Work Study. In North America there were several disciplines, the more comprehensive of which was industrial engineering.

"A couple of the larger companies, Dunlop being one of them, had on-the-job training programs for industrial engineering

232

which was matched with going to university at night. I applied to Dunlop for the simple reason that it was a British company and I felt that I would receive credit for my officer's training and experience back in England. They wanted applicants to have basic undergraduate degrees before becoming trainees. Dunlop hired me for the trainee program and I worked there for two years. Then, I was hired by the W. H. Gage Company as a supervisor of their methods and standards department."

Tom went to the extension department of the University of Toronto for four years, obtaining a certificate in industrial management. By that time, Tom had enough training and experience to apply for admission to the American Institute of Industrial Engineers. He has since achieved senior membership status in that organization.

Getting North American Experience

For the next ten years, in addition to his regular work, Tom lectured every Monday night at the Extension Department of the University of Toronto. With his background in industrial engineering, which is the study of work input and how materials are handled in the workplace, he set his sights on a career in management consulting and sought a broad range of experience to prepare for it.

Apart from applying at Dunlop as a trainee in industrial engineering and then at W. H. Gage as a manager of methods and standards, Tom remembers, "I did not have to apply for another job in the subsequent thirty-odd years that I have been in business. All of the other jobs that I have had came as a result of recruitment firms seeking me out.

"From Gage, I went to Hallmark Greeting Cards [which in Canada was called Coutts Hallmark Greeting Cards] as their manager of process engineering. Then I went to the corporate offices of Union Carbide, essentially as their chief of industrial engineering. My title was manager of operations improvement. All jobs were in Toronto.

"Over the years I continued to do a variety of external activities and lecturing work. I presented papers at a variety of universities, including Georgia Tech and Duke University. Union

Carbide sent me down on a two week lecture course to Brazil to make a presentation at their venture partner in that country."

Tom Savage holds a Certificate in Management from the Canadian Institute of Management. He became president of the Toronto branch and subsequently president of the National Council and Chairman of the Advisory Board. He was appointed a Life Member in 1972.

Making It at ITT

With his good position at Union Carbide and his activities with the University of Toronto developing young managers and helping executives in their career development, plus his work with the Canadian Management Institute, Tom Savage had a full and satisfying life, so he was not overly enthused when a "head-hunter" called him from New York. Tom did manage to be polite enough to find out about the position. They wanted to know if Tom would be interested in coming to work for the major communications conglomerate, ITT.

The ITT requirements in Canada came as a result of their aggressive acquisitions program of the late 1960s and 1970s. Virtually every acquisition in the United States brought with it a Canadian subsidiary or branch plant. Although not necessarily by design, ITT obtained a significant but diverse presence in Canada, a presence that at least needed some co-ordination, if not restructure. After extensive talking back and forth, Tom Savage joined ITT in October, 1968 as Operations Staff Executive. Tom spent nine months learning the ropes from the executive ITT had sent to Toronto. Tom then took over as Director of Staff Operations - Canada and immediately started putting his stamp on the Canadian ITT.

There was much sensitivity in Canada at that time regarding foreign multinationals and conglomerates in general and American companies in particular. Tom felt that the twenty-five or so businesses that ITT had acquired needed to be restructured into a single corporate identity to present to the regulatory bodies and to the business community at large. This restructuring involved a very complex two to four years of work and a re-organization of a whole variety of individual holdings into one

234

single ITT Canada Limited. Tom was appointed President in 1970 and was designated Senior Officer for Canada in 1978. He is currently Chairman of ITT Canada Limited and Senior Officer - Canada ITT Corporation.

In 1992, Tom Savage was appointed Chairman of the Board of North America Trust Company, again as a result of another unsolicited approach. This recruiter was representing a client who had just bought a trust company and was looking for a non-executive chairman. Tom laughed and told him that he didn't really have the right person because he was not a financial person. The representative had done his homework and said he was fully aware of Tom's area of expertise but his people still wanted to talk to him.

As a result of the ensuing conversations, Tom came to an agreement that he would take on the chairmanship on a part-time basis, if he could work out a proper arrangement with ITT. Tom put together a transitional plan with ITT that showed how the changeover would take place after his retirement, who would take over and how the company should be structured.

After much discussion with the vice-chairman and chairman, both agreed that it would be good for both parties. North America Trust is headquartered in Toronto. It is a wholly owned subsidiary of North American Life Insurance, which is a Canadian company established in 1881 with assets under management of $16.1 billion and life insurance in force of $77.9 billion.

Extracurricular Activities

Tom Savage is the Chairman of the Board of Governors for West Park Hospital and a Director of Acklands Limited. Tom tells us, "Before that I was the President of the West Park Hospital Foundation, leading the Foundation's campaign to provide funds for research, education, equipment, programs and services not fully funded by government agencies. I am also Chairman of the Advisory Board of the Boys and Girls Clubs of Canada and a Director of the RP Eye Research Foundation."

Tom is an active member of the Policy Committee of the Business Council on National Issues. He is the Business Co-

Chair of the Canadian Labor Market and Productivity Center. According to Tom, "We have completed several significant projects which have produced important recommendations, some of which have become policy. Some of these policies have become the framework for individual provinces to examine issues and set up programs for retraining and dealing with employment redundancies as a result of technological change and economic downsizing.

Tom Savage is also a member of the Dean's Advisory Council of the Faculty of Management, University of Toronto. He has been director of the Canada Ireland Fund since its inception. This Fund, which is non-political and non-denominational, raises moneys to support initiatives which promote peace, culture and charity throughout Ireland -- North and South.

Irish Connections

Tom's mother died in Belfast a few years ago. His sister and brother-in-law and their family live in County Down. He has a brother living in England since the end of World War II. Tom was back in Northern Ireland in June of 1993 and spent a week visiting the University of Ulster and a variety of different people, including the Northern Ireland Industrial Development Board. Tom works on behalf of the University of Ulster to find positions in Canada for some of the students who are on international marketing programs as part of their second year. They go out and work in an international business environment and Tom tries to find spots for them.

Tom tells us, "My best memories of growing up in Belfast center around the Boys Brigade organization. It is a boys' church organization attached to all the churches. I was a member of the 11th Boys Brigade attached to St. Paul's [Church of Ireland] on York Street. I was baptized Presbyterian but grew up Church of Ireland. I attended Belfast Model and Belfast High schools where I was scouted for my soccer playing abilities. I played soccer with them until I joined the army. I actually was a gym instructor for them after I came out of the service.

"The association with the 11th Boys Brigade was probably the fondest memory I have from Belfast because I met and was beneficially influenced by some absolutely fine people. And in terms of my personal development, our minister, the Reverend C.H.P. [Chip] Lyndon, probably made the most significant contribution. Of all the people I met in my life, he probably had the greatest influence on me."

Over the past ten or so years, one of the extra-curricular activities that has been most important to Tom is his work with the Northern Ireland Partnership in Canada. This is an initiative that began several years ago in Belfast when senior members of the business community felt that their response to the situation in Northern Ireland had to be the preservation of growth and prosperity of economic activity, so they got together and founded the Northern Ireland Partnership. This is an non-political, non-denominational group. Its purpose is to assist the Northern Ireland Industrial Development Board (NIIDB) with economic initiatives and new investments in Northern Ireland.

From that modest beginning, the Northern Ireland Partnership has become a somewhat international activity with Partnership activities in Great Britain, Canada, Australia, South Africa and laterally in France. As Chairman of the Partnership in Canada, Tom leads a group of some eighty expatriate Ulster men and women who have dedicated themselves to assisting the director of the NIIDB for North America in his efforts to generate investments in Northern Ireland from Canada. This group of men and women are individuals with senior positions in business and industry and/or significant contacts with several aspects of the business community. They are committed to raising the profile of Northern Ireland as a place for investment from which to address the European market.

Through these activities, Tom has developed relationships with Jackie Redpath and Sean Curran of the Greater Shankhill Development Agency and the Phoenix Trust respectively, both of which work to address the severe unemployment problems in West Belfast. In addition, these activities have brought him in contact with Dr. Ian Adamson who heads the Somme Association in Belfast, an organization dedicated to bringing young people from both North and South of the border and both religious communities together on an extended basis and to provide an opportunity for them to meet and interact one with the other. Tom Savage is a patron of both the Phoenix Trust and the Somme Association.

Tom's wife of eighteen years is Canadian-born Evelyn Phyllis. Between them, they have four children. Tom has three children by his first wife, two girls and a boy. Both girls are married and his step-daughter is also married. They have seven grandchildren.

Tom says that he "never found it difficult to intermix with the two Irish cultures. I grew up in a household that had no sort of partisanship, certainly not in the context of religion. My father had an extensive military background and served in both wars and my mother was a military nurse most of her life. I think those backgrounds brought a much broader and more enlightened attitude toward people, politics and religion. I benefited significantly from those attitudes."

Tom Savage was made a Commander of the Order of the British Empire on June 16, 1990 in recognition of his work for Northern Ireland. He is equally comfortable in Ireland and in Canada and has used his considerable talents and influence to the benefit of both countries.

Belfast-born Tom Savage, who molded ITT Canada's many diverse operations into a cohesive administrative organization in a few short years. Tom serves on many boards, including the Canada Ireland Fund, the Boys and Girls Clubs of Canada and the Northern Ireland Partnership.

Pathfinders

For more than three centuries the Celts have been pouring into North America. They settled everywhere, the Eastern cities, the Middle West, the Great Plains, the Spanish Possessions, the Oregon Territory and the Canadas. In each area they left their imprint -- from the mountain peaks to the valleys and from the railroad towns to the big cities. Communities such as Limerick, Maine; Derry, New Hampshire; Listowel, Ontario; Cork, New Brunswick; Dundalk, Maryland; Ulster, New York; Shamrock, Texas; Sheridan, Wyoming; St. Patrick's Peak, Oregon; and Dublin, California became established.

Capt. John Smith is credited with having led the first party of white men overland to California in the 1820s. Smith, a native of County Offaly, immigrated to America at an early age. He joined the American Fur Company and ultimately became chief trader at the company's Green River post. He crossed the Sierra Nevada range at the head of a party of forty trappers for the American Fur Company. In 1827, on his return trip, he and most of his party were wiped out by Indians.

Two Irishmen, Peter O'Reilly and Patrick McLoughlin, headed west to Nevada and discovered the Comstock Lode, which was fabulously rich in gold and silver deposits. Davy Crockett, the great American frontiersman, was the son of a County Derry immigrant. Crockett's life came to an end at the siege of the Alamo.

Leander McNally, the son of immigrants from County Down, became a legendary folk hero of the Texas Rangers in the late 1800s. He is credited with putting an end to cattle rustling by Mexicans. He lead forays into Mexico to recover thousands of stolen cattle.

Dr. John McLoughlin, born to a County Donegal father in Canada in 1784, is regarded by many as the "Father of Oregon" for the important role he played in the development of the Pacific Northwest. After a distinguished career with the Hudson's Bay and North West trading companies, he chose to become an American citizen following the 1846 treaty which divided the Oregon territory between Britain and the United States.

Following are the stories of three individuals and their roads to success. John Sheridan Kilkenny and the Irish of Morrow County came from the Carrigallen area of County Leitrim. They braved their way across the great American continent in the late 19th century to the Heppner area of Oregon where they became sheep ranchers. These early pioneers began the Irish colony of Morrow County, Oregon by encouraging their friends and relatives back in County Leitrim, through assisted passage, to come and work on the ranches. These workers, in turn, put the power of their earning into ranches of their own and continued the tradition of providing the cost of transportation for their fellow countrymen. In time, the sheep ranching expanded and the Irish community of Morrow County grew into a permanent settlement. Judge John F. Kilkenny's father, John Sheridan Kilkenny, was one of the early Morrow County sheep ranchers. Judge Kilkenny shares with us some of the early experiences of the Irish community of Morrow County.

Irish immigrants were prepared and willing to undertake any challenge to sustain themselves and their families. In the process of trying anything at hand, they found liberty and interests far beyond what had been available to them in Ireland. Out of expediency came opportunity which led to ambition and possibilities beyond their wildest dreams. Often it was the second or third generation that attained the dream, but it was the effort of the first generation that paved the way.

John Holland designed and built the first submarine for the American Navy. His is a success story that probably would not have happened if he had remained in Ireland. He certainly had no intention of furthering Britain's domination of the high seas.

Henry Ford's family story is not typical for survivors of the Irish Famine. The Fords had relatives already established in Dearborn, Michigan who helped them get settled on their own farm. William Ford wanted his son, Henry, to remain on the farm. Henry persisted against his father's wishes, pursuing instead his fascination with mechanics and engines.

Judge John F. Kilkenny
And the Irish of Morrow County

Judge John F. Kilkenny, an Irish-American, has been a judge since being appointed by President Dwight Eisenhower in 1959. He was ninety-two years of age when interviewed for this book in his chamber at the courthouse in Portland, Oregon. Judge Kilkenny gives a "legal" opinion that the origin of the name "Oregon" can be traced to a band of Irish led by the great Michael Patrick O'Regon who discovered the territory long before the advent of the North American Indian. To the naysayers, the judge responds that the "burden of proof" is theirs.

Be that as it may, the fact remains that the Irish played an important part in the development of Oregon, beginning with those who accompanied Lewis and Clark in opening up the Oregon Trail, to the railroad builders and the latter day sheep-ranchers and homesteaders who settled Morrow County and the surrounding areas of Oregon.

The towns of Heppner and Pendleton in eastern Oregon are populated mainly by people of Irish extraction and the countryside abounds with such names as Casey, Cassidy, Clancy, O'Connell, Curran, Doherty, Dolan, Darcy, Doyle, O'Flaherty, Fitzgerald, Heffernan, O'Meara, O'Reilly, O'Rourke, Kilkenny, Monahan, Mahoney, Moore, Carthy, Quinlan, Quinn, Sheridan, Skelly, Summers, Walsh, Shields, Ryan and others. Today, there are many Irish families in the area, running businesses, operating sheep farms and involved in every area of local activity.

The Coming of the Irish to Morrow County

The beginning of the Irish influx into the Heppner area can be traced to William (Bill) Hughes, a native of Tipperary. Bill Hughes had been a very successful businessman in California, operating as a merchant and stockman. He arrived in the Heppner area in 1870. He had heard about the abundant land available and the rich bunch grass which provided year-round grazing.

Bill Hughes was followed by Charlie Cunningham and then by Felix Johnson, Jeremiah Brosnan, Michael Kenny, Patrick and James Doherty. John Kilkenny and his cousin James Carty came in 1890. Bill Hughes played a large part in establishing the Irish community, making money available to new arrivals so they could buy their homesteads and get started. He also made money available so the new settlers could bring relatives and friends out from Ireland.

The new settlers came in sailing ships, then by rail, oxcart, wagons and on foot over the Oregon Trail. It was not unusual for the Irish immigrants to spend several months from the time they left home in Ireland until they arrived in the wilds of Oregon.

These Oregon Irish paid their dues. An example is the family of Pat and Fred Mutch. They had five sons, Dan, Con, Jack, Emmett and Vincent, in the armed forces during World War Two. A grandson, Joseph, also served.

The story of the Summers family is a testimonial to the indomitable Irish spirit. Michael Summers, who was born in County Kilkenny, immigrated to New Orleans in 1856. Michael married a Tipperary girl, Mary Ellen MacCormack. Michael died in 1860, and in 1863 Mary Ellen took her three young children and set off for Oregon. In time, the children of Mary Ellen prospered and multiplied and they now number in excess of four hundred. They have distinguished themselves in the fields of education, politics, religion and engineering.

Settling Down in Morrow County

According to Judge Kilkenny, the early population mix of the Irish in Morrow County was eighty-five per cent male and fifteen per cent female. This meant that many of the men remained bachelors and lonely. Living in a wilderness area added to their loneliness. However, there were some enterprising males who saved up enough money to make a trip back to the old country, capturing a colleen and bringing her out to the far ends of America to a life of farm chores, hard work and beautiful country.

This traffic back and forth resulted in a great flow of Irish from Leitrim and Longford counties, home of many of the original settlers who returned to pick out wives, or relatives to work their spreads. Judge Kilkenny recounts how his own father, John Sheridan Kilkenny, managed to get himself a wife. John read an

243

John Sheridan Kilkenny and his wife, Rose Ann. John Kilkenny, born in the Carrigallen area of County Leitrim, immigrated with his cousin, James Carty, to Morrow County, Oregon in 1890 where they went into sheep ranching. Below, their son, Judge John F. Kilkenny of the United States Court of Appeal for the Ninth Circuit.

obituary notice of the death of Luke Farley, who had lived in the eastern United States and who was mourned by his widow. Being an enterprising fellow, he wrote the widow asking if she would be interested in a new life in Oregon. After a spell, he heard back and before long this lady, Rose Ann Curran, arrived in Oregon and they were married in 1898. On learning that Rose Ann had a sister in Ireland, John's cousin, Jim Carty, returned to Ireland and brought her back as his wife.

As the stories of the Morrow County Irish got around Leitrim and Longford, a steady flow of immigrants made their way west, sponsored by Bill Hughes and others like him. Many of them came as indentured servants, with the fare paid from Ireland to Oregon. Many of the immigrants worked as laborers on the sheep ranches and were content with that life. Others, like the Kilkennys, the Kennys and the McCabes, accumulated large spreads and ran major sheep farms.

As soon as the settlers arrived, they were entitled to homestead a parcel of land. This involved a commitment to build and occupy a home. There was some skulduggery involved in this procedure as a husband and wife would often have separate homesteads. They would erect a cabin on each property to fulfill the commitment, but would live together. When the government people came on their inspection tours, there was no shortage of good solid citizens to verify that the cabins were indeed lived in by the homesteader.

The migration from Ireland to Morrow County dried up in the 1920s with the coming of the Great Depression and the subsequent tightening up of immigration requirements, due in part to the scarcity of jobs. The towns of Heppner and Pendleton remain thriving Irish communities where the descendants of the original settlers treasure their Irish heritage.

Judge John F. Kilkenny

United States Federal Judge John F. Kilkenny is the son of John Sheridan Kilkenny, who was born in County Leitrim on May 14, 1870, and Rose Ann Curran. The Judge was born in Heppner, Oregon on October 26, 1901. His grandfather was Peter Kilkenny and his grandmother was Mary Ann (Sheridan) Kilkenny. The

Judge's father claims a family relation to the famous General Phil Sheridan, the Civil War hero. Sheridan had spent part of his early military career in Oregon fighting the Indians and keeping the area safe for settlers.

Like every other youngster in Morrow County, Judge Kilkenny had a basic elementary education in the traditional one-room school which housed eight grades. He grew up on a sheep farm, with a spread of about forty thousand acres and over ten thousand head of sheep, plus assorted cattle, horses and pigs. While things were not as rough in his youth as when his dad had started (the run-ins with cowboys who wanted to run the sheep-men out of the territory were behind him), nevertheless, there were still terrible winters, brush fires and floods.

John Kilkenny managed to convince his dad that he wanted to attend Columbia Preparatory School (now the University of Portland). His scholarship there earned him admission to Notre Dame University. On his way to seek entry to Notre Dame, John Kilkenny was funneled off on the train to Chicago with six hundred live lambs in his charge. His job was to escort the lambs to the slaughterhouse at the Chicago stockyards and then report to Notre Dame.

After getting the smell of the lambs washed out, John Kilkenny presented himself at Notre Dame without his papers. He had to wait around until they were forwarded from Columbia in Oregon. "Admission standards were not as stringent then," the Judge says, "so I was accepted."

John Kilkenny was a pretty good high school football player, so he was able to make Knute Rockne's famous football squad. This was in the days of the Four Horsemen and the Gipper -- later made famous in a movie featuring Ronald Reagan and Pat O'Brien. Knute Rockne became a mentor-father to the young John Kilkenny, picking him up from games and practices and driving him home to his lodgings and at other times, taking him to his own home. Bad knees as a result of football injuries shortened the football career, but the future judge went on to get a law degree from Notre Dame. After graduation, John Kilkenny joined the Pendleton law firm of Raley, Raley and Steiwer. Later, he became a partner in the firm of Raley, Kilkenny and Raley. In

1959, President Dwight Eisenhower appointed John F. Kilkenny to the United States District Court for the District of Oregon. President Richard Nixon then elevated him to the United States Court of Appeal for the Ninth Circuit in San Francisco.

In 1971, Judge Kilkenny took senior status under federal law. Following open heart surgeries in 1979 and again in 1983, the judge reduced his workload, concentrating on those cases selected as suitable for disposition on the briefs and without oral argument.

In recognition of such an eminent career as a lawyer and judge, as well as the outstanding service to community, state and nation, the United States Congress on December 21, 1984, renamed the post office and federal courthouse in the old hometown of Pendleton the "John F. Kilkenny United States Post Office and Courthouse."

A Proud Irishman

Extremely proud of his Irish ancestry, Judge Kilkenny served for fifteen years as vice-president of the American-Irish Historical Society. This interest in Gaelic history led him to create the Kilkenny Fund, an endowment devoted to the acquisition of books and materials on Irish, Scottish and Pacific Northwest history. To date more than five hundred volumes, most of them located in the library of the Blue Mountain Community College, bear the label of the Kilkenny Fund. In addition, Judge Kilkenny has himself published articles on Irish history in *The Oregon Historical Quarterly*. He wrote *Shamrocks and Shepherds*, a history of the Irish of Morrow County, Oregon.

Judge Kilkenny was married to Virginia Brannock in Pendleton, Oregon on October 14, 1931. They celebrated the sixtieth anniversary of their marriage in 1991. To this union were born Michael John Kilkenny and Karen Margaret (Kilkenny) Klosterman, who awarded the Judge and his wife with nine grandchildren and, thus far, seven great-grandchildren. Among his favorite activities with family and friends, both before becoming a judge and afterwards, has been traveling throughout the United States, the South Pacific and Ireland.

Henry Ford
The Man Who Put America on Wheels!

"I invented nothing new, simply assembled into
a car the discoveries of other men behind whom
were centuries of work. Had I worked fifty or ten
or even five years before, I would have failed. So
it is with every new thing. Progress happens when
all the factors that make for it are ready and then
it is inevitable. ..."   -- Henry Ford

H enry Ford, mechanical wizard, inventor and founder of the
worldwide Ford Motor Company, was the grandson of John
and Thomasina Ford of County Cork, Ireland who were evicted
from their tenant farm near Bandon during the potato famine in
1847.   Their eldest son, William, who would become Henry's father, was twenty-one at the time. When disaster struck, he convinced his parents that the family should leave Ireland and immigrate to America. The Fords packed their meager belongings and
headed for the Port of Queenstown and there boarded a ship for
the New World.

William took on the role of leader of the family retinue
which included his brothers, Henry and Samuel, his sisters,
Rebecca, Jane, Nancy and Mary, and his parents. On the journey
crossing the Atlantic, the Fords encountered tragedy when
Thomasina became ill of fever and died. She was buried at sea.

Unlike so many of their fellow countrymen who got off the
ship in Boston or New York, the Fords continued overland to
Detroit and from there to the small neighboring town of Dearborn.
There to greet them upon their arrival were John's brothers,
Samuel and George, who had immigrated to the United States
years earlier and had acquired sizable farms of land. Dearborn was
still a frontier town when the Fords arrived there in 1848. The
area around was a dense wilderness.

The Fords were not as concerned about the lack of comforts as they were in acquiring their own land and achieving self-
sufficiency.   Soon after he arrived, John Ford managed to
purchase eighty acres.   William worked with his father to clear

the land, and he did carpentry work to help pay off the three hundred and fifty dollars the eighty acres had cost,

A close by neighbor of the Fords in Dearborn was fellow countryman Patrick O'Hearn who had arrived from Fairlane, County Cork in the 1830s. Patrick and his wife, Margaret, did not have any children of their own, so they adopted three-year-old Mary Litigot when her father, an immigrant from Belgium, died as the result of an accident.

Mary had reached her teenage years when William Ford began working for O'Hearn. Mary was attending the local Scotch settlement school and William, fourteen years her elder, fell in love with her. He waited until she graduated and married her in 1861. As a wedding gift, Patrick O'Hearn sold William ninety of his prime acres at a low price, with the understanding that he and his wife would live with the newlyweds.

William and Mary's first child, a boy, died at birth early in 1862. On July 30, 1863, their second child was born and they named him Henry after one of William's brothers. Seven other children would follow. William faced tragedy once again when his ninth child died at birth and, shortly after the birth, Mary also died. His sister, Rebecca Flaherty, came from Detroit to help him look after the young children.

Of the seven children that survived, none gave William more anguish in rearing than Henry did. Mechanically inclined from an early age, Henry was obsessed with things mechanical and showed little interest in school or working the farm. William did not disapprove of his son's interests in mechanics, but he was disappointed when Henry showed little interest in farming. William often reminded Henry that he himself had gone from poor Irish immigrant to prosperous farmer.

Soon after he turned seventeen in 1880, Henry landed his first job with the Michigan Car Company, a manufacturer of railroad boxcars. His starting wage was a dollar and ten cents a day. The job lasted for only six days. He was fired for solving a mechanical problem which the foreman and several employees had unsuccessfully worked on for several days. The foreman, feeling threatened, canned Henry. With his mechanical skills, Henry had no difficulty in finding another job around the Detroit area.

249

Above, Henry's parents, Mary Litigot and William Ford. Born in County Cork, William immigrated to Dearborn, Michigan at age twenty-one. Below, Henry and his wife, Mary, on the quadricycle -- the first car Henry built. Standing next to them is their grandson, Henry Ford II.

He next went to work for a small machine shop making valves. There he learned how to read blueprints. His pay was a mere two dollars and fifty cents a week which wasn't enough to pay for his room and board. He moonlighted, doing watch repairs to make ends meet. Next, Henry went to work for the Detroit Dry Dock Engine Works where he had an opportunity to work on motors, his forte. He quickly became an accomplished mechanic. He enrolled in business courses at Goldsmith Business College in Detroit.

In 1884, Henry met and fell in love with Clara Bryant, whom he married in 1888. Six months after they were married, the couple moved into an apartment in Detroit and Henry went to work for the Detroit Edison Company. Their only child was born on November 6, 1893. Henry named him Edsel after his old high school friend, Edsel Ruddiman. Henry Ford rose rapidly at Edison and eventually was made chief engineer at $1,000 a year.

About this time, the gasoline-operated vehicle was being developed in Europe and America. Henry became very interested in its development and he kept abreast of its progress through mechanic magazines. Soon he was undertaking his own experiments, working on his own model of a gasoline engine in a shed in the backyard of the house he and Clara were renting. With his friend, Jim Bishop, he developed an ingenious quadricycle powered by a gasoline engine that was ready to be tested.

After midnight on June 4, 1896, Henry rolled his "baby carriage" out of the barn. What happened next was told by Henry many times over during his lifetime: "It was raining. Mrs. Ford threw a cloak over her shoulders and came outside. Mr. Bishop had his bicycle ready to ride ahead and warn drivers of horse-drawn vehicles, if indeed any were to be met at such an hour. I set the choke and spun the flywheel. As the motor roared and sputtered to life, I climbed aboard and started off. The car bumped along the cobblestones of the alley as Mr. Bishop rode ahead on the bicycle to warn any horse-drawn vehicles. We went down Grand River Avenue to Washington Boulevard. Then the car stopped. We discovered that one of the ignitors had failed. When we had repaired it, we started the car again and drove home. Both

Mr. Bishop and I went off to bed for a few winks of sleep, then Mrs. Ford served us breakfast and off we went to work as usual."

Henry's obsession with developing the "horseless carriage" began to pay dividends. In 1899, the mayor of Detroit and some friends put up $15,000 to form the Detroit Automobile Company, with Henry as chief engineer and partner. The car was an idea whose time was rapidly approaching and Henry was working on a prototype of the famous Model T Ford with its four-cylinder engine generating twenty horsepower. The Ford Motor Company was formed. The Model T went into production and was soon capturing everyone's fancy. Ford, it was said, had hit the mother lode of the automobile Gold Rush.

Over the years, the Ford Motor Company expanded its operations into a world-wide operation, with plants in Canada, the United Kingdom and Europe, along with several United States locations.

Henry's Sentimental Side

In 1912, Henry, Clara and Edsel went to England for talks about expanding his operations into England. Afterward, Henry took Clara and Edsel to Ireland and visited the place where his father, William, had been born. All that was left was a crumbling structure.

Henry Ford had become a celebrity with the American public. His house on Edison Street became a tourist attraction as the curious would gather outside to catch a glimpse of him. He decided he needed privacy, so he had built for himself and his family an edifice resembling a Norman castle out in Dearborn along the shore of the Rouge River. He called it *Fairlane* after the little Irish town in County Cork where his grandfather, Patrick O'Hern, had been born. Henry always retained his sentimentality for Ireland. He built an assembly plant in Cork and transferred his tractor operations there.

John Phillip Holland
Inventor of the Modern Submarine

John Phillip Holland emigrated from his native Ireland to the United States in 1873. Holland was an extraordinary man with a natural aptitude in mechanics and mathematics who had spent his early years dreaming of undersea craft and flying machines. Among his few possessions when he arrived in the United States was a drawing of his first submarine. After studying all the available information on submarines and influenced by Robert Fulton's earlier innovations on underwater craft, Holland spent the next several years working on the problems of submarine construction and navigation.

Growing Up in Ireland

John Phillip Holland was born in the Village of Lisconnor in County Clare in 1841, the second of four sons born to John Holland Sr. and Mary Scanlon. His father was employed by the British Coast Guard Service. Young John attended Macreehy National School and the Christian Brothers' Secondary School in Ennistomy.

The family moved to Limerick in 1853 and there John entered the Order of Christian Brothers. Holland took his initial vows and was sent for further training to the Order's famous school in Cork where he came under the influence of Brother Dominic Burke, a noted science teacher and the founder of vocational education in Ireland. Brother Dominic recognized the youth's drafting, mathematical and mechanical skills and encouraged him to develop them.

Holland trained to become a teacher, a profession that would afford him the chance to satisfy his curiosity about the natural world. When poor health forced him to give up teaching for two years, he rested, sketched and studied. He resumed his teaching duties when his health improved and went on to become an accomplished science and music teacher. It was while teaching in Dundalk, County Louth in 1869 that Holland first started to work seriously on the principles of submarines. According to local tradition, he experimented with a clock-driven submarine model in a large tub filled with water.

His brother, Michael, active in the Fenian separatist movement in Ireland during the 1860s, fled to the United States after several of the leaders were arrested. Holland's mother and older brother, Alfred, joined Michael in the United States in 1872. John, still experiencing poor health, withdrew from the Christian Brothers Order and followed his family to America, arriving in Boston in November of 1873.

From Teacher to Inventor

Shortly after he arrived in Boston, John Holland suffered a broken leg when he slipped on an icy street. He used his recuperation time to restudy the principles involved in submarines. Finding that his ideas had not changed substantially from his earlier efforts, he concluded that his solutions for submarine navigation must be correct. But first he had to find a job to support himself. He landed a job with the Christian Brothers as a lay teacher, which took him to St. John's Parochial School in Paterson, New Jersey.

Two years later, he began working on his submarine plans again. About this time his brother Michael, an active member of O'Donovan Rossa Circle No. 159 of the Fenian Brotherhood, introduced him to two of the leaders, O'Donovan Rossa and Jerome Collins.

At the same time the father of one of his students convinced Holland to submit his submarine plans to the United States Navy. At the Navy's Torpedo Station, Captain Edward Simpson told him the whole scheme was impractical. Somewhat irked, Holland replied that the captain had no experience navigating by compass under water, to which Captain Simpson retorted, "no one would go down in such a craft" and he advised Holland to drop the whole matter. Furthermore, he told Holland that to put anything through Washington was uphill work. Holland was to find the last words prophetic.

Holland's first real break came with the dramatic rescue of Irish political prisoners from the British Penal Colony in Australia in 1876 by the New Bedford whaler *Catalpa*. He was present at the

Battery in New York Harbor when the Fenian leaders received the prisoners and it was there he was introduced to John Devoy and John Breslin of the Fenian Executive Committee. He repeated for them the submarine proposal he had earlier made to Rossa and Collins, telling them that a submarine offered great potential to the Fenians in their strike against John Bull.

Devoy took the matter up with the Trustees of the Fenian Skirmishing Fund, which had been launched in 1875 to campaign for contributions to free Ireland. The Trustees appointed John Breslin, the daring leader of the *Catalpa* rescue, to look into the submarine proposal. A practical chap, as well as an adventurer, Breslin needed some concrete evidence that Holland's paper dream could in fact work. So Holland constructed a thirty inch model of his submarine which he demonstrated to a small group of Fenians at Coney Island. Satisfied that Holland was something of a mechanical genius, the Trustees of the Skirmishing Fund decided to financially support Holland in the building of his first submarine. Details surrounding the project were kept quiet.

The *Holland I*, by which it became known, was launched on May 22, 1878 at Paterson, New Jersey. A small crowd was on hand to see the "strange lozenge-shaped mass of metal about fourteen feet long, topped with a circular turret." At first she floated free, then something went wrong and she sank. After two more days of alterations, she was tested again and sank again, this time due to faulty riveting. After more adjustments, there was a successful total immersion of the *Holland I* witnessed by O'Donavan Rossa and other Fenian leaders. Holland succeeded in staying under the water for one hour.

The *Fenian Ram*

The Trustees of the Fenian Skirmishing Fund were satisfied with the *Holland I* demonstration and agreed to finance the building of a larger craft. Later called the *Fenian Ram*, it would be a three-man boat with a pneumatic gun, armed for combat and capable of breaking any enemy blockade -- a formidable weapon against the British navy, so thought the Fenians.

Holland left the classroom to devote his full time to building the *Fenian Ram*. It had to be built in secrecy and Holland had to convince New York's old and reputable Delamater Iron Works to build his craft without divulging his backers. They had little confidence that the craft would float but they agreed to build it at a cost not to exceed $20,000 cash. Work began on May 3, 1879.

The *Fenian Ram* was rolled out for trial runs on July 3, 1883. The porpoise shaped craft was thirty-one feet in length and six feet in beam. She used an improved version of Brayton's newly developed twin-cylinder gasoline engine, meeting specifications laid down by Holland. Constructed of iron, Holland estimated her "ramming power" sufficient to smash the plating of a ship's bottom. The long tapered bow and stern each held a sealed compressed air reservoir for positive buoyancy. Between each reservoir and the crew's control room were separate water ballast compartments.

Holland and his engineer took the craft down and they emerged without difficulty. Next, they carried out tests in deeper water to determine if she would perform under her own power while remaining under water. With some minor adjustments, the *Ram* performed as Holland thought she would. He proved that he was well ahead of his time in his ability to maintain a fixed center of gravity and longitudinal stability.

Work got underway on a third submarine designed to incorporate improvements in navigation. In the meantime, dissension arose among impatient members of the Fenian Brotherhood who wanted more action for the money they were spending. There were lawsuits and the Trustees and Holland came under attack.

Then, on a dark November night in 1883, Breslin and some of his Fenian buddies did the unthinkable. Forging Holland's signature, they stole the *Ram* and the new craft and with both in tow, proceeded up New York's East River. The turret had not been completely closed in the new craft and she sank. The *Ram* was taken to the Brass Foundry of James Reynolds in New Haven where attempts to run tests in the busy harbor were banned because they were a "menace to navigation."

Holland complained to Devoy about the covert action of Breslin and his friends. When Devoy ignored his pleas, Holland, knowing the scoundrels would be unable to successfully operate the *Ram* without him, stated, "I'll let her rot on their hands." He never again bothered with his Fenian backers. In 1916, the *Fenian Ram* performed its last service in the cause of Irish independence when it was exhibited at a Madison Square Garden bazaar to raise funds for the victims of the Easter Uprising. Today, she stands in West Side Park, New Jersey as a tribute to the genius from County Clare.

Overcoming Obstacles

The stolen *Fenian Ram* marked the end of a chapter, but Holland was more determined than ever to continue in his mechanical endeavors. He turned to his American engineering friends, Vanderbilt Bergen and Charles Morris. He met Navy Lieutenant William Kimball and was introduced to Lieutenant Edmund Zalinski of the Fifth U.S. Artillery, who was by far the best submarine man in the United States, if not in the world. Zalinski offered him a position in his Pneumatic Gun Company and Holland accepted.

Zalinski, a well known inventor of military devices, and Holland established the Nautilus Submarine Boat Company to construct Holland's fourth submarine. Holland had new features he wished to test and Zalinski wanted to prove the merits of his pneumatic dynamics gun. However, things did not go well with this venture. A launching accident resulted in a hole in the new craft's hull. Holland was unhappy with the engine and with Zalinski's armament. On top of everything, a settlement of the Sino-French War ruined any hopes for marketing the submarine and the Nautilus Submarine Boat Company went out of business in 1886.

At the time, submarine development was going ahead in Europe. In the United States, there were efforts to persuade the Secretary of the Navy to open a competition for an experimental submarine. Finally in 1888, the United States Navy Department, with two million dollars available to it, announced an open competition for design of a submersible craft. Holland entered and his design was selected. However, when the Cramps Shipbuilding Company could not guarantee to meet all specification requirements, the Selection Board in Washington withdrew its agreement and asked that a new design be sought.

257

A further delay occurred when the newly elected Harrison Administration reappropriated submarine funds for other marine construction. Four years later in 1892, when Cleveland replaced Harrison as President, the interest in submarines resumed and on March 3, 1893, Congress passed an appropriation to cover re-opening the competition for an experimental submarine. Before he could submit his design, Holland had to borrow the $349.19 needed to cover fees and material expenses. This design was to become the guide for the construction of Holland's fifth submarine.

John Holland had been struggling with the Navy for seven years when his company, the John P. Holland Torpedo Boat Company received the $200,000 government contract on March 3, 1895 for Holland's fifth submarine, later to become known as *The Plunger*. The lean years were over.

The *Plunger* and the *Holland VI*

Holland's fifth submarine was built at the Columbian Iron Works in Baltimore. It was a huge craft, eighty-five feet long and eleven and one-half feet in diameter. But all did not go well with the *Plunger*. Holland, surrounded by Navy brass who constantly demanded senseless modifications in conflict with his theories, became frustrated.

Meanwhile, his partner recognized Holland's genius and he proposed that control of the Holland Torpedo Boat Company be consolidated. Holland was given a non controlling share of the company stock and was named manager. All submarine patents and inventions were registered for and became the property of the company.

Holland became famous. He was also happy when his company granted his request to build a sixth submarine, which would become known as the *Holland VI*, under private contract, free from all the government red tape. In the meantime, Lt. Kimball had succeeded in getting Congress to authorize the Navy to build two more submarines if the *Plunger* was successful.

The *Holland VI* was built at Nixon's Crescent Shipyard in Elizabethport, New Jersey during 1896-1898. Legend has it that it took its first successful dive on St. Patrick's Day. To sell his sub-

258

marine to the government, Holland offered to take his craft into Santiago Harbor in Cuba (the Spanish-American War was on then) and sink Admiral Cervera's Spanish fleet there. Washington turned the offer down.

In 1900, the *Holland VI* was purchased by the Navy for $150,000. The United States became the second major power, after France, to adopt submarines as part of its Navy. Six more submarines were ordered, to be delivered in 1902 and 1903.

Holland began having trouble controlling the destiny of his inventions when new financial interests took control of his company and his foreign patents. He was no longer skipper of the *Holland VI* when the Navy took it over. The Electric Boat Company, which took over his company, demoted Holland from general manager to chief engineer and brought in new technically trained engineers. With less control and less to occupy his time, Holland resigned.

Holland had amassed no fortune and his shares, less than one per cent of the company, were worth only $50,000. He had, however, a loyal group of friends, some minor unassigned patents and the exclusive rights to his new type high speed submarine.

In 1905, Holland incorporated the John P. Holland Submarine Company to build his new submarine. The Navy showed no interest so he looked to Europe for sales but the foreign shipyards had heard that sales of his patent rights to others legally barred them from participating. The Electric Boat Company had filed suit against Holland claiming that he had assigned to it all his inventions during his lifetime, and that he had agreed to never use his talents in competition. The court dismissed the suit but the damage was done. His financial backers were frightened away.

John Holland withdrew from public life and found comfort in his wife and five children. Holland became interested in community life and became a member of the American Irish Historical Society. He died at his home in Newark on August 12, 1914 at seventy-three. Within two months of his death, German U-boats torpedoed three British destroyers off the Dutch coast. The submarine was destined to play an important role in the navies of the world.

Builders and Organizers
of the Labor Movement

In the early 19th century there were trade journeymen's associations that were local in character and had no collective bargaining rights with employers. It was a time when any attempt by workers to collectively increase their wages was regarded under common law as a criminal conspiracy. For example, in 1806 eight cordwainers (bootmakers) were charged and convicted for the crime of "a combination and conspiracy to raise their wages" after they had refused to accept wage cuts unilaterally imposed by the master cordwainers. This doctrine of criminal conspiracy was applied in a number of subsequent cases and it acted as a check on unionism until it was set aside in 1842 in a Massachusetts case.

Between the 1820s and the 1850s, Irish laborers were the largest source of unskilled labor in building America's vast canals, public works and railroads systems. Irish immigrants also provided much of the unskilled labor for coal mining, an industry where low wages, poor working conditions and exploitation of the workers was appalling. Those early impoverished immigrants somehow endured an inhospitable environment. Their grim circumstances were ignored and individual protest of their miserable working conditions was largely ineffective. In time, exploitation fueled their fighting passion and out of their organizing efforts the first industrial unions were born.

About the time of the Civil War, militant Irish miners were in the forefront of organizing efforts to combat the unhealthy and dangerous conditions of the mine workers in the anthracite coal fields of Pennsylvania and surrounding areas. Their exploitation by the mine operators reminded them of the hardship they had endured at the hands of absentee landlord agents before they left Ireland. Some workers resorted to using the same terrorist tactics they had used in Ireland against the landlords. A secret society, known as the "Molly Maguires," embarked on a wave of violence against the mine operators until a number of suspected ringleaders were arrested, convicted and executed. While the

Molly Maguire episode demonstrated that violent confrontation with management would not be tolerated, it reinforced the idea that the only way the mine workers could have their grievances resolved was through a united front. The Irish soon provided many leaders both in the United States and Canada.

In 1865, John Siney organized the first anthracite miners union in the Anthracite Coal Fields of Pennsylvania. John was born in Bornos, Queen's County, Ireland in 1831. He immigrated to Schuylkill, Pennsylvania in 1863 and worked in the coal mines. Siney chaired the convention at Youngstown, Ohio in 1873 that founded the first national miners union, one of a succession of mining unions which was replaced by the Knights of Labor. He was elected president of the union three times.

Terence Vincent Powderly, the son of Irish immigrants, was the most powerful labor leader in the 1880s. He was a driving force in the Knights of Labor, the forerunner of industrial union-ism, which he built into an organization that represented some 700,000 union members in the United States and Canada. He was elected on the Greenback Labor party ticket as Mayor of Scranton, Pennsylvania and President McKinley later appointed him Commissioner General of Immigration in 1897. The Knights of Labor accepted everyone as members except lawyers, bankers, stockbrokers and professional gamblers. Thomas McMahon emigrated from County Monaghan in 1887 at the age of 17. His union activity began in 1889 when he joined the Knights of Labor. From 1921 to 1937 he served as president of the United Textile Workers of America. He was also a founding member of the Congress of Industrial Unions (CIO) in 1934.

The American Federation of Labor (AFL) was largely the creation of the Irish. Founded in the late 1800s by Peter J. McGuire, the son of Irish immigrants, and cigar maker Samuel Gompers, the AFL drew its inspiration from many of the exploited craftsmen's associations (bricklayers, plumbers, carpenters and others) that had existed in various forms since the late eighteenth century. Peter McGuire is also credited with having Labor Day instituted as a holiday in the United States and Canada.

Frank McNulty emigrated with his parents from Londonderry in 1876. He became a journeyman electrician and joined the International Brotherhood of Electrical Workers (IBEW). In 1903, he was elected international president of the IBEW and served in that post until 1918. He also served as vice president of the AFL. Later he served as congressman from the 8th Congressional District of New Jersey.

Frank Duffy emigrated from County Monaghan in 1881, became a member of the Carpenters' International Union and served as its general secretary-treasurer for forty-eight years. He also served as vice-president of the AFL from 1918-1940 and was a member of the United States labor delegation to the 1919 Paris Peace Conference.

Daniel Joseph Tobin emigrated from County Clare in 1890 and became a motorman for the Boston Street Railway Company. He later went to work as a driver for a meat packing company where he joined the Teamsters Union. In 1907, he was elected general president of the Teamsters and served in the post until 1952. Tobin also served as AFL vice-president from 1933 to 1952. He was the United States delegate to the International Labor Organization in 1939. He also served as an administrative assistant to President Roosevelt in 1940.

Thomas W. Gleason, the son of Irish immigrants, quit school in the seventh grade at age fifteen and went to work on the New York docks. He joined the International Longshoremen Association (ILA) in 1919, became actively involved in union organizing and was elected ILA president in 1963 and served in that post for many years. He became an AFL-CIO vice-president in 1969. Martin Durkin, also the son of Irish immigrants, served as president of the Plumbers International Union, and as vice-president of the AFL before he became President Eisenhower's first secretary of labor in 1953.

When the CIO was formed in 1934, Irish-Americans played a significant part. Philip Murray, the son of an Irish immigrant coal miner, emerged to govern the CIO. Murray had emigrated with his father from Scotland in 1902. He shoveled coal for three dollars a day in Westmoreland County, Pennsylvania, became active and rose rapidly in the United Mine Workers' Union. In 1936, County Kerry-born Michael Quill came up from the subways of New York to organize the Transport Workers Union (TWU) and affiliate it with the CIO. Quill served as president of the TWU until his death in 1966. Joseph Beirne became president of the Communications Workers Union in 1949 and two years later led his union into the CIO where he became a vice-president.

Throughout most of the latter part of the twentieth century until his death in 1980, Irish-American George Meany was the most powerful labor leader in North America. He transformed the labor movement by bringing together the CIO and the AFL into a powerful cohesive organization. With an unparalleled career in United States labor history, Meany rose from journeyman plumber to rendezvous with eight United States presidents.

Meany was born in the Irish section of lower Harlem at 125th Street and Madison Avenue in 1894 to Michael Meany and Anne Cullen. The Meanys had emigrated from County Westmeath in the 1850s. George left school at age fourteen and went to work as an errand boy. He decided that he wanted to work at his father's trade and in 1917 became a full fledged member of Plumbers Local 463 in the Bronx. His union career began when he was elected to his local union's executive board at age twenty-five, starting his meteoric rise to presidency of the AFL-CIO.

Likewise in Canada, the Irish played a significant part in the growth of unionism. Daniel O'Donoghue came to Canada with his parents in 1852 at the age of eight and went on to become one of Canada's most honored and respected union leaders. O'Donoghue, often referred to as the Father of Canadian Labor, began his career as an apprentice to a printer. In 1866, he got a job with the *Ottawa Times* where he helped organize the Ottawa Typographical Union. In 1874, he became the first trade unionist elected to the Ontario Legislature, where he pushed for progressive legislation to improve the standard of living and the working conditions of the laboring people.

Pat Conroy, born in Glasgow in 1900 to Irish parents, immigrated to Drumheller, Alberta in 1919, where he started as an apprentice coal miner at fifty cents a day. He joined the United Mine Workers' Union and rose through a succession of union positions to become vice-president of District 18. When the Canadian Congress of Labor was established in 1940, he was

Irish-Canadian Robert (Bob) White, President of the Canadian Labor Congress and fiery spokesman for 2.2 million Canadian union members.

elected a vice-president and one year later he became secretary-treasurer and chief administrative officer. He became an executive member of the International Confederation of Free Trade Unions upon its formation in 1949. Following his resignation as secretary-treasurer of the Canadian Congress of Labor in 1951, Conroy was appointed labor attaché to the Canadian Embassy in Washington, a post he held until 1972. His services during World War II were recognized by the award of Member of the British Empire.

Bob White, elected president of the Canadian Labor Congress in June of 1992, is the fiery spokesman for 2.2 million Canadian workers. White, who was born in Ballymoney, County Antrim, got his start in union politics and organizing with the United Auto Workers (UAW). In 1959, he was elected president of UAW Local 636 and the following year he was appointed UAW international representative with responsibility for union organizing throughout Canada.

White was at the center of one of the most dramatic moments in Canadian labor history when, in 1984, he led a successful drive to have the Canadian UAW disaffiliate from its American parent. The following year, White emerged as the first president of an independent Canadian Auto Workers union, a position he held for three terms until his election to the CLC. In recognition of his exceptional service to Canadian workers, Bob White was given the Order of Canada Award.

John Lawe emigrated from County Roscommon in 1949 and got his first job as bus cleaner from the New York Fifth Avenue Coach Company. For seventeen years, he drove a bus in New York City and became active in Local 100 of the Transport Workers Union (TWU). In 1966, he was on the TWU negotiating committee which led to a citywide transit shutdown and the jailing of union president Michael Quill and several top union leaders. In 1985, John Lawe became president of the TWU and served in that post until his death in 1989.

Joseph R. Lavin immigrated to New York from his native County Roscommon in 1907, where he went to work for the Long Island Railroad. He became keenly interested in union activities upon joining the Brotherhood of Railroad Trainmen

(BRT) in 1911. He was elected chairman of the Long Island Railroad negotiation and grievance committee in 1918 and served in that capacity until his election as vice-president of the BRT Grand Lodge in 1940. He served in that post for eighteen years until his retirement in 1958. He has the distinction of being the first Irish Catholic to be elected to the Grand Lodge of the Brotherhood of Railroad Trainmen.

Peter Brennan served as vice-president of the New York State AFL before he became President Nixon's Secretary of Labor in 1973.

The story of Mother Jones shows what determination, courage and faith can do. She was the undisputed leader in demanding social justice for children, mothers and miners. The stories of Thomas Donahue and Martin Durkin tell of the accomplishments of two Irish-Americans in building the American dream.

The Irish have had a far greater impact on building the labor movement in North America than any other group. With dogged determination, courage and a sense of humor, they changed the workplace, improved working conditions and forced management to treat their employees as individuals with rights.

Mother Harris Jones
"The Most Dangerous Woman in America"

Mary Harris "Mother" Jones was one of the most persuasive and dramatic figures of the American labor movement during its historic struggle. A self-described "hell raiser," her fiery rhetoric and bold encounters with the coal mining and textile barons of her day was an inspiration to countless coal miners and sweat shop workers across America. From the 1890s, when she first became prominent, through the 1920s, Mother Jones was said to have been the most beloved individual in the American labor movement. To employers and politicians, she was "the most dangerous woman in America."

Mary Harris Jones was born in Cork City, Ireland in 1830 into a poor family. Her father, Richard Harris, immigrated to the United States in 1835 and after obtaining his naturalization papers, sent for the rest of the family. His work as a laborer with railway construction crews took him to Toronto, Canada, where Mary attended school to become a teacher and a dressmaker. After she finished her training in Toronto, she moved to Monroe, Michigan where she taught at a convent school, run by the Servants of the Immaculate Heart of Mary, for a short time. Then she opened a dressmaking business in Chicago because, in her own words, she "preferred sewing to bossing kids around." Again on the move, Mary turned up in Memphis, Tennessee where she took up teaching again in a parochial school. In 1861, she met and married iron molder and union leader George Jones.

In the yellow fever epidemic of 1867, George Jones and Mary's four children died. Mary remained in Memphis nursing the sick. When the epidemic was over she returned to Chicago and again went into the dressmaking business with a partner. As if trouble were following Mary around, she lost everything four years later in the great Chicago Fire of October 1871.

Joins in the Labor Movement

Homeless and destitute, Mary Jones became interested in the rising labor organization, the Knights of Labor. According to her own accounts, she became an organizer. She soon emerged as a crusader on behalf of the labor movement. From her own experience in the loss of her husband, children and all of her possessions, Mary knew first hand the plight of workers, most of whom were immigrants who had been recruited in Europe to work in the mines, the mills and the factories of a newly emerging industrial America. It was an era when the huge resources of the United States were being developed and millions of immigrants were flooding into America's heartland.

Working conditions were appalling, particularly in the mining and the textile industries. In the mills, children as young as ten worked from twelve to sixteen hours a day at ten cents an hour. Many establishments would not hire a woman unless she came with a family of kids. Solidarity efforts by workers were resisted by mine operators and factory owners with the use of force by the police. Scabs were used to replace striking employees. Beginning in the 1890s, Mary Jones embarked on her crusade to fight for justice in the workplace using the motto, "Pray for the dead and fight like hell for the living."

Once she heard of a strike, she packed her few belongings in a traveling bag and head out to support and encourage the striking miners. She was in Pittsburgh for the 1877 railroad strike and in 1892 to witness the battles between Pinkerton detectives and striking steelworkers at the Homestead works. On one occasion, she was arrested for allegedly advocating violence during the coal strike at Clarksburg, West Virginia. In court she told the judge that she would never publicly encourage violence, saying to him, "Your Honor, you have been forty years on the bench and you would know when someone is lying." To which the prosecutor jumped up shouting, "Your Honor, there stands the most dangerous woman in the country today. She called your Honor a scab, but I will recommend leniency if she will leave the state and never return." The judge took Mary into his chamber and after lecturing her and denying that he was a scab, he acquitted her. The miners, "her boys," affectionately called her Mother Jones.

One of Mother Jones's most poignant campaigns was in 1903 when some 75,000 textile workers went on strike in

Kensington, Pennsylvania. Over 10,000 of the mill workers were children, few of them were over ten years of age. There were boys with missing fingers and young mothers who had to bring their babies to work with them. Mother Jones, appalled at what she saw, accused the owners of building their "Philadelphia mansions on the broken bones and quivering hearts of the children." She was so upset, she organized a march of the children from Philadelphia to New York to dramatize their plight and demand changes to child labor laws.

In towns along the way she held meetings at which she put the children on display to show the horrors of child labor. At Trenton, New Jersey, the mayor told her that she couldn't hold a meeting there because he couldn't provide sufficient police protection for her and the children. Mother Jones angrily shot back, "These little children have never known any sort of protection, Your Honor and they are used to going without it." He let her hold the meeting.

At Princeton University in New Jersey Mother Jones spoke to a large gathering of faculty and students. Pointing to a ten year old child who was stooped over like an old man from carrying heavy bundles of yarn she said, "Here's a textbook on economics."

In New York, her request for permission to march up Fourth Avenue to Madison Square was denied by Police Commissioner Ebstein because she and her marching children were not citizens of New York City. Confronting Mayor Low she said, "Permit me to call your attention to an incident which took place in this nation just a year ago. A piece of rotten royalty came over here from Germany, called Prince Henry. The Congress of the United States voted $45,000 to fill that fellow's stomach for three weeks and to entertain him. His brother was getting four million dollars in dividends out of the blood of the workers of this country. Was he a citizen of this land? And it was reported, Mr. Mayor, that you and all the officials of New York entertained that chap. Was he a citizen of New York? Well, Mr. Mayor, these are the little citizens of the nation and they also produce its wealth. Aren't they entitled to enter your city?"

The mayor called the police commissioner and soon Mother Jones and her army of little folk were marching up Fourth

County Cork-born Mary Harris "Mother" Jones, a pioneer American socialist, was a living example of working class direct action in the forefront of the American labor movement.

Avenue accompanied by the police. In a speech to a large gathering at Twentieth Street she spoke of the horrors of child labor in the textile mills and showed them some of the children.

Support from the newspapers and politicians helped Mother Jones to push ahead with her crusade for child labor laws. Mother Jones's efforts were not in vain. The Pennsylvania Legislature soon enacted a Child Labor Law which forbade children under the age of fourteen from working in the mills.

Her exploits on behalf of America's workers became legendary. She organized miners' wives and children to march in support of their striking husbands and dared the soldiers to bayonet them. She was at Cripple Creek in Colorado and witnessed hundreds of mine strikers being taken out of Colorado and dumped into Kansas and told never to come back; others were thrown into stockades.

She fought for the three miners -- Charles Moyer, William Haywood and George Pettibone -- who were kidnapped from Colorado and taken to Idaho where they were lodged in jail and charged with the murder of the governor. They were acquitted. Every effort was made to keep Mother Jones away from areas where there was a strike. She outwitted the guards and the soldiers, often by getting the porters and trainmen to smuggle her on board the train outside the town before it was due to leave and dropping her off a mile or so outside the town where the strike was in progress.

In West Virginia, she was arrested, tried and sentenced to prison for twenty years on a trumped up charge of murder. When the editor of the *San Francisco Bulletin* got wind of the story, he exposed what had happened and sent his wife to Washington to intercede with the government on Mother Jones's behalf. She never served the sentence.

Mother Jones was in the fighting zone during a strike at the Copper Queen mine in Bisbee, Arizona when the mine operators accused the strikers of setting fire to the mill. The military was called in and over a thousand miners were herded into boxcars at gun point and taken out into the Arizona desert and dumped there without food or water and told never to come back. She ventured as far north as Victoria, British Columbia, where union members were on strike, and into the Mesabi iron range in Minnesota to help out the strikers.

Mother Jones spent seventy years of her life traveling throughout the United States preaching solidarity to half-starved miners, helping their families, nursing the sick, and agitating for child labor laws. She was repeatedly driven out of mining communities, enjoined by the courts, locked up in jails and even threatened with assassination, but she fearlessly pursued her crusade for the miners.

Mary Harris "Mother" Jones died in November 1930. Following a requiem mass at St. Gabriel's Church in Washington, her body was removed to the miners cemetery in Mount Olive in Southern Illinois not far from St. Louis. She was laid to rest next to "her boys" who were shot in an 1898 gun battle with strike breakers in the nearby town of Virden. So ended the long and dauntless life of the little immigrant Irishwoman who spent her life fighting to better the plight of the workingman.

Induction into Labor's Hall of Fame

On January 28, 1993 Mary Harris "Mother" Jones was inducted into the Labor Hall of Fame in Washington, D.C. "The most dangerous woman in America" finally had her place of honor beside such labor greats as Samuel Gompers, John L. Lewis and George Meany and her old friend, Eugene V. Debbs. Speaking to an overflow audience in the Frances Perkins Auditorium, Secretary of Labor Robert Reich said of her, "...Her voice was a clarion call of support for beleaguered miners in West Virginia, Colorado and Pennsylvania, and she mounted massive crusades against the evil of child labor." United Mine Workers' President, Richard Trumka, said of her, "It is especially appropriate to commemorate the life of Mother Jones at the one agency of our government whose mission it is to make her dream of dignity and fairness and economic justice a reality that every American worker can share."

It is fitting that Mother Jones receive labor's highest honor. She risked her life time and time again with no thought of reward. Always a humble person, she probably would have balked at such an honor for herself, if she were alive.

272

Thomas Reilly Donahue
Labor Statesman

Thomas Reilly Donahue holds the second most powerful
position in American labor. His election to the office of
secretary-treasurer of the giant American Federation of Labor and
the Congress of Industrial Organizations (AFL-CIO) in 1979,
came at a time when the American labor movement was in crisis.
Membership in 1975 had stood at an all time high of twenty-two
million; in 1979 it was falling sharply. New technology in the
workplace, loss of industrial competitiveness and shifting worker
demographics meant a bold new approach was needed.

In the face of the crisis, Donahue was chosen to head a
blue-ribbon committee to develop new strategies for future avenues of growth for America's unions. As a result of initiatives
adopted by the committee, the face of the movement was
modernized. Union membership stablized and public support for
unions has increased over the intervening years.

Growing Up in the Bronx

Tom was born in the Bronx on September 4, 1928, the
youngest of four children. After attending parochial school and
Mount St. Michael's Academy in the Bronx, Tom received a
Bachelor of Arts degree in labor relations from Manhattan College
in 1949. He went on to Fordham University Law School and
received a law degree in 1956. During his undergraduate student
years, Tom worked as a doorman at Radio City Music Hall, bakery
worker, truck driver, auto mechanic's helper, school bus driver,
elevator operator and wire lather.

His Career

Tom Donahue began his labor career while still in college,
first as a part-time organizer for the Retail Clerks International
Association and later in organizing for the Elevator Operators
Union. While attending law school, he held a number of positions in Local 32B of the Service Employees International Union,
then the second largest local union in the United States. Next, he

spent three years in Paris as labor-program coordinator with the Free Europe Committee, the parent organization of Radio Free Europe, handling liaison with West European trade unions and trade unionists in exile from countries in Eastern Europe.

After returning to the United States, Donahue worked for the Service Employees International Union until he was named assistant secretary of Labor for Labor-Management relations by President Johnson in 1967. In 1973, George Meany, then president of the AFL-CIO, selected Tom to be his executive assistant. When Meany resigned in 1979, Lane Kirkland, who was the secretary-treasurer, was elected the office of president and Tom was elected to replace him as secretary-treasurer.

His Interest in His Heritage

Tom Donahue is not only a great labor leader, but also is recognized as a champion advocate for Irish causes. His paternal grandfather emigrated from Kilmuckridge, County Wexford, near the ancestral home of the Kennedys. His paternal grandmother, Margaret Reilly, came from Mullagh, County Cavan, where his cousins still run the dairy farm that has been in the family for nearly 150 years.

Born into a home with a strong Irish heritage, Tom Donahue developed a lifelong interest in Irish affairs. He helped organize the Irish Cultural Society at Manhattan College. He marched for years in New York's St. Patrick's Day parades. He co-founded the Irish American Labor Coalition which put Ireland on the agenda of the American labor movement. One result was formal AFL-CIO backing for the McBride Principles that require equal rights in the workplace in Northern Ireland.

In 1990, Tom Donahue led an AFL-CIO fact-finding mission to Belfast. It found continuing job discrimination and upon their return called for fair employment safeguards in United States contracts with Northern Ireland firms. During other visits to Ireland, Tom and his wife, Rachelle, visited his grandfather's home in Kilmuckridge and his grandmother's hometown of Mullagh in County Cavan.

The American Irish Historical Society awarded Tom Donahue its 1990 Gold Medal for his extraordinary contribution to the American labor movement and his courageous leadership in defense of fair employment and human rights in Northern Ireland.

Thomas Reilly Donahue, an American labor stateman, is secretary-treasurer of the powerful American Federation of Labor-Congress of Industrial Organizations. Donahue is an outspoken defender of Irish causes.

Martin Patrick Durkin
Distinguished Unionist and
Secretary of Labor

It was the day after Thanksgiving when Martin Patrick Durkin, President of the powerful Plumbers and Pipefitters Union, received a telephone call from the White House. Herbert Brownell said he was calling for Republican President-elect Eisenhower, who wanted Durkin for the post of Secretary of Labor. Astounded at the invitation, Durkin said, "Do you know I am a lifelong Democrat?" Brownell replied that he was aware that Durkin had supported Eisenhower's opponent, Adlai Stevenson, in the election. Martin Durkin, the highly respected labor official, joined what became known as Eisenhower's Cabinet of millionaires and a plumber, as Secretary of Labor in early 1953.

As a condition of accepting the appointment, Durkin got assurances from the President that the administration would push Congress to remove some of the harsher anti-union clauses in the Labor-Management Relations Act (Taft-Hartley). Taft-Hartley, enacted in 1947, was in response to wartime strikes by the coal miners and a postwar rash of industry-wide walkouts. The unions adamantly opposed the restrictions this legislation had placed on the right to strike and on the "closed shop" which forced employers to hire only workers that were members of a union.

As Secretary of Labor, Martin Durkin set in motion the machinery for amending the Taft-Hartley Act. Working closely with George Meany of the AFL-CIO and other union leaders, Durkin drafted a proposal of nineteen amendments to the law which the White House approved and readied to submit to Congress on July 31, 1953. But the proposal wasn't sent to Congress as planned. That same day Senator Taft, one of the authors of the original law, died. President Eisenhower, out of respect for the senator, decided to delay submitting the package to congress until a later date. The delay bought time for the forces opposed to the proposed changes to lobby the president into with-

276

drawing his support. Several weeks later, President Eisenhower told Durkin that he could no longer support the amendments.

Feeling betrayed, Martin Durkin resigned as Eisenhower's Secretary of Labor on September 10, 1953, nine months after he was appointed.

Growing Up in Chicago

Martin Durkin was born on March 18, 1894, the first of eight children -- four boys and four girls -- to County Mayo emigrants, James Joseph Durkin and Mary Kate O'Higgins. He grew up in the stockyards area of South Chicago. Four of the children died while they were still quite young. Martin's youth was much like that of other children in the area who played ball on the vacant lots of South Chicago.

The Durkins struggled to make ends meet. The elder Durkin worked twelve hours a day, seven days a week, as a stationary fireman in a factory, and every other week he had to put in a straight twenty-four hour shift. The long hours, dreadful working conditions and meager pay that James Durkin earned would influence the thinking of his son in later years when he became active in the labor movement.

Martin Durkin finished school at fourteen and started working full time to help support the family. In his first job he worked fifty-four hours a week and earned four dollars. At age fifteen, he got a job in one of the slaughter houses in the Chicago stockyards. About this time, Martin enrolled in night classes and soon became a steam fitter's helper. After six years as an apprentice, he joined the steam fitter journeymen's ranks. His two surviving brothers also became steam fitters. His career was interrupted by World War I. He enlisted in the United States army and served in France in the Sixth Cavalry Corps.

Distinguished Career

After the war, Martin returned to Chicago and his trade as a steam fitter. He became active in union affairs and in 1921 became the business agent for Steam Fitters Local Union 597. That same year he married Anna McNicholas, a Chicago girl whose parents were also born in County Mayo, Ireland.

277

Martin Durkin, president of the Plumbers and Pipefitters International Union and President Dwight Eisenhower's first secretary of labor in 1953. Below, his granddaughter, Mary Durkin, budget and finance director for the United States Federal Mediation and Conciliation Service.

Martin Durkin went on to become president of Local 597. Under his leadership, it became the largest Steam Fitters Local in the United States with a membership of 9,000. In 1927, he was elected vice-president of the Chicago Building Trades Council. During that time, Al Capone's hoodlums were attempting to infiltrate and take over the trade unions, and Martin furiously and effectively fought them off.

In 1933, Martin was appointed to the post of Director of Labor for the State of Illinois. He served in that post for eight years under three Governors, Democrats Henry Horner and John H. Spell and Republican Dwight Crane.

During his time as director of labor for Illinois, Martin Durkin contributed to the establishment of a state unemployment compensation system and to the regulation of minimum wage and maximum hours for women and children. He was effective in establishing a state mediation and conciliation service and in having safety legislation enacted. He had training programs introduced for workers and he cracked down on certain employment agencies who were taking advantage of workers during the Great Depression. According to an article in the February 7, 1953 issue of *Colliers Magazine*, Governor Horner called Durkin's appointment, "The best appointment I ever made." He called him "a man of high character and ability who never had a breath of scandal during his eight years in office."

After leaving State office in 1941, he returned to the Plumbers and Pipefitters Union where he was elected its international secretary-treasurer. In 1943, he became international president of the union. For the next nine years he served in the union's top job and earned the reputation of a successful leader and labor statesman.

After resigning the position of Secretary of Labor, Durkin returned to his post as president of his union. One year later he collapsed in Los Angeles from what was determined to be a brain tumor. He died a year later.

Martin Durkin's granddaughter, Mary Durkin, resides in Washington, D. C. where she is budget and finance director for the Federal Mediation and Conciliation Service (FMCS), a federal government agency. Mary is active in the Sheridan Circle, an association of Irish-Americans in Washington, D. C. which provides a forum for the exchange of ideas, knowledge and activities relating to Irish culture and economic concerns. Since its founding in 1990, the Sheridan Circle has attracted a cadre of distinguished speakers from Ireland and the United States, including Ireland's Prime Minister, Albert Reynolds; Senator Eugene McCarthy; former United States Ambassador to Ireland, Margaret Heckler; Mary Harney, Minister of State, Ireland's Department of the Environment; Ambassadors Padraig MacKernan and Dermot Gallagher, Irish envoys to the United States; Sir Kenneth Bloomfield, former head of the Northern Ireland Civil Service; Dermot Earley, Deputy Military Advisor to the Secretary General of the United Nations and a host of others. These speakers have helped to enlighten the Circle's membership on current issues confronting Ireland, Europe and the United States. Mary served as the Circle's President in 1992-1993 and was on the welcoming committee of Irish-Americans for President Mary Robinson's visit to Washington in May of 1993.

Heroes and Warriors

The Irish are a great race of fighters. In ancient Ireland the feats of heroes and warriors such as Cuchulain and Fionn MacCool are recounted in the great Irish epics. The Tain Bo Cuailgne provides a great basis of legendary lore. King Brian Boru later became a legend when he succeeded in driving the Vikings out of Ireland at the battle of Clontarf in the year 1014. Since the Norman invasion of Ireland in 1169, the Irish struggle against English rule has created numerous heroes such as Wolfe Tone and Robert Emmet.

Throughout the 17th and 18th centuries, Irish officers and soldiers distinguished themselves on many of the battlefields of Europe. Irish brigades, reinforced by tens of thousands of Irishmen over the years, were conspicuous fighting forces in the armies of France, Spain and Austria. Many Irish adventurers and their descendants achieved fame and fortune fighting for their adopted lands in Europe and in South America.

Ambrosia O'Higgins is one example. Born in Ballinary, County Sligo in 1720, he fled Ireland as a youngster to Spain. Educated in Cadiz, he later made his way to Chile where he engaged in trade between Europe and South America. He went on to become Governor of the Spanish Province of Chile in 1789. His son, Bernardo O'Higgins, born in Chile in 1778, led a revolt against the Spanish which succeeded in Chile becoming an independent country. Bernardo is called the Father of Chile.

Irish officers and soldiers distinguished themselves alongside George Washington during the American War of Independence. Colonel John Fitzgerald of Wicklow was Washington's Aide-de-Camp and was known as the finest horsesoldier in the Colonial army. Richard Montgomery, Andrew Donnelly and Andrew Lewis, natives of County Donegal, were distinguished officers in the Revolutionary Army. They commanded troops in the War of Independence under Washington. Montgomery was killed in the attack on Quebec in 1775. Montgomery County in Maryland was named after him. In March 1783, the British frigate *Sibylle,* and the *USS Alliance* under the command of John (Saucy Jack) Barry, fought the last battle of the American War of Independence. The fight ended with both ships sailing off in different directions. The land war had ended some weeks earlier with the American Colonies gaining their independence from Britain.

John Barry was seventeen when he slipped away to sea from his home in Rosslare, County Wexford and sailed for America. He was born in the village of Ballysampson in 1745. When John was very young, his family moved to Rosslare, where he was exposed to the seafaring life. At age ten, John Barry sailed as a cabin boy on a ship out of Wexford for Jamaica. His second voyage was to Philadelphia where he caught the eye of a gentleman called Morris, of the trading firm of Willing & Morris. Morris signed him on as a cabin boy and over the next few years he rose to become a first mate in the company's service. At age twenty-one in 1766, John Barry was master of his own ship, the schooner Barbados, and in a few short years he built up a sizable shipping business. About this time he met and married Mary Cleary, who also came from County Wexford.

In 1776, when the American Colonies erupted in revolt against England, Barry was first approached by the British, but as he put it in his Wexford accent, "I spurned the eydee of being a traitor." He was then approached by the Revolutionary Naval Committee and was given the task of fitting out a fleet which consisted of two vessels, the *Lexington* and the *Reprisal.* He was put in charge of the *Lexington*, with the rank of Commodore, the first ever to hold that rank in the American Navy.

Barry's first successful encounter at sea was against the English vessel the *Edward.* The *Lexington* with its seventy guns proved too much for the English crew who fought gallantly before the surrender. Barry sailed proudly back to port with the first capture of an enemy ship in the American War of Independence.

This feat and others during the Revolutionary War won Barry the reputation of a skilled fighting seaman. In 1778, Barry was given command of the thirty-two-gun *Raleigh,* which he had to beach to prevent its capture after a nine-hour battle with the British. With his next command, the *Delaware,* Barry wreaked havoc on the British in another encounter. Commanding the

282

Alliance on a return trip from France, where he had taken revolutionary officers to seek French help for the American Revolution, Barry captured two British vessels, the *Atlanta* and the *Trepassy*. He was injured in this encounter.

In 1794, he was sent into the Mediterranean against the Algerian pirates. Four years later in 1798, when hostilities arose against France, he was given command of the United States navel forces in the Caribbean. Later, he was promoted to commodore in charge of navy operations. He died in Philadelphia in September of 1803 at age fifty-eight. The American people had a memorial built commemorating him in Wexford town in 1956.

Then there was Thomas Francis Meagher who had been tried in Ireland by the British for high treason and was formally sentenced to be hanged at Clonmell in 1848. His sentence was commuted to banishment for life to Tasmania. In 1852, he escaped to the United States where his considerable military ability enabled him to rise to the rank of general in the Union Army during the Civil War.

Meagher made history at Fredericksburg in 1862, leading the Irish Brigade on repeated assaults against the Confederate lines, which caused General Robert E. Lee to remark, "...They ennobled their race by their gallantry on that desperate occasion..." Of the 1,200 men he led into that fateful battle, only 280 survived. The battle honors of the Irish Brigade in the Civil War also included Chancellorsville, Yorktown, Oak Ridge and Gettysburg.

Major-General Patrick Cleburne of the Confederate forces during the Civil War was regarded by the leaders of the Confederate States as second only to the great Stonewall Jackson. Cleburne died at the Battle of Franklin and was buried in Polk Cemetery near Columbia, Tennessee, far away from County Cork, Ireland where he spent his youthful years.

Wild Bill Donovan's heroic exploits as colonel of New York's Fighting 69th Regiment during World War I earned him the Medal of Honor. It was the same Bill Donovan who, in World War II, was commissioned to set up and run the Office of Strategic Services (OSS), the predecessor organization of the Central Intelligence Agency (CIA).

There were the Sullivans, five brothers who grew up in the 1930s in a working class neighborhood of an Iowa city. During WW II, all five enlisted in the U.S. Navy and, because they wanted to be together, were assigned to the cruiser USS *Juneau.* All were drowned when their ship was sunk off Guadalcanal. They are memorialized in the movie, *The Sullivans,* and the navy named a destroyer, *The Sullivans,* after them.

Another hero of World War II was a young Irish-American chaplain by the name of John Patrick Washington, whose father immigrated from County Roscommon. Father Washington and three fellow chaplains of different faiths gave their lives in a desperate attempt to save the lives of their fellow passengers after their ship, the *Dorchester,* with 638 troops aboard, was hit by a torpedo in the North Atlantic in 1943.

Since the United States Congressional Medal of Honor was first awarded in 1863, there have been more than two hundred and fifty Irish-born who have earned this recognition for military heroism. No other nationality has come close to winning so many. Among the recipients of the Medal of Honor was a Texas sharecropper's son, Audie Murphy. Born in 1924, he was the most decorated hero of World War II. He received the Medal of Honor for heroism during an encounter with the Germans in Eastern France in January 1945. He received twenty-seven other decorations, including the Distinguished Service Cross, the Silver Star with Oak Leaf Cluster, and the Croix de Guerre with Palm.

The stories of the three Irish generals that follow are illustrative of the significant contribution made by the Irish in the countries of their adoption. Brigadier General Hugo O'Conor is credited with being the founder of Tucson, Arizona which was a Spanish Territory at the time. He later became governor of Chile. General Philip Sheridan who fought on the Union side during the Civil War, and General Patrick Cleburne, who fought and died fighting with the Confederates, were two valorous Irishmen who distinguished themselves in many battles. The loss of the five Sullivan brothers in the sinking of the USS *Juneau* in World War II is every mother's nightmare, times five. It is a naval story that will never be forgotten.

Commodore John Barry
Father of the
United States Navy

Bronze memorial to Commodore John Barry, Father of the American Navy, stands in Wexford Town, Ireland. County Wexford-born Barry went to sea as a cabin boy at the age of ten and went on to become the first commander of an American warship during the American War of Independence.

The Minstrel Boy

The minstrel boy to the war has gone,
   In the ranks of death you'll find him,
His father's sword he has girded on,
   And his wild harp slung behind him.
"Land of song!" said the warrior bard,
   "Though all the world betrays thee,
One sword, at least, thy rights shall guard,
   One faithful harp shall praise thee!"

The minstrel fell! -- but the foeman's chain
   Could not bring his proud soul under;
The harp he loved ne'er spoke again,
   For he tore its chords asunder;
And said, "No chains shall sully thee,
   Thou soul of love and bravery!
Thy songs are made for the pure and free,
   They shall never sound in slavery!"

-- Thomas Moore
1779-1852

286

Brigadier General
Hugo (Hugh) O'Conor
Founder of Tucson and Governor of Chile

Hugo (Hugh) O'Conor was born in Dublin in December of 1734 to Daniel and Margaret Ryan O'Conor. Bearer of a royal and honored name, tracing an ancestry through the O'Conor Dons of Connaught back to Turlogh Mor O'Conor who died in 1156, Hugo joined the rebellion against the English invaders. When it failed, Hugo O'Conor went into exile. He became part of that exodus which started after the siege of Limerick in 1691, when the "Flight of the Wild Geese" (as the exiles were called) saw the Irish flee to France and Spain and enter the service of the Irish Brigades in those countries,

Hugo O'Conor was luckier than most exiles. He joined the army of Spain and through his royal blood was accepted for officer training. He joined an Aragon regiment and in 1763 was posted to Cuba, then a Spanish colony. He served under his cousin, Field Marshall Alexander O'Neill. Soon promoted to major, Hugo was inducted into the Order of the Knights of Calatrava, a most select group.

Eager for action, Hugo became part of the Army of New Spain (as Spanish America was then called) and he was posted to Mexico City. From there he went to Texas where he filled in for the Spanish Governor who had been recalled. Tiring of administration work, Hugo sought an active service posting. He was promoted to lieutenant colonel and put in charge of the campaigns against the Apache and Comanche Indians who were still occupying a major part of what is now the southwestern United States and northern Mexico. The Spanish had established a chain of presidios or garrison forts through Mexican territory north into what are now Arizona, Texas and New Mexico, to protect settlers from Indian attacks.

Most presidios had been erected hurriedly and were not in the most strategic places for defense and sustenance, so O'Conor was given the job of relocating them. He fought many battles with the Apache tribes. The new garrison locations cut off the route used by marauding Apache warriors on their forays against the Spanish. One new location, which was laid out by O'Conor himself, became the foundation of modern day Tucson, Arizona. By December 1775, Spanish troops had been moved from Tubac and were garrisoned at the new presidio. The walls and buildings of Tucson were not finally completed until 1783.

Being in poor health after his four years of active service, O'Conor asked to be relieved of his command. For his gallant work on behalf of Spain, Hugo O'Conor was promoted to Brigadier General. Soon after, he became Governor of Chile and played a part in building that country into a modern nation.

Some reports have Hugo O'Conor dying abroad, but one of his surviving descendants confirms that a tomb in the old grave-yard in Castlerea, County Roscommon, ancient home of the O'Conor Don, is inscribed: "Sir Hugo O'Conor, Knight of Calatravia and Brigadier General in his Majesty's Service and Governor of Chile."

The O'Conor Dons

The O'Conor family provided Ireland with many of its High Kings, including the last, King Rory O'Conor, who died in 1175. Clonalis House in Castlerea is the ancestral home of the O'Conor family which traces its lineage back for sixty-six generations.

Clonalis House is presently occupied by Piers David O'Conor Nash, who became the present head of the O'Conor family upon the death of his uncle, Father Charles O'Conor, S.J. Fr. O'Conor had no brothers and when he died the male line title went to his sister and subsequently to her son, Piers David O'Conor Nash. The present family head is seven generations removed from Brigadier General Hugo O'Conor.

One of the O'Conors, a Charles O'Conor of Mount Allen, County Roscommon, and his son participated in the 1798 rebellion of the United Irishmen. When the rebellion failed, they fled to New York where they joined Charles's other sons, Thomas and Denis, who were already living there. Thomas published an Irish-American newspaper, *The Shamrock*. His son, Charles, became one of New York's most able and influential lawyers and is re-

288

garded as the father of the New York Appellate Court. In 1872, his name was placed in nomination for the presidency of the United States, becoming the first Catholic to have that distinction.

Tucson

Tuscon became part of Mexico in 1821 after Mexico won its independence from Spain. In 1854, Tucson was annexed by the United States as a result of the Gadsden Purchase. Arizona, where Tucson is located, became the forty-eighth state in 1912.

Modern Tucson is a flourishing city of some 800,000 people with a thriving Irish community. Recent census figures show some 19,000 residents of Pima County claim Ireland as their land of origin and another 50,000 consider themselves as having some Irish background. The Irish have played an important part in Tucson's history and its politics. Irishman Jim Corbett was Mayor of Tucson for many years and was defeated for this office by fellow Irishman Lewis C. Murphy, who ran the mayor's office for sixteen years. Murphy's grandparents came from County Cork.

General Phillip Sheridan

Up from the South at break of day,
Bringing to Winchester fresh dismay,
The affrighted air with a shudder bore,
Like a herald in haste, to the chieftain's door,
The terrible grumble, and rumble, and roar,
Telling the battle was on once more,
And Sheridan twenty miles away.

--From "Sheridan's Ride," by Thos. Buchanan Read

General Phillip Sheridan rose from simple beginnings to the highest military command in the United States Army. He was an obscure army captain who soared to prominence during the Civil War, becoming the most famous and honored union cavalry commander of that campaign. He made military history in Missouri and in Mississippi where he fought in many of the battles, including Booneville, Perryville, Stones River, Cedar Creek, Missionary Ridge and Chickamauga. He led the Shenandoah Valley campaign and was present at Wilmer McLean's house in Appomattox when Lee surrendered to Grant. Sheridan had an army-wide reputation for being a deliberate and careful commander who had the best scouts of any union general in the civil war. After a brief but stormy period in Louisiana during Reconstruction, he went out West where he became a fearsomely effective and highly controversial leader in operations against American Indians, crossing paths with Sitting Bull, Crazy Horse and Geronimo.

He was an unimpressive little man, five feet, five inches tall. Abraham Lincoln humorously described him as a "brown chunky little chap, with a long body, short legs, not enough neck to hang him and such long arms that if his ankles itched, he could scratch them without stooping."

His Irish Roots

Sheridan was born on or about March 6, 1831, somewhere along the path his immigrant parents traveled from their ancestral home in County Cavan, Ireland, via Albany, New York, to Somerset, Ohio, where he grew up. His *alma mater* accepts Albany, New York as his birthplace. His mother told the Chairman of the Sheridan Monument Association that her son had been born at sea on the voyage over, but she also had told Sheridan himself earlier that he was born in Albany. Sheridan himself is reported to have claimed he was born in New York City, supposedly because he wanted to run for the office of President of the United States.

He was the third of six children. His older sister, Rosa, died at sea on the trip over. His parents, John and Mary Meenagh Sheridan, were second cousins who had been tenant farmers in Ireland before immigrating to America. Upon arrival, the family stayed for a short while in Albany, New York with Sheridan's uncle, Thomas Gaynor, before heading west to Ohio.

The family settled in the little town of Somerset, a Catholic community about forty-three miles southeast of Columbus. The elder Sheridan soon rose from laborer to free-lance railway contractor. Sheridan's older brother, Patrick, died suddenly at age twenty-one. Sheridan and his two younger brothers found employment in a succession of Somerset stores during their teenage years.

At age eighteen, Phil Sheridan received an appointment to West Point through the recommendation of his congressman, Thomas Ritchey. He graduated from the Academy in 1852, thirty-fourth on the roll of graduates recited by Superintendent Robert E. Lee. Disqualified for duty in the more prestigious ranks, Sheridan was assigned to the First Infantry Regiment, then garrisoned at Fort Duncan, Texas.

An incident occurred while he was at West Point which came within a whisker of ending his military career before it started. In 1851, at the end of his first-class year, Cadet Private Sheridan was given a preemptory order by Cadet Sergeant William Terrill, when something about Terrill's tone irritated Sheridan. He cursed the sergeant while at the same time lowering his rifle and lunging his bayonet. This shocking breach of discipline gave the flabbergasted Terrill no choice but to report the matter. The next afternoon, Sheridan ran into Terrill and again attacked him, striking him a pelt on the side of the head. Sheridan was placed under house arrest and after a hearing was suspended for a year. Nine months later, he was back at West Point and for the duration of his term succeeded in harnessing his Irish temper until he graduated.

Oregon Territory Assignment

In November 1854, Sheridan was promoted to Second Lieutenant and transferred to the Fourth Infantry Regiment at Fort Redding, California where he replaced his academy classmate John Bell Hood. In command of a small group of dragoons, Sheridan set about routing Yakima Indians and their allies who were hostile to the white settlers along the Columbia River. He served at Fort Yamhill and Fort Hoskins.

While he was serving at Fort Hoskins, Sheridan found himself a female companion. Her name was Sidnayoh, the daughter of Chief Quatly of the Willamette Valley Klikitats. To her white friends she was known as Frances. Such an arrangement was not unusual for lonely young officers at distant posts.

The Civil War

The attack on Fort Sumter resulted in many southern army officers resigning their commissions to follow their home states into rebellion. Among them were Sheridan's old West Point superintendent, Robert E. Lee, and his fellow classmate, John Bell Hood. For Sheridan and other young officers who had remained for years at the same first rank, the storm of resignations was a godsend. After eight years without a promotion, Sheridan was quickly raised to the rank of Lieutenant in March of 1861 and he received his captain's bars two months later. With the war underway, the ambitious Sheridan was worried that it would end before he had a chance to make his mark. Finally, in September 1861, his orders came instructing him to report to Jefferson Barracks, Missouri to join the newly created Thirteenth Infantry Regiment commanded by fellow Ohion Brigadier William Tecumseh Sherman.

On April 15, 1862, Sheridan received orders to report to Major General Henry Halleck in Tennessee. Sheridan had always considered this appointment the turning point in his military career. On May 27, 1862, Captain Phillip H. Sheridan was appointed Colonel of the Second Michigan Regiment Cavalry of the Army of the Mississippi led by the brilliant Major General William Rosecrans of Cincinnati.

His first skirmish was at Boonesville against the Confederates led by General Chambers. The day after the battle, Rosecrans praised the coolness, determination and fearless gallantry displayed by Colonel Sheridan and the officers of his command. He recommended that Sheridan be made a brigadier general. With his general's star, Sheridan found himself commanding three infantry brigades of twelve regiments and two artillery batteries. The Battle of Stones River was a triumph for Sheridan. He not only withstood the initial offensive of the Confederates, but also managed to delay their advance for two crucial hours while Rosecrans set up a new position. General Grant would say about Sheridan's performance at this battle, "It was from all I can hear about it a wonderful bit of fighting. It showed what a great general can do even in a subordinate command; for I believe Sheridan in that battle saved Rosecrans' army." After Stones Ridge, General Rosecrans urged that Sheridan be promoted to Major General. This was a great endorsement for someone who only seven months earlier had been a mere captain.

Sheridan helped to win a victory at Chattanooga, one that confirmed Grant's unrivaled status as the Union's preeminent man-at-arms. Crowned by such laurels, Grant soon headed East to greater renown and Phil Sheridan followed. Sheridan was given charge of the cavalry corps of the Army of the Potomac. At Winchester, he attacked Rebel forces under Jubal Earley and three days later routed them at Fisher's Hill. Sheridan pursued Earley to the southern end of the Shenandoah Valley, breaking the Confederates' hold on the valley for good and, in the process, became the scourge of the Shenandoah Valley.

General Phillip Sheridan is credited with leading the cavalry charge which crumpled the Confederate lines at Appomattox in the waning hours of the war and it was Sheridan who signalled Grant that Lee was waiting at the Appomattox Court House to surrender his army.

The Indian Campaigns

After the Civil War, Sheridan was given the task of clearing and restoring Texas and Louisiana in the so-called "reconstruction" of those states. President Andrew Johnson reassigned him from that post in 1867, placing him in charge of the Army of the Missouri Territory and giving him the task of making that huge area safe for the white settlers who were then pouring onto the Great Plains. That mission accomplished, Sheridan headed north against the Sioux tribes and their leaders, Chiefs Sitting Bull and Crazy Horse. It was during this campaign that Sheridan's subordinate, General George Custer, and his force of 261 men were wiped out by the Sioux at the Battle of the Little Big Horn.

Commanding General of the Army

When Sherman retired in 1884, Sheridan inherited the position of commanding general of the army. Also in 1884, the nation prepared to elect a new president. Chester Arthur, who had assumed the presidency when Garfield was shot in 1881, decided not to seek reelection. Sheridan was mentioned as a possible candidate but remained on the sidelines. He had supported Republican Grant four years earlier. James Blaine lost the election to Grover Cleveland, who became the first successful Democratic candidate since before the Civil War.

Soon after Napoleon III declared war on the allied German states, Sheridan made a trip to Europe and visited political and military leaders in London, Brussels and Berlin. During the same trip, he made a sentimental journey to Ireland.

In 1887, Sheridan's health started to decline. After Sheridan returned home, in March of 1888, from touring the proposed site of Fort Sheridan north of Chicago, he suffered a massive heart attack. Congress voted to make him a four-star general, a rank which only Grant and Sherman had held before him. The first and last order Sheridan made as general of the army was to promote his brother, Michael, and two others to colonels on the general staff. On August 5, 1888, Sheridan suffered another heart attack and died at Nonquitt, south of New Bedford. Sheridan was laid to rest in Arlington Cemetery near the front door of Robert E. Lee's old home.

General Patrick Cleburne
Confederate Hero

Many brilliant stories have been written about the gallantry of the Irish who fought on the Union side during the American Civil War. The Irish Brigade, under Wexford-born Brigadier General Thomas F. Meagher, distinguished itself on many battlefields from Fredericksburg to Chancellorsville to Gettysburg. The Irish also fought on the Confederate side, but the story of their feats is not as well known, essentially because they were on the vanquished side and the losers seldom fare as well historically as do the conquerors.

However, one story has lived on. It tells of a great Irish-born combat soldier in the Army of Tennessee, named General Patrick Cleburne. For his "gallant and meritorious service" at the Battle of Richmond he received an official vote of thanks from the Congress of the Confederate States. His division formed the first line of attack against General Grant's army at the Battle of Shiloh. Pat Cleburne was called the best division commander in Bragg's army. He stalled Sherman's forces while defending Missionary Ridge at the battle of Chattanooga.

As the war dragged on, Cleburne, recognizing the superiority of the North's military resources, advocated recruiting blacks into the Confederate army. He maintained that blacks (accustomed to obedience from youth) would, under the command of their masters, make better soldiers for the South than they had proven to be under different principles of organization for the North.

Cleburne insisted that it was the duty of the Southern people to waive considerations of property and prejudice and use this powerful source of manpower. His proposition to a conclave of generals was hushed up immediately.

It was unthinkable, to all Southerners, that a slave could be turned into a soldier; they feared that freeing part of the race would mean freeing it all. One year later, after Cleburne had been killed, the Confederate Congress passed a bill permitting blacks into the army.

General Patrick Ronayne Cleburne's brilliant career came to an end when he was killed leading his troops at the battle of Franklin on November 30, 1864. General W. Hardee, his commanding officer, said that Cleburne's death was a greater loss to the Confederate cause than that of any other Confederate leader except Stonewall Jackson. In eulogizing him, Hardee called him an Irishman by birth, a Southerner by adoption, a lawyer by profession, a soldier of the British army by accident, and a patriotic soldier of the Confederate armies.

His Early Years

Pat Cleburne was born near Cork city in 1827. His father, the son of a country gentleman in Tipperary, was a medical doctor for the dispensary districts of Ovens and Ballincollig. His mother was a Ronayne from Queenstown (now Cobh), County Cork. Patrick was the youngest of three sons. He attended medical school for a short period, hoping to follow in his father's footsteps, but soon decided that he wanted a military career instead. Because his father was unable to purchase an officer commission in the British army, Pat enlisted as a private. At age twenty-one, he decided he wanted to immigrate to America, and with the help of some friends, purchased his way out of the British army.

Cleburne was practicing law at Helena, Arkansas when the Civil War broke out. He enlisted as a private and was soon made captain of his company. Promoted from one rank to another, he rose to the commission of Major-General.

After the Battle of Franklin, Cleburne's body was buried in the Polk cemetery near Columbia in Tennessee, one of the most beautiful spots in the valley of the Tennessee River. The story is told that on his way to Franklin, a few days before the battle, Pat Cleburne stopped at this spot and while gazing at its beauty turned to a staff member and said, "It is almost worth dying to rest in so sweet a spot."

Pat Cleburne's two brothers also fought in the Civil War. His youngest brother was killed fighting on the Confederate side in southwestern Virginia. The other brother was in the Union Army. It has been said that Cleburne believed that the Irish, who had espoused the Union cause, lacked consistency and morality. On the one hand, they invoked the sympathies of the world on behalf of the oppressed people of Ireland and, on the other, supported the enslavement of the Southern people.

The Saga of the Sullivan Brothers
World War II Tragedy

The loss of the five Sullivan brothers with the sinking of the U.S.S. *Juneau* was the greatest single blow suffered by one family in the history of the United States Navy.

Less than three weeks after the Japanese attacked Pearl Harbor on December 7, 1941, the five Sullivan brothers of Waterloo, Iowa enlisted in the United States Navy. A condition of their voluntary enlistment was that they not be separated. Although it was against Naval policy to have all the boys serve together, the policy was relaxed and the five brothers, George, Francis, Joseph, Madison and Albert, became part of the crew of the United States cruiser *Juneau.*

The *Juneau* was part of a flotilla of thirteen light cruisers and destroyers sailing with reinforcements for the United States marines on Guadalcanal in the South Pacific, when she was sunk by Japanese torpedoes in an area known as Torpedo Junction. This channel was patrolled by Japanese submarine commanders as American ships had to pass through this area on their way back to base.

The *Juneau* exploded when the torpedo hit and four of the Sullivans were killed instantly. The fifth brother, George, managed to hang on to a life raft, but eventually was drowned in the cold, shark infested waters. There were only ten survivors of the *Juneau* crew. Since the *Juneau* disaster, the policy of not allowing members of the same family to serve together has been strictly enforced.

There was only eight years' difference among the boys. Albert, the youngest, was twenty when he met his death and he was the only brother who was married. Albert and the former Katherine Rooff had one son, James, born February 13, 1941. George, the oldest, was twenty-eight, Francis was twenty-seven and Joseph and Madison were twenty-four at the time of the disaster.

The Sullivan family came from Cork. The boys' father, Thomas F. Sullivan, was born at Harpers Ferry, Iowa on March 10, 1883. He worked as a brakeman and conductor for the Illinois

Central Railroad from 1914 until he retired in 1954. Thomas and Alleta (Abel) Sullivan were married in 1914 and lived in Waterloo, Iowa. Alleta passed away on April 23, 1972.

Michael Magee, a genealogist from Waterloo, Iowa, shows that Thomas Sullivan Sr., the boys' grandfather, immigrated to America in 1849 with his brother Owen. They settled in Taylor Township, Allamakee County, Iowa. Thomas and his wife Bridget were the parents of six children.

Striking Back -- U.S.S. *The Sullivans*

The U.S.S. *The Sullivans* was launched in April of 1943. Alleta Sullivan, mother of the five Sullivans who lost their lives, christened the ship. Also attending were Mr. and Mrs. Patrick Sullivan of San Francisco who had five sons in the service as well, but not serving together.

The destroyer was soon active in the fleet. It helped sink a Japanese cruiser in Leyte Gulf; participated in the invasion of the Marianas and Caroline Island; took part in the capture of the Philippines and in the first carrier sweep of Tokyo. *The Sullivans* also shot down a Japanese dive bomber and helped in the rescue of two damaged American warships. After playing a significant role in the war in the Pacific, *The Sullivans* was retired and now rests in the Naval Park in Buffalo, New York. However, the United States Navy is determined not to let the Sullivan name and the exploits of the famous Sullivan Brothers fade away. A new Navy vessel, also to be named *The Sullivans*, will be commissioned in 1995 and plans are being made to have this new ship make a courtesy call into Bantry Bay in County Cork, traditional home of the Sullivans of Ireland.

A Nation Mourns the Sullivan Tragedy

When news of the sinking of the *Juneau* and the death of the five Sullivan brothers was made public, reporters and photographers descended on 98 Adam Street in Waterloo, Iowa, home of the Sullivans. The family received letters and cards of condolence from all around the world. President Franklin D. Roosevelt sent personal condolences to the family and later visited with them to express the sorrow of the nation at the great loss. Purple Heart medals were awarded posthumously to all the brothers and presented to their parents.

There is a Sullivan Park in Waterloo, Iowa which was dedicated in September of 1964. The memorial in the park is shaped as a pentagonal dais and topped with a shamrock insignia from the U.S.S. *The Sullivans*. Each of the five facets is inscribed with the name of one of the brothers.

The Sullivan brothers photographed with Jack Dempsey in his restaurant on Broadway shortly before they set sail for the South Pacific on the Juneau.

The Sullivan brothers -- (from the left) Joseph, Francis, Albert, Madison and George -- who lost their lives during World War II when their cruiser, the U.S.S. Juneau, was sunk off Guadalcanal in the South Pacific. Below, their parents, Alleta and Thomas Sullivan, photographed shortly after they received the tragic news of their sons' deaths. (Photo courtesy Waterloo Public Library)

Statesmen and Politicians

Nowhere did the Irish achieve so much as in politics. Fourteen United States presidents were of Irish ancestry. Andrew Jackson (Old Hickory), the 7th President (1829-1837) was the son of Irish immigrants. His father was born near Carrickfergus in County Antrim. His mother, Elizabeth Hutchinson, was also from Co. Antrim. The Jacksons settled in the Carolinas where Andrew was born. Jackson served as a major-general in the war of 1812, defeating the British at the Battle of New Orleans. It has been said of Andrew that he would boast to his friends, "I was born in America, but I was conceived in Ireland."

James Knox Polk, the 11th President (1845-1849), was born in Mecklenburg County, North Carolina. Polk's ancestors came from Londonderry.

James Buchanan, the 15th President (1857-1861), was the son of the Buchanans from Omagh, County Tyrone who immigrated to Franklin County, Pennsylvania where he was born on April 23, 1791. It was during his last year as president that South Carolina held a convention to decide whether or not to secede from the Union.

Andrew Johnson, the 17th President, succeeded Abraham Lincoln and served as president from 1865 to 1869. He was born of poor parents in Raleigh, North Carolina on December 28, 1808. A tailor by trade, he was illiterate until he married Eliza McCardle who taught him to read and write. His ancestors emigrated from County Antrim in the eighteenth century.

Ulysses S. Grant, the 18th President (1869-1877), had Irish ancestors. His mother, Hannah Simpson, came from Dungannon, County Tyrone. Before becoming President, Grant was the great Northern military hero of the Civil War. As Supreme Commander of the Union forces, he directed the campaign which brought about the surrender of the Confederate army.

Chester A. Arthur, the 21st President, assumed the presidency upon the assassination of James Garfield. He served from 1881 to 1885. He was born in Fairfield, Vermont in 1830, the son of a Baptist minister. His father, William, came from Dreen,

Cullybackey, County Antrim, immigrating to the United States with his family in 1816. It was during Arthur's Administration that the Federal Civil Service was reformed,

Grover Cleveland served as the 22nd and 24th President. Cleveland was born in Caldwell, New Jersey on March 18, 1837, the son of a Presbyterian clergyman. His mother's family, the Neals, were from County Antrim. From New York sheriff to mayor to governor to president, his ascent was meteoric. As sheriff of Erie County, New York, Cleveland supposedly placed the rope and sprung the trap-door for two convicted criminals.

Benjamin Harrison, the 23rd President (1889-1893), was grandson of William Henry Harrison, the 9th President. Born in North Bend, Ohio in 1833, Harrison's maternal ancestors, the Irwans, came from the North of Ireland. It was during Harrison's presidency that the White House was wired for electricity.

William McKinley, the 25th President (1897 to 1901), was born in Niles, Ohio in 1843. He was the great-great-grandson of James McKinley who immigrated to America from Dernock, County Antrim in the 1700s. William McKinley was shot down by an assassin's bullet on September 6, 1901 in Buffalo. During his Administration, the United States acquired Puerto Rico, the Philippine Archipelago and Guam. Hawaii was also annexed in 1899.

Teddy Roosevelt, the 26th President (1901 to 1909), assumed office upon the assassination of President McKinley. His mother, Martha Bullock, descended from a family that had emigrated from County Antrim. His father's mother, Margaret Potts Burnhill, was born in County Meath.

Woodrow Wilson, the 28th President (1913 to 1921), was born on December 28, 1856 in Staunton, Virginia, the son of a Presbyterian minister. He also served as governor of New Jersey and president of Princeton University. His grandfather was born in Dergalt, near Strabane, County Tyrone.

John Fitzgerald Kennedy was the 35th President, serving from 1961 to 1963. At 43, he was the youngest man ever elected President and the first Catholic. Kennedy was born in Brookline, Massachusetts on May 29, 1917. He was a World War II hero. Eight of his great-grandparents emigrated from Ireland's shores to

303

the United States in the nineteenth century. John F. Kennedy became the first serving United States president to visit Ireland when he went there in 1963. He visited the old farmstead at Dunganstown, County Wexford, from which his paternal great-grandfather, Patrick Kennedy, had emigrated over a century before. He was given a tumultuous welcome everywhere he visited. He told the people of Wexford, "I am glad to be here. It took 115 years to make this trip and 6,000 miles and three generations. ..." Five months later, President Kennedy was felled by an assassin's bullet while riding in a motorcade in Dallas, Texas.

Richard M. Nixon, the 37th President of the United States, served from January 29, 1969 to August 9, 1974, when he resigned rather than face an impeachment trial in connection with the Watergate scandal. He was born on January 9, 1913 in the town of Yorba Linda, about thirty miles inland from Los Angeles. His maternal great-great-grandfather, Richard Milhous, born at Timahoe, Queens County, had immigrated to North America in 1729. The Nixons were also of Irish origin. His wife, the former Thelma Catherine Ryan, was one of seven children born in Ely, Nevada on March 16, 1912. Her father nicknamed her Pat because she was born on the day before St. Patrick's Day. She was brought up on a small ranch south-west of Los Angeles. She attended the University of Southern California where she graduated with honors. The couple met in 1938 when both were trying out for a part in a play called *The Dark Tower*. Pat was teaching business at Whittier High School at the time. While in the White House, the Nixons owned an Irish setter named Timahoe after the town in Ireland where the Milhous family came from.

Ronald Wilson Reagan served as the 40th President, from 1981 to 1989. His ancestors hailed from Ballyporeen, County Tipperary where his great-grandfather, Michael O'Regan, was born in 1829.

With their political *savoir-faire*, their leadership talents and their strong command of the English language, the Irish began forming broad based political alliances with other immigrant groups following the Civil War. The Irish built political machines which helped elect them to political office, first at the city level, next at the state level and finally at the federal level. Tammany

Hall, the leading political machine in New York, was taken over by the Irish in the 1850s. One of Tammany's great bosses, Richard "Boss" Corker, was born in Clonakilty, County Cork. When he retired from politics in 1903, he returned to live in Ireland.

By 1886, the Irish had won a majority of the seats on the Boston City Council and in 1901, Irish-born Patrick Collins was elected mayor. He was followed as mayor by several other Irish-Americans, including "Honey" FitzGerald and James Curley. In 1880, Irish-born William R. Grace was elected mayor of New York, the first Catholic to hold the job. He became a reformer of New York's corrupt politics dominated by Tammany Hall and its Irish-American leader, "Honest John" Kelly.

Many State Governors were Irish. Sir Thomas Dongan, appointed governor of New York in 1682, was the first Catholic governor of an American colony. He established what are basically the current boundaries of New York State.

The discovery of gold at Sutter's Mill in 1847 started the trek westward of hordes of eager prospectors to California. Among those who headed west, lured by the possibility of making his fortune, was John G. Downey who left his native Roscommon in 1849 with only ten dollars in his pocket.

Four years before Downey's arrival in California, the Black Bear Revolt had occurred. Settlers in the Sacramento Valley had proclaimed California a republic independent of Mexico and had raised the black bear and star flag at Sonoma. A month later, United States forces took possession of Monterey and claimed possession of California for the United States.

Downey settled on the Santa Gertrude Ranch near Los Angeles in 1850 where he engaged in cattle raising, a talent he had picked up from his father, Dennis Downey, who was in the cattle raising business back in County Roscommon. Downey also dabbled in real estate and became active in California Democratic politics.

He was elected Lt. Governor of California in 1859, on a Democratic ticket with Governor Milton S. Latham. Governor Latham resigned two days after his inauguration to fill the vacancy caused by the death of Kilkenny-born Senator David C. Broderick. Downey succeeded Latham as Governor, serving out the remainder of his term until January 10, 1862. After his unsuccessful gubernatorial election attempt in 1862, Downey returned to his ranch in Los Angeles County near the present-day City of Downey.

It was during Downey's term in office that the Civil War started. There was a movement by some California leaders at the time to establish an independent Pacific Republic, should the Union be dissolved. However, this idea was quickly crushed. A mass meeting, attended by 14,000 people in San Francisco on February 22, 1861 in support of the Union, ended the movement for a separate Pacific Republic. Sympathy for the United States government gained momentum and on May 17, 1861 the California Legislature pledged the State's support to the Union cause.

It was during Downey's administration that the first Pony Express mail arrived in San Francisco; also, the Central Pacific Railroad Company of California and the first transcontinental telegraph line linked the east and west coasts of the United States. Downey died in 1894.

James E. Boyd emigrated from his native County Tyrone to Ohio in 1844 and later to Nebraska. He worked as a grocery store employee and as a carpenter before being elected to the Nebraska House of Representatives in 1866. He was elected Mayor of Omaha in 1881 and again in 1885. Boyd was elected Governor of Nebraska in 1892. Francis Parnell Murphy served as New Hampshire's governor from 1937 to 1941. He was the son of Irish immigrants Patrick and Ellen Murphy. Mike O'Callaghan was Nevada's governor from 1971 to 1978. Mike, the son of Ned O'Callaghan and Olive Barry, was a decorated war hero, receiving the Silver and Bronze Stars for gallantry in the Korean War.

An extraordinary number of Irish-Americans have served in the United States Senate over the years. Among them was David Broderick, born in Kilkenny in 1820. He immigrated to America with his parents. His father was a stonecutter by trade and he worked on renovating the capitol in Washington. David didn't care much for the stonecutting trade and he headed to California on the first news of the gold rush. There he read law, entered politics and was elected to the United States Senate. Broderick, an outspoken opponent of the extension of slavery, was killed in a duel with a pro-southern "fire-eater" during the 1859 election.

Mike Mansfield served in the Senate from 1952 to 1977 and was Senate Majority Leader for many years. Born of Irish Catholic parents in New York's Greenwich Village, Mike grew up in Great Falls, Montana. He left school at age fourteen and served in the United States navy during World War I. After the war, he enlisted in the army and later joined the Marines.

After he separated from the service in 1922, he went to work in the mines in Butte. Encouraged by his wife, Maureen, he attended the Montana School of Mines. He later attended the University of Montana in Missoula, where he earned his bachelor's and master's degrees. After he graduated, he taught Far Eastern and Latin American history at the Missoula campus.

Mike Mansfield began his political career in 1942 when he was elected to the United States House of Representatives. He was relected to four more terms in the House and in 1952, was elected to the United States Senate, where he served until he retired in 1977. He served as Senate Majority Leader from 1961 to 1974. After his retirement from the Senate in 1977, Mike Mansfield was appointed Ambassador to Japan by President Carter and was reappointed by President Reagan in 1981. Mike retired from official public service in 1983, after serving thirty-four years in congress and six years as an ambassador.

Millions of words and scores of books have been written about America's political dynasty, the Kennedy family. Three of four sons served in the United States Senate. Jack was Senator from Massachusetts when he ran for President in 1960. Ted was elected Senator from Massachusetts in 1961, following Jack's election to the presidency. Robert left the Johnson administration in 1964 and successfully ran for the Senate from New York State. He represented that State until his assassination in 1968.

Senator Daniel Patrick Moynihan's grandfather, Jack Moynihan, emigrated from County Kerry in the late nineteenth century and went to work for the Standard Oil Company in the oil and gas fields of Ohio, Pennsylvania and Michigan. Daniel Patrick was born in Tulsa, Oklahoma on March 16, 1927, but grew up in New York. He attended Tuft University, where he received his bachelor's and doctoral degrees. He gained distinction for his writings on urban problems and poverty. He entered the London School of Economics on a scholarship in 1950. Upon returning home in 1953, Pat threw his support behind Averell Harriman's race for governor of New York and accompanied Harriman to the State Capitol in Albany after the election.

Moynihan went to Washington with the Kennedy Administration in 1961 as Assistant Secretary for Labor. In 1966, he left Washington to teach at Harvard and was enticed back to Washington in 1969 as an adviser to President Nixon, responsible for running the Urban Affairs Council. In 1973, Moynihan was made ambassador to India and in 1976, ambassador to the United Nations. He has served in the Senate since 1977.

In the House of Representatives, the Speaker's chair has been occupied by Irish-Americans John McCormack and Thomas (Tip) O'Neill. Tip O'Neill, a Boston Irishman, served as Speaker of the House from 1977 to 1986, at which time he retired from politics. Tip began his career in Massachusetts in 1936 and became Speaker of the State Legislature in 1948. In 1952, he was elected to the United States House of Representatives and embarked on a course that paralleled his state political career.

Many of the Justices that served on the United States Supreme Court were of Irish extraction. Among them were Joseph McKenna of California (1898-1925), Frank Murphy of Michigan (1940-1949), James Francis Byrnes of South Carolina (1941-1942), William J. Brennan, Jr. of New Jersey (1956-1990) and Anthony Kennedy of California (1988-).

Canadian Political Leaders
The Irish have also made a significant contribution to Canada's political development. Thomas D'Arcy McGee fled Ireland to avoid sedition charges by the British government, and in a few short years he became a Father of Canadian Confederation. Irishman Edward Whelan also has the distinction of being called a Father of Canadian Confederation. Robert Baldwin, the grandson of a County Cork settler in Upper Canada, headed the first Liberal government of a United Canada in the

1840s. Another leader of the federal Liberal party was Edward Blake, whose family came from County Galway. Brian Mulroney, the grandson of Irish immigrants, became Canada's 18th Prime Minister.

Many Provincial Premiers were Irish. County Tyrone-born John Foster McCreight, whose father served as the last Speaker of the Irish House of Commons prior to the union of 1801, became British Columbia's first Premier in 1871. He was born in Caledon, County Tyrone in 1827. His family was part of the ascendancy, the group that dominated political and social life in Ireland. His mother, Elizabeth Foster, was the daughter of the Bishop of Clogher and niece of John Foster, the last Speaker of the Irish House of Commons prior to the union in 1801.

McCreight was an experienced lawyer, respected both socially and professionally. He worked harmoniously with Lt. Gov. Joseph Trutch to establish essential procedural matters such as the selection of the Speaker and representatives. He lost a vote of confidence in the legislature during the opening of the second term and he immediately resigned, along with his colleagues.

McCreight continued to be active in the legislature in a quiet way and he was one of the first to speak out for "Better Terms" in Ottawa's treatment of the province. In 1873, he became Q.C. and in 1880, he was appointed to the Supreme Court of British Columbia. Concurrently, McCreight had to serve as a County Court Justice in the Cariboo, a virtual purgatory for him.

In 1883, Judge McCreight took up residence in New Westminster, happy to be finished with duties in the interior. Surprising many of his colleagues and friends, McCreight became a Roman Catholic in 1883 and remained so the rest of his life. He retired from the bench in 1897 and died in England, where he had spent the last years of his life, on November 18, 1913.

John Hart was born on a farm near Mohill, County Leitrim on March 31, 1879. After attending Ross school in Mohill, he found little in Ireland except to continue in the footsteps of his father, running the family farm. John wasn't overly enthusiastic about a career in farming, so at the age of nineteen he set out for Victoria, British Columbia. He arrived in the provincial capital in 1898. He was greeted by his two sisters, who had earlier emigrated to British Columbia to look after an uncle, Michael Hart, who had built a prosperous cannery business on Vancouver Island.

John was not sure what he wanted to do when he arrived. Among other things, he thought of heading for the Yukon to try his luck in the gold mines. Finally, he decided to stay in Victoria and he applied for a job with the Bank of Montreal. The job paid fifty dollars a month, which seemed like a fortune to a young lad of nineteen off the farm in Ireland. However, there was one hitch; he would have to wait six months for a vacancy. He then took a job with the Robert Ward Company at a starting wage of ten dollars a month. He worked with Ward for five years, and after spending another six years with the Rithet Company, John started his own business -- Gillespie, Hart & Company -- a financial house.

John Hart married Harriet McKay in 1908. Harriet was the daughter of Donald McKay, who was part of the older Hudson's Bay Company establishment. The marriage made the Victoria establishment accessible to John, and although a Catholic and an Irishman, he was totally accepted into its inner circle.

With the outbreak of war in 1914, he joined the British Columbia Coast Regiment when it was called up for duty. He was in active service for two years, when he was released to run for office in the provincial election. Hart was an ardent supporter of Liberal Party leader Harlan Carey Brewster, who succeeded to the provincial premiership in 1916 upon the resignation of Premier Bowser. In 1917, Brewster rewarded Hart with the Ministry of Finance portfolio, which he held for seven years. He shared responsibility for the Ministry of Industries for two of these years as well.

In 1924, John Hart retired from politics and spent the next nine years managing the Vancouver office of Gillespie, Hart and Company. He reentered the political arena in 1933 and regained his Victoria seat in the provincial legislature. Premier Pattullo invited him to reassume his old Ministry of Finance portfolio. British Columbia's financial situation was in a mess and Hart had to immediately set about restoring a near bankrupt province. His first budget provided for a program of public works, creating a deficit of two million dollars. When the B.C. government failed to get much needed funding from Ottawa in 1935 to boost its economy, Hart went and borrowed seven million from New York bankers. On another occasion, when the Ottawa government balked at permitting an American company to build ships at a federal shipyard, he threatened to acquire the federal land on the grounds that the province had never given full title to the Dominion.

Hart advocated publicly in 1941 that the Liberals form a coalition with the Conservatives to prevent the Socialists from assuming office. He had also become disenchanted with Premier Pattullo's "Fight Canada" policy and parochialism. Pattullo dismissed him from the cabinet, but a few months later, at a Liberal Convention on December 2, 1941, John Hart defeated Pattullo for the leadership of the Liberal Party, and the lad from County Leitrim assumed the Premiership of British Columbia a week later. Two days earlier, the Japanese had bombed Pearl Harbor and there was great fear that west coast cities would be bombed.

During Hart's administration, orders were issued to all Japanese to leave coastal regions and relocate in the interior of the province. While this policy may have blemished John Hart's record somewhat, it was otherwise unblemished. Hart advocated construction of the Alaska highway, promoted a resettlement scheme, setting aside one million acres of land for farms for veterans, and pushed for government activity in developing hydro electrical power. Perhaps his greatest achievement was the execution of the Dominion-Provincial tax sharing agreement.

He served as Premier for six years. He resigned the Premiership in 1947, but continued to retain his legislative seat. Prime Minister Mackenzie King offered him the Ambassadorship to Ireland, but his wife's ill health precluded him from accepting any diplomatic post. He was elected Speaker of the Assembly in 1948. He was extremely proud of this honor because it showed that he had the respect of his fellow members. He was invited, in 1951, at the age of seventy-one, to assume the post of Lieutenant-Governor. He declined out of concern for his wife's ill health. John Hart died in 1957, after a distinguished career in British

311

Columbia political life, where he had the enviable record of having never lost an election race.

In the following profiles, we look at the lives and times of three prominent North American leaders of Irish ancestry, Thomas D'Arcy McGee, Ronald Reagan and Brian Mulroney.

Thomas D'Arcy McGee
A Father of Canadian Federation

It was past midnight when Parliament adjourned and the members headed home. As D'Arcy McGee walked the short distance along Sparks Street to Mrs. Trotter's boardinghouse, where he lodged while attending Parliament sessions, he was felled by an assassin's bullet.

McGee, a gifted speaker and orator, had given his most memorable speech just hours before on the floor of the Canadian House of Commons, on April 6, 1868. He had spoken eloquently on the independence and relationship of the Canadian provinces under the Union of Confederation:

"....Its single aim from the beginning has been to consolidate the extent of British North America with the utmost regard to the independent power and privileges of each province and I, Sir, who have been and am still its warm and earnest advocate speak here not as a representative of any race, or of any province, but thoroughly and emphatically a Canadian, ready and bound to recognize the claims of my Canadian fellow subjects from the farthest east to the farthest west, equally as those of my nearest neighbor or the friend who proposed me on the hustings."

McGee, a man of great vision and determination, did not live to accomplish all of his dreams for Canada; but in his short life he won the distinction of becoming a great Canadian statesman. While he readily admitted that he owed his undivided allegiance to the Canada he helped bring together, he said that he could not deny a divided affection between Ireland and the country he adopted.

An Irishman by Birth

Thomas D'Arcy McGee was born at Carlingford, County Louth, on April 13, 1825, to James McGee and Dorcas Catherine Morgan. In 1842, D'Arcy immigrated to America where he landed a job in Boston with the *Boston Pilot*. Within two years he was the paper's editor. His speeches, lectures and writing attracted the attention of Daniel O'Connell back home, and he was invited to join

313

the editorial staff of the *Dublin Freeman's Journal*. Soon he was influenced by men like Thomas Davis, John Blake Dillon and Charles Gavan Duffy, who had founded the *Nation* newspaper in Dublin to revive nationalism among the Irish. In sympathy now with the Young Ireland Movement, D'Arcy accepted an invitation to join the *Nation*. He had returned to Ireland with lofty ambitions to serve Ireland as a poet and scholar, but the passion of nationalism began burning within him. Circumstances made him, in turn, a propagandist, a conspirator and then he was heading towards becoming an armed rebel.

The year was 1847 and the leaders of the Young Irelanders were making plans for a rebellion against England, but it faltered. The authorities rounded up some of the leaders; others went into hiding. They had failed because they were unable to muster a fighting force; the clergy had turned the people away from supporting it. McGee, one of the leaders, was in Sligo selling the idea of rebellion when he heard the news. The authorities were hot on his heels. He headed for Londonderry where his good friend, Bishop Maginn, supplied him with a clerical black suit and a Roman collar. In disguise, McGee boarded a ship, the *Shamrock*, heading for America.

A Canadian by Choice

In New York, he started the *New York Nation*, a paper that was very successful, until he got on the wrong side of Bishop Hughes for criticizing the Irish Catholic clergy's position on the role of the Young Irelanders. McGee then left New York for Boston and founded the *American Celt*. He continued his revolutionary fervor until 1852, when he suddenly changed his political philosophy, turned against everything revolutionary and passed "from a Republican to a Monarchist, from an ardent liberal to a quietest conservative, from holding that politics are independent of the Church, to subjecting to it the whole conduct of life, public and private." This turnaround position did not sit well with his old friends of revolutionary days.

McGee had made several previous trips into Canada and had liked what he saw there. He had traveled through parts of Upper Canada, had visited Peterborough, a community of two thousand very poor Irish settlers who had emigrated in the early 1820s through the help of Canadian Peter Robinson. Robinson had sought and obtained assistance from the Imperial government for the emigrants in the form of passage, livestock and supplies, with the government of Upper Canada supplying the land. Despite the hardships and the primitive life endured by these settlers, they seemed happy and content on their farms in the backwoods.

McGee believed he saw in Canada a land where the Irish emigrant might find a decent life. He contrasted what he saw in Canada with what he had seen in the cities in the United States. There, according to McGee, the immigrants were trapped in the slums of the cities where they got off the boat. McGee never got over the shock of the horrible tenements he saw when he lived in New York and Boston. He believed that the Irish were more adaptable to a rural lifestyle than to the cities, and through his newspaper, *The American Celt*, he strongly promoted the advantages Canada had to offer to the immigrating Irish. He became disenchanted with life in the United States and moved to Canada in the spring of 1858, settling in Montreal, which had a large Irish population.

In Montreal, McGee started the *New Era* newspaper. He entered politics and was elected to Parliament for a Montreal seat in the 1858 general election. McGee soon threw his support in favor of confederation for Canada. He envisioned and championed the cause of an independent and united Canada from sea to sea. With his fiery oratory and his prolific writings, he popularized the idea throughout Upper and Lower Canada and in the Maritime Provinces. His dream for a united Canada moved towards reality in 1867 when the British North America Act was passed by the British Parliament, giving Canada Dominion status.

For Thomas D'Arcy McGee, poet, visionary, orator, writer, politician and Canadian statesman, it was ironic that he had escaped death in Ireland for his part in the attempted Rebellion of 1847, in which he played a prominent role and for which he could have been executed, to meet a violent death in peaceful Canada, where he was on the side of the established government.

Thomas D'Arcy McGee did not die in vain. He is honored in Canada as one of the Fathers of Confederation and he is a hero in his native Ireland. The name, Thomas D'Arcy McGee, has the historic ring associated with the great heroes of Ireland, such as Owen Roe O'Neill, Red Hugh O'Donnell, Wolfe Tone, Robert Emmet and Michael Collins.

In Ireland, Thomas D'Arcy McGee is remembered as a poet and nationalist. His memory also lives on in Canada, where his monument adorns the Parliament Building in Ottawa. Descendants of D'Arcy McGee's half-brother, John, can be found in Ontario and British Columbia. Thomas D'Arcy McGee, a great-grandnephew of D'Arcy's, is a judge in Vancouver. The judge's father, also named Thomas D'Arcy McGee, lives in Victoria. Another descendent, Frank McGee, lives in Toronto. For several years, he was a member of the Canadian Parliament and is now a citizenship judge. His father, also Frank, was one of Canada's most outstanding hockey players when he played for the Ottawa Senators in 1903-1906. He served in the Canadian army during World War I and was killed in action in the Somme offensive in 1916. He is in the Hockey Hall of Fame.

"Am I remembered in Erin; I charge you to tell me true. Has my name a sound or memory in the scenes my childhood knew?" Thomas D'Arcy McGee asked this wistfully in a poem he wrote shortly before his assassination in Canada. (Photo courtesy Public Archives)

Ronald Wilson Reagan
Actor, Union Leader, Governor and President

Ronald Wilson Reagan, the 40th President of the United States, loves to tell Irish stories. On his first visit to Ireland while he was still governor of California, he tells of visiting a graveyard and coming across an inscription on a tombstone which fascinated him. The inscription read:

> Remember me as you pass by,
> For as you are so once was I,
> But as I am so will you be,
> So be content to follow me.

To which, according to Reagan, another Irishman had added,

> To follow you I am not content,
> I wish I knew which way you went.

Ronald Reagan's great-grandfather, Michael Reagan, was born in Ballyporeen, County Tipperary in 1829. At age twenty-one, he crossed over to London, England where he married an Irish girl, Catherine Mulcahy, in 1852 at St. George's Catholic Church. Michael listed his occupation as laborer. Two years after they were married, the President's grandfather, John, was born. In 1858, the Reagans left London and headed for America, by way of Canada. They settled in Whiteside County in Illinois and hired out as farm laborers. In time, John met and married a Canadian of Irish descent. The youngest son of their marriage, John Edward "Jack," was the President's father.

Ronald Reagan was born in a small three-bedroom apartment over a general store in Tampico, Illinois on February 6, 1911. The family moved to Dixon, Illinois (about 100 miles from Chicago) in 1920.

Ronald Reagan attended Eureka College, graduating from there in 1932 with a degree in economics. During his college years, he was active in the school's dramatic society where, ac-

318

cording to himself, the acting bug really hit him. When he graduated in 1932, Reagan wanted more than anything else to be a radio sports announcer. Jobs were scarce everywhere; the depression was taking its toll and his first job at Montgomery Ward's only lasted a few days. After an unsuccessful job-hunting trip to Chicago, he found work as a sports announcer with WOC Radio Station in Davenport. From there he went to WHO Radio Station in Des Moines, Iowa, where he spent the next four years as a sports announcer. At WHO, he broadcast the Chicago White Sox baseball games and in the springtime, he would travel to Southern California to observe the team's practice.

In 1937, while attending the Cub's spring practice in Los Angeles, Reagan took a screen test, which resulted in Warner's Film Studio giving him a seven year contract at $200 a week. During his early years at Warner's, Reagan was cast mostly in "B" movies. His big break came in 1940 when he was cast for the part of George Gipp -- the immortal Gipper -- in the classic movie, *Knute Rockne, All American.* The movie was about the legendary coach, Knute Rockne, of Notre Dame. The same year he played the Gipper, Reagan married Jane Wyman. He had no sooner finished making this movie, when he was cast as Custer in *Santa Fe Trail* with Errol Flynn. Reagan appeared in fifty-three movies throughout his movie career. He became active in the actors' union -- the Screen Actors' Guild -- and served six terms as its president, after he was first elected in 1947. He married Nancy Davis in 1952.

Ronald Reagan switched his political affiliation to the Republican Party in 1962. Four years later, he won the first of two terms as Governor of California on the Republican ticket, winning by almost one million votes over his opponent, Pat Brown. During his governorship, Reagan had to deal with mass protests on university campuses over the war in Vietnam. He ordered the National Guard in to quell the disturbances on the Berkeley campus.

On November 4, 1980, Ronald Reagan was elected President of the United States. A week after his inauguration, there was a welcoming home greeting on the White House lawn for the fifty-two hostages who had been freed by Iran. On March 30, 1981, tragedy struck the President when he was shot by a lone gunman outside the Washington Hilton Hotel where he had just given a speech at a convention of the Construction Trades Council. A bullet had lodged in his lung and his life was in danger. He quickly recovered and was back in the White House within two weeks. In 1984, he was re-elected President by a landslide electoral and popular vote -- 525 electoral votes, the highest ever won by a candidate.

President Reagan was the third president to visit the birthplace of his ancestors while he was in the White House (President Kennedy and President Nixon had previously visited there). He helicoptered from Dublin to Ballyporeen, where he was given a *céad mile fáilte* of a welcome. In Ballyporeen, he visited the church and examined the handwritten entry recording the baptism of his great-grandfather in 1825. He walked through the town, meeting the locals and shaking their hands. He dropped in at a pub that had been named after him and had a pint with the lads, including many of his distant relatives. While he was visiting the town, President Reagan was introduced to a young man in his middle twenties who bore a remarkable resemblance to the President -- his eyes, hair and whole facial structure.

The visit to Ballyporeen was a warming and emotional experience for Reagan. In his autobiography, *Ronald Reagan, An American Life,* he tells of walking down the narrow main street of the little town, retracing his great-grandfather's footsteps as he set out in pursuit of a dream. Thinking also of his grandfather, whom he had never met, and of his father, Jack, and the Irish stories he used to tell, and the drive he'd always had to get ahead, he thought to himself, "What an incredible country we live in, where the great-grandson of a poor emigrant from Ballyporeen could become president."

President Ronald Reagan addressing a crowd during a visit to the village of Ballyporeen, Couny Tipperary. His great-grandfather had emigrated from Ballyporeen during the Great Famine. Below, the president samples a pint of Guinness with the lads at a local pub.
(Photos courtesy of President Reagan Library)

Martin Brian Mulroney
Prime Minister of Canada 1984-1993

Martin Brian Mulroney, a fourth generation Canadian of Irish descent, reached the highest elected office in Canada in 1984, when he became the country's prime minister. During his term as prime minister, Brian Mulroney fought unceasingly to keep Canada together. A big sprawling land, Canada has two founding peoples -- the French and the English -- and as the country developed, the cultural differences became the source of friction, with some factions in Quebec talking about making that province a sovereign nation. Mulroney, who was born in Quebec, and who was fluently bilingual in French and English, first proposed the Meech Lake Accord, and later the Charlottetown Accord, designed to constitutionally keep Quebec within Canada while respecting Quebec's status as a distinct society.

Brian Mulroney was first elected to federal office in 1983, winning a byelection in Central Nova, in Nova Scotia. Just prior to the by-election, Mulroney had been elected leader of the Progressive Conservative Party. At that time, the Conservative Party had several divisive factions and was in disarray. Also, it had been out of office for many years. Mulroney molded it into a united party. He turned the party into a winner and in the process, made Canada a leader in world affairs.

In his first election as party leader, Brian Mulroney won a majority government and went on to lead Canada for over eight years, until voluntarily retiring as Prime Minister on February 24, 1993. Mulroney played a major part in cementing and broadening friendly relations between the United States and Canada. His Shamrock Summit with then United States president, Ronald Reagan -- himself an Irish American -- where they both joined in a chorus of "When Irish Eyes Are Smiling" at the 1985 summit meeting in Quebec, gave Americans a better understanding of the common heritage of Canada and the United States.

Under Mulroney, Canada was able to sign a Free Trade Agreement with the United States, allowing the free flow of goods and services back and forth between the two countries. This

Prime Minister Mulroney, President Reagan, their wives and friends join in a rendition of "When Irish Eyes Are Smiling" during their Shamrock Summit in Quebec City in 1985.

agreement helped Canadian companies gain access to the huge American market. He also initiated the talks leading up to the North American Free Trade Agreement (NAFTA), which aims to incorporate Mexico into a trading partnership with Canada and the United States.

Always a good friend of the United States, Mulroney was one of the first to back President George Bush's "Desert Storm" operation against Saddam Hussein in Iraq. He was a frequent fishing buddy of President Bush at his summer place in Kennebunkport in Maine.

Growing up in Canada

The Mulroney family history in Canada is in the classic "Log Cabin To White House" tradition, except in this case it is from a tent on the North Shore of the St. Lawrence River in Quebec to 24 Sussex Drive in Ottawa - the traditional home of Canada's Prime Ministers.

Brian Mulroney was born in Baie-Comeau, Quebec in March of 1939 to Ben and Mary Mulroney. He was one of six children. His mother was the former Mary Irene O'Shea, whose family had come over from County Kilkenny to settle in Canada.

The marvel in the Mulroney story is that he came from a place so small and so remote that hardly anyone in Canada, or anywhere else, had heard of it, until he became Prime Minister of Canada -- a true rags to riches story. Usually it takes old family ties and good connections to become the top man; Brian Mulroney started at the bottom of the totem pole.

Instead of heading to Boston and New York, like the Kennedys, the Reagans and the O'Neills, Brian Mulroney's paternal ancestors stayed on the boat to Quebec, via the St. Lawrence River. His great-grandfather, Pierce Mulroney, who had emigrated from Leighlinbridge, County Carlow at the age of fourteen in the 1830s, settled at Ste. Catherine de Portneuf. Pierce Mulroney's grandfather, also named Pierce, was an innkeeper down the road a bit at the Royal Oak Inn

Mulroney's father, who was an electrician by trade, came to the Baie-Comeau area of Quebec in 1936 when he got word that a new paper mill was to be built there, promising jobs. Brian Mulroney tells the story of how his dad, Ben, told his wife, Mary, "I'll go down there for six months, make piles of money and send for you." He didn't make a pile of money, Brian Mulroney said, "but he made six children and had to stay."

The paper mill was built to feed the presses of the *Chicago Tribune*, then owned by Irish-American Robert McCormick. When Ben Mulroney got to the mill site, there was no accommodation and there were no roads into Baie-Comeau. He slept in a tent while helping build the mill and the town, and stayed on working at the mill as an electrician. He did not live to see his son's greatest triumph -- becoming Prime Minister of Canada.

When he was just fourteen years of age, Brian left home to attend boarding school. After graduating, he went on to St. Francis Xavier University in Antigonish, Nova Scotia and got his B.A. (Honors) in Political Science. In 1963, he received a law degree from Laval University in Quebec City, and in 1972, he was made a partner in the law firm Howard, Cate, Ogilvi in Montreal.

In 1973, Brian Mulroney married the former Mila Pivnicki; the couple has four children -- Caroline, Ben, Mark and Nicolas.

Brian Mulroney was made president of the Iron Ore Co. of Canada in 1977, a huge iron mining and shipping conglomerate with operations in Newfoundland and northern Quebec. The mines supplied iron ore concentrates and pellets to the steel mills in the United States.

Going Home

Brian Mulroney's trip to Ireland with his wife Mila and his children in 1991 was, as he himself described it, "a very special and personal experience for me and my family. To return to Ireland, the land of my roots is a genuinely moving experience. To be privileged to do so at this time, while serving as the Prime Minister of Canada, is a particular cause of joy."

Mulroney visited Leighlinbridge in County Carlow, home of his ancestors, where he had an emotionally filled time among his own. Before leaving Leighlinbridge, the Prime Minister said to the people of his home town, "Please accept my heartfelt thanks, and that of my family, for your kindness and generosity. We shall long remember the warmth of your welcome and will keep this day in our hearts forever: God Bless."

Talking to a gathering in Dublin Castle, Mulroney said "In the seven years I have been Prime Minister of Canada, I have been privileged to visit many countries and participate in many official functions around the world. But no visit and no official function has been more meaningful for me than this one, here in St. Patrick's Hall in Dublin Castle. For more than eight centuries, Dublin Castle was a symbol of the subjugation of the Irish people, and then in 1922 it became a symbol of their liberation. Today, in my mind's eye I can still see my mother, whose family came from Kilkenny, ironing the children's clothes and humming "The

Mountains of Mourne," and "Macushla" -- ballads of a land she had never seen, yet loved so deeply. In her simple Irish way she showed the pride of her Irish heritage and passed on to us the Irish culture, literature and music, on a continent so far away from Ireland's shores."

On February 24, 1993, Brian Mulroney decided to quit politics to devote more time to his young family and to pursue private business interests.

In Religion

The Irish have dominated the upper echelons of the Catholic Church in the United States since the second half of the nineteenth century. Beginning in the 1860s, the church's leadership became predominantly Irish. Of the sixty-nine Episcopal offices that existed in the United States in 1886, thirty-five were held by Irish. Of the remainder, fifteen were held by Germans, eleven were held by French and eight by English.

In New York and other northeastern cities, where the Catholic population was experiencing a rapid growth from the influx of immigrants, the church embraced an extremely conservative and inward course under an Irish hierarchy, To the Church, the Catholic community's relationship to the larger American society was not considered a matter of immediate concern. The conservative Irish hierarchy concerned itself primarily with organizing new parishes and building churches and schools. Many Irish Catholics in the Northeast, primarily in New York, had begun to identify with the upper-middle-class strata of society and were quite comfortable with conservative clerics such as Archbishop John Joseph Hughes and his successors, Archbishops John McCloskey and Michael Corrigan. Hughes, born in County Tyrone in 1797, became the first archbishop of New York in 1842. John McCloskey, whose parents emigrated from County Derry, became the first American cardinal in 1875.

In the years following the Civil War, as Irish Catholic immigrants moved into the mainstream of American life, entering politics, labor unions and social-reform movements, the Northeastern conservative leadership of the Church faced new challenges. A progressive element within the Church, led by James Cardinal Gibbins of Baltimore and Archbishop John Ireland of St. Paul, took on the role of redefining the emerging Church's social policies and definitions in a pluralistic American society. They encountered strong opposition to any liberalization of the Church's position from Archbishop Corrigan of New York and Bishop Bernard McQuaid of Rochester, the bulwarks of the conservative viewpoint. Corrigan and McQuaid were not altogether comfortable with the political freedom evolving from the American system of government. It was alien to what the Church had, for centuries, dealt with in Europe. They wanted to keep Catholics within the confines of the Catholic community and away from contact with the non-Catholics in secular organizations. Gibbin and Ireland, on the other hand, argued that withdrawal of American Catholicism from participating in American society would be counterproductive, and a dereliction of the Church's responsibility to fulfill its role in the larger community.

Corrigan and McQuaid warned that Catholics mixing with non-Catholics in fraternal societies or labor unions were in danger of sin. They saw moral danger in the emerging Knights of Labor and its Catholic leader, Vincent Powderly. They even went so far as to ask the Third Plenary Council in Baltimore in 1884 to make a request to Rome for a decree condemning the union as a secret society. Cardinal Gibbins, presiding at the Council, pleaded against the motion, saying he believed that Church condemnation of the Knights would run the risk of alienating the half million Catholics who were members. Gibbins managed to have the issue assigned to a committee on secret societies, which bought the progressives time to plead their case with Rome.

The progressives finally prevailed when Pope Leo XIII decided in Gibbins's favor. The Pope's decision was a setback to Corrigan and the conservative clerics, but it barely dampened their efforts to build a powerful conservative constituency within the Catholic Church, which has maintained its voice down through the years, primarily in the Archdiocese of New York. Cardinal Gibbins and Archbishop Ireland, leading the progressive clerics, struggled on tirelessly against the "uncompromising dogmatism" of Archbishop Corrigan and the conservative clerics. Along the way progressives suffered some setbacks, but over time they triumphed on many major issues and succeeded in giving a progressive character to Catholicism in America.

Born in Baltimore in 1834, James Cardinal Gibbons was taken to Ireland when he was three. He returned to live in the United States when he was nineteen. His meteoric rise in the church began when, at thirty-four, he was made bishop of North Carolina. Later, he served as bishop of Richmond, Virginia and in

1877, he was elevated to the Archbishopric of Baltimore, a large and thriving community of Germans and Irish Catholics. Gibbins is regarded as the greatest leader the Catholic Church has produced in America.

John Ireland was born in County Kilkenny in 1838. He immigrated with his family to the United States during the great famine, later settling in St. Paul, Minnesota in 1852. He studied for the priesthood in France and fourteen years after he was ordained, he was made bishop of St. Paul. Ireland was a great orator. He believed that the Church needed an atmosphere of political freedom to safeguard its own liberty.

Irish clerics also played a prominent role in the emerging Catholic Church of English Canada, In 1791, Upper Canada was carved out of the Quebec territory to satisfy the demands of English colonists who settled there following the American War of Independence. For several years there were no priests to serve the English speaking Catholics of Upper Canada, until an Irish cleric, Father Edmund Burke, arrived on the scene.

Father Burke was born in Maryborough, Queens County, in 1753. As the penal laws were in effect, Father Burke was sent, at a very young age, to a seminary in Paris for his education. Upon his return to Ireland, he asked his friend, Archbishop Carpenter of Dublin, to send him out to Canada where there was a great need for priests.

For eight years, Father Burke was the only priest to serve a five hundred mile area, roughly between what is now Detroit, Michigan and Kingston, Ontario along the St. Lawrence River. It took tremendous endurance to survive the hazards of traveling through dense forest and the long journeys by land and water. He made repeated requests to Quebec's Bishop Hubert to send additional English speaking priests to the neglected Catholic soldiers (most of whom were Irish), who guarded the numerous posts in Upper Canada. His appeals ran into opposition from the Colony's English establishment, who wanted to establish the Anglican Church as the official church. The French Catholic hierarchy of Lower Canada did not want to disrupt its relationship with the English. Eventually, through repeated letters to

Rome, to powerful friends in Europe, and in particular to Archbishop Troy of Dublin, this situation was remedied,

At the request of Lt. Governor Simcoe of Upper Canada, Father Burke was assigned to Fort Miami, forty miles west of Detroit, to serve a group of one hundred French Canadian Catholics and a large group of Huron Indians. In February of 1795, he reached Fort Miami and his first act was to stop the sale of rum to the Indians. This created so much bad feeling that he had to have an armed guard with him at all times, even in his sleeping quarters. His second act was to request the Bishop of Quebec to send two missionaries to service the isolated forts, but there was no help for several years.

Father Burke was called back to Quebec, where he was made professor of philosophy and mathematics in the seminary. He longed to get back to the missions and in 1791, he was assigned as a parish priest to Sts. Peter and Lawrence on the Island of Orleans, where he remained for three years.

In September of 1798, Father Burke found that four companies of Catholic soldiers, under Colonel John Macdonald, were ordered to attend Anglican services. This order was seemingly to keep the soldiers sober and out of public houses. Father Burke insisted the practice be stopped at once. Around this same time, Comte de Puisaye, a refugee from the French Revolution, had settled some forty immigrants on Yonge Street in York (Toronto). The Comte had also been unsuccessful in getting a priest to join them, and Father Burke spent what time he could administering to this group

Father Burke's next assignment was Halifax, Nova Scotia. Despite repeated attempts by New England Puritans to destroy the settlement of Catholics in Nova Scotia, the community remained steadfast. It was the oldest settlement of Catholics in Canada, older than Quebec by at least ten years. It had survived oppression and hardship at the hands of New England fanatics and United Empire Loyalists who had brought to Nova Scotia an intense hatred of the Catholic Church. At the time, Nova Scotia had the only penal code in America where Catholics could not become teachers, could not hold land and could not be elected members of Parliament.

Father Burke infused new life into the church in Halifax. He persevered and built a Catholic school, against strenuous opposition. He was effective in convincing Rome to create English dioceses separate from Quebec, and he became Titular Bishop of Zion and Vicar-Apostolic of Nova Scotia. He built St. Mary's Cathedral in 1820. Bishop Burke died on November 20th, 1820.

Among the clerics of the Protestant persuasion who rose to prominence in North America was Francis Makemie, who founded American Presbyterianism. Francis Makemie was born in Rathmelton, County Donegal in 1685. He followed a business career in Ireland before immigrating to the American colonies, where he was ordained into the Presbyterian ministry. In 1706, Makemie founded the Presbytery of Philadelphia, the first in America, which united the scattered churches in Maryland, Pennsylvania, Virginia and New York.

The Sporting Irish

The early Irish immigrants to North America were so busy trying to find a place to live, or trying to find work, that they had little time for the sporting life. As they gradually got a foothold in the New World and became more secure, they naturally turned to sports.

In the beginning, the Irish took to boxing. In the fisticuffs profession, some of the more notable were Peter Maher, Mike McCoole, Bob Fitzsimmons, John L. Sullivan, Jim Corbett, Jack Dempsey and Gene Tunney. Peter Maher was from Galway and his greatest fight was against Bob Fitzsimmons on March 2, 1892. Mike McCoole, born in Thurles, Tipperary in 1837, was heavyweight champion for a short time.

One of the most popular of the Irish boxers was John L. Sullivan, the "Boston Strong Boy." Sullivan became world champ on February 7, 1882 against fellow Irishman Paddy Ryan. It was during Sullivan's boxing career that the Marquess of Queensberry rules in fighting became popular. Out of the ring, Sullivan, supposedly a good natured person, was now and then predisposed to a little braggadocio. One of his famous lines was, "My name is John L. Sullivan and I can beat any sonofabitch alive."

Sullivan was born in Roxbury, Massachusetts in 1858. His father came from Tralee and his mother was from Athlone. His most memorable fight was against Jake Kilraine. The fight lasted seventy-five rounds before Kilraine's corner threw in the towel, by which time Sullivan had broken every rib in Kilrane's body, had broken his nose, split both lips and had given him a black eye. Overcoming his weakness for booze, Sullivan embarked on a temperance crusade.

Sullivan lost his title on September 7, 1892, in twenty-one rounds, to Gentleman Jim Corbett. Jim Corbett was born in San Francisco on September 21, 1886 of Irish parents. He was one of twelve children. After defeating Sullivan in 1892, he retained the world championship for five years.

Jack Dempsey, "the Manassa Mauler," learned his boxing in bars, in mining camps and in the hobo jungles of America. He first won the world championship in 1919 by defeating Jess Willard -- a six foot-five inch giant. During this historic fight, Dempsey knocked Willard down seven times in the first round, broke his jaw bone and knocked out six of his teeth. Willard, who had killed a man in the ring in a previous fight, had enough and his corner ended the fight before the fourth round. Dempsey remained world heavyweight champion until 1926, when he lost the title to fellow Irishman Gene Tunney. Dempsey's ancestors came from County Kildare.

The Irish in North America have taken to ice hockey in the same enthusiastic way that young people in Ireland take to hurling. Ice hockey and hurling have a lot in common -- including mayhem -- one with a hockey stick and the other with a hurley stick! It is at hockey that the Irish have excelled, from J. Ambrose O'Brien, who founded the Montreal Canadiens on December 4, 1909, through the Conachers, the King Clancys and the glorious Bobby Orr, to the present day greats such as Brendan Shanahan and Owen Nolan.

The Montreal Canadiens (then called the Montreal Maroons), the premier team for years in hockey, was founded on December 4, 1909 by Irish-Canadian sportsman J. Ambrose O'Brien, then a resident of Ottawa. Over the years, Montreal has had many players of Irish extraction on its roster, with the illustrious Lionel Conacher, known as the "Big Train," as one of the more notable. Lionel Conacher was named Canada's greatest all round athlete of the first half of the twentieth century. Not only was he a great hockey player, he also made a name for himself in professional football. Lional Conacher is now an honored member of the Hockey Hall of Fame.

The Conachers were one of hockey's first families, with Lionel "Big Train" Conacher being the most famous. Lionel was the eldest of ten children. Their grandmother, Elizabeth Black, came from County Wicklow and the family settled in the Toronto area before 1900. Lionel played hockey for the Pittsburgh Hornets, New York Americans, Montreal Maroons and Chicago Blackhawks. He played in the National Hockey League (NHL) from 1925 through the 1937 season. Lionel Conacher went on to become a Member of the Canadian Parliament. Charlie Conacher, brother of Lionel, played for the Toronto Maple Leafs and was an all-star right winger from 1933 through the 1936 season. Charlie Conacher led the league in scoring five times. He is also in the Hockey Hall of Fame.

Another famous name in ice hockey was King Clancy, who was just 5' 7" tall. He was one of the NHL's premier defensemen in the league's early days. Clancy played for the original Ottawa Senators in 1922 and was on the Stanley Cup winning team of 1927. He was transferred to Toronto in 1931, and was on three Stanley Cup winning teams with the Maple Leafs.

King Clancy's family left County Sligo during the Great Famine for Boston and moved from there to Bruce County, Ontario where King Clancy was born in 1903. After his playing days were over, he became a referee. He ended his career as coach and then as special advisor to Maple Leafs' owner Harold Ballard.

A modern day Irish notable in ice hockey is Brian Patrick (Pat) Quinn, president and general manager of the Vancouver Canucks. Quinn's path to the NHL was filled with sweat, fisticuffs and a pugnacious determination to give the best at all times. In his youth, Pat entered a seminary to study for the priesthood, but his vocation gave way to junior hockey. Pat played nine years in the NHL as a defenseman with such teams as the Toronto Maple Leafs, the Atlanta Flames and the Vancouver Canucks. He began his coaching career with the Philadelphia Flyers. During his first year he was named coach of the year after the team went into the championship with a thirty-five game unbeaten streak.

One of the greatest ice hockey players of all time was Robert Gordon (Bobby) Orr, whose style of play, combined with his speed and his great anticipation, changed the game of ice hockey forever. Bobby Orr was a defenseman and defensemen are expected to stay within their own end to prevent the forwards on the other team from scoring. Bobby Orr was the first really successful rushing defenseman and his great speed allowed him to get back into his own end of the ice if the other team broke out.

Bobbie Orr was born in 1943 in Parry Sound, a small town in Ontario's lake country. Bobby Orr's ancestral home was in Ballymena, County Antrim where his grandfather was born. Bobby was only fourteen when he left Parry Sound to play junior

334

hockey for the Oshawa Generals. A gifted athlete, his progress in junior hockey was followed with great interest by the NHL.

Orr began his NHL career with the Boston Bruins in 1966 and in 1969, he scored the winning goal to give Boston its first Stanley Cup championship since 1941. He won many awards during his career including the Rookie of the Year Calder Trophy, the Art Ross Trophy previously awarded only to forward players, and the Conn Smythe Trophy for the most valuable player in the Stanley Cup playoffs. After twelve years with the Bruins, Orr hung up his jersey at the end of the 1978-1979 season. He remains the idol of millions of hockey fans in Canada and the United States, where Orr memorabilia has a wide spread market.

Boston, a city with a large, well established Irish community, has always been a hotbed of hockey enthusiasts. Its rink, known in hockey circles as the Zoo, is one of the most feared places to play for any visiting team. In recent years, with the coming of Bobbie Orr, Boston has gained back some of its yesteryear luster, finishing at or near the top of its division just about every season.

When coached by Don Cherry (Grapes to his friends and enemies alike!), accompanied with his redoubtable mutt (Blue), and with foam and invective streaming from both mouths, Boston "Gawdens" was no place for the faint hearted. With players like Terry O'Reilly digging in the corners, and bruisers like Cam Neely flattening opponents and putting the puck in the net, and Gerry Cheevers keeping the other side off the score sheet, Boston was a jumping place.

Today, hockey's roster is teeming with Irish names. Pat Quinn runs the whole shebang at the Vancouver Canucks operation. The Patrick family, long associated with the New York Rangers, were in on the founding of the National Hockey League. Frank McGee, a descendent of Thomas D'Arcy McGee, is among numerous Irish-Canadians who have made it to the Hockey Hall of Fame. Two Belfast born players, Owen Nolan of the Quebec Nordiques and Brendan Shanahan of the St. Louis Blues, were top picks in the draft. Shanahan is one of the best all-around players in the NHL and Owen Nolan is expected to keep the Nordiques' team in the top ranks of the league for years to come.

This book barely touches on what the Irish have achieved in sports. The two stories which follow bring a warmth to the heart and a smile to the lips at the audacity of Ned Hanlan, who mastered a skill by necessity and made it pay, and the inimitable Danny Gallivan, the voice of the Montreal Canadiens for many years, who set the standard of hockey broadcasting for all those who came later.

National Hockey League Hall of Famer King Clancy (left) and his cousin Bill Clancey. The spelling of the family name got mixed up over the years.

Irish-Canadian Bobby Orr, perhaps the greatest hockey player who ever laced on skates, in one of his most memorable moments. In what is one of hockey's greatest action photos, Bobby is shown after scoring the overtime goal which put the Boston Bruins into the Stanley Cup Final.

Brendan Shanahan, a native of Belfast, County Antrim, is one of the stars of the St. Louis Blues and one of the best all-round players in the National Hockey League. Brendan and his family live in Mimico, Toronto. Brendan started his hockey career by skating on the frozen ponds in Ontario and going through St. Michael's (St. Mike's) College in Toronto -- famous for producing many hockey stars over the years. Brendan maintains a summer residence in Ireland.

Don Cherry's (Grapes to his enemies and friends alike!) sartorial splendor is matched only by his flamboyance and his desire to see every North American (especially Irish) kid get a crack at the National Hockey League. Don's family came from County Cork.

Ned Hanlan
Canada's First World Champion

When he was just five years old, Ned Hanlan had rowed across Toronto Harbor and when he was sixteen, he entered his first rowing competition. Before he retired in 1880, he was champion of Ontario, the Maritime Provinces, the United States, Great Britain and the world.

Ned Hanlan's parents, John and Ann Hanlan, emigrated from County Cork and they were so poor they squatted on Mudd's Landing on Toronto's Centre Island. With schooling interrupted just about every day, Ned had to leave school early so he could earn some money by rowing people back and forth from the Island to Toronto, taking trippers to the modest hotel that his parents had managed to acquire. Growing up on the water and rowing every day helped develop the skills and endurance which were to stand Ned in good stead the rest of his life.

Ned won his first rowing race when he defeated the well known Tom Louden on Hamilton Bay. The public was astounded that a young unknown could defeat one of the premier oarsmen in Canada. He defeated Louden again, on August 15, 1874, in a race for the Lord Dufferin Medal, the highest award Ontario had to offer in rowing. In 1875, Hanlan defeated all challengers and became Ontario Champion.

With his fame spreading, a group of Toronto businessmen formed the Hanlan Group to fund his races and arrange meets for him. This group entered Ned in the famous Schuylkill River Regatta in Philadelphia in 1876. With the Hanlan Group doing all the financing and arranging all the travel, Ned was supposed to go into serious training for this event. However, Ned had other ideas. With his dad's hotel now doing a brisk business, Ned decided that he would do a little rum running, supplying drink to people who lived outside the hotel's license area.

This kind of shenanigans landed him in trouble with the law and a warrant was issued for his arrest. Ned's backers concealed him in the Toronto Rowing Club. The police found out and came to pick him up. Ned was warned of their approach and scooted out the back door down to the dock, where he grabbed a rowing shell and headed out into Lake Ontario, with the law in hot pursuit. Exhibiting his best racing form, Ned soon outran the cops and before their astounded eyes, he soon caught up with a passing steamer. Then, grabbing a rope ladder which was dangling over the side, he hauled himself on board, bound for the United States.

Ned got to Philadelphia in time for his big race, to the great relief of the Hanlan Group. This was his first international race and he started what was to become a favorite gambit. He would row like crazy, build up a good lead and then stop rowing, until his competition almost caught up with him. Then, he would turn on the speed and leave them all behind.

In the Philadelphia race, Ned set a new record for the five-meter course, completing it in 21 minutes 9.5 seconds. Ned received a hero's welcome when he got back to Toronto. Even the police were proud of him. He was the first Canadian ever to win an international event. This was in the days before baseball, hockey or basketball, and in a time when rowing was one of the world's premier sports.

With his new fame, Ned became a big celebrity and in 1877, he married Margaret Sullivan of Pictou, Nova Scotia. Margaret was to accompany Ned on all his races all over the world. That same year, 1877, Ned won the Canadian Championship by defeating Wallace Ross by a whopping thirty boat lengths, an unheard margin of victory for such a competitive event.

The Hanlan Group then challenged the American rowing champion, Ephriam Evan Norris, to a row-off on June 24, 1888. This event attracted a lot of interest from Toronto and fifty-four well-heeled citizens made the trip to the United States and wagered $300,000 on Ned. He did not disappoint his backers and he made a lot of Torontonians happy. Winning that race made Ned the American Champion.

With his fame spreading, a match was arranged to row off against John Hawdon, Champion of England. On May 5, 1879, in a race on the River Tyne over eight kilometers, Ned pulled away very fast, leaving the Englishman far behind. Getting up to his old tricks, Ned stopped rowing, to the consternation of the spectators, until Hawdon almost caught up with him. Then he sped off again, winning the race by five lengths. It could have been by a greater margin, except for Ned's showboating. On June 16, 1879, in a race for the Championship of England, Ned rowed the course fifty-five seconds faster than any previous rower. He was now Champion of Canada, America and England.

Ned Hanlan raced for the World's Championship in England in 1880. There was heavy betting on Ned. Two days before the race, punters were lined up for blocks trying to get their bets on Ned. The race was run on the historic Thames River in London. This win made Ned Hanlan, the Irish emigrant's son, World Champion of rowing and Canada's first superstar.

Ned retired from rowing at age forty-two to help Mary raise their six boys and two girls. He ran for political office and was elected a Toronto Alderman. Ned Hanlan passed away in 1908 and ten thousand mourners turned out to say their good-byes to Canada's premier athlete.

To honor his memory, the city named Hanlan's Point on Centre Island for Ned, and eighteen years after his death, Toronto erected a bronze statue on the grounds of the Canadian National Exhibition. Ned Hanlan won an astonishing three hundred consecutive races during his heyday, a record unmatched in any sport. Ned is also remembered by patrons at Ned Hanlan's Great Canadian Sporting Saloon at Eglington Avenue and Mount Pleasant in Toronto, where the Irish Rovers have gathered a great collection of his memorabilia.

The Incomparable Danny Gallivan
Voice of the Canadiens for 32 Years

His excited voice resounding over the airwaves, "an enormous save, a cannonading shot," were parts of the flowery language and eloquent terminology the late Danny Gallivan brought to hockey. Danny Gallivan, once named Montreal's Irishman of the Year, brought a love of language to the game, and as his voice rose and fell with excitement, the millions of listeners to *Hockey Night in Canada* would become caught up in the thrill of the game.

His "Here comes the Hawks" (as the Blackhawks would cover over the blueline into Montreal territory) would cause your spirits to sink, until Danny would scream "Robinson poke-checks the attacker and passes off to Savard and Savard does his spin-nerama and clears the puck ahead to the Rocket, who is in the clear." The fans of the Habs (Montreal) would clap their hands and shout with joy -- such was the power of Danny Gallivan's hockey broadcasting style.

Year after year, the country was captivated by Gallivan's colorful style, and even the dullest game sounded like the final game of the Stanley Cup playoffs. Danny Gallivan was at the mike for over 1,800 NHL broadcasts, and every game seemed fresh and different from any other game he had covered.

He retired from hockey broadcasting after the 1984 Stanley Cup finals, won by the Edmonton Oilers. During his time as the Montreal Canadiens' play-by-play announcer, the Canadiens won the Stanley Cup sixteen times. For his services to hockey, Danny Gallivan was inducted into the Hockey Hall of Fame in 1980, and he also won the Foster Hewitt Memorial Award.

Danny Gallivan's family were Nova Scotia Irish. He was born in Sydney, Nova Scotia on April 11, 1919 and he served in the Canadian Armed Forces in Europe during World War Two. He retired from hockey broadcasting in 1984 and spent his remaining years playing golf and on speaking engagements.

Danny Gallivan was married to the former Eileen McPhee. The Gallivans had four children, one son and three daughters.

Epilogue

No longer do the Irish leave Ireland as the impoverished emigrant of yesteryear. Like the missionaries of medieval times many now leave in the service of their country working through the United Nations peacekeeping efforts and assisting relief efforts in Third World countries.

In reviewing the varied fields which attracted the Irish, it is amazing how the necessity of earning a living led them into fields of endeavor not previously considered, or open to them. This pattern occurred from the early days right down to recent immigrants. Once they had their feet in the door, many rose to the top of their chosen fields. Large numbers became entrepreneurs in small businesses, some establishing immense wealth.

The Irish maintained their culture through their church and by congregating in communities where they lived close to each other. An important aspect in preserving their heritage was the fact that, unlike other European immigrant groups, almost as many women as men immigrated and they passed on their beliefs and ideas to their children. They maintained their contacts with families in Ireland.

A pattern of success has become clear from the interviews of the people in this book. The combination of hope, confidence and imagination, driven by the unlimited opportunities in their adopted lands, stirred an ambition beyond anything they had previously experienced. Their approaches to getting a job were varied. They used each job as a springboard to their next objective; they all had a goal from which they could not be deterred. In the process, they enriched their own lives and the lives of those who follow.

Thank You Ireland is a tribute to the sons and daughters of Erin who made the North American Continent their home while keeping a special place in their hearts for the green and misty isle from whence they came.

Selected Bibliography

Adams, William Forbes. *Ireland and Irish Emigration to the New World, From 1815 to the Famine.* Baltimore, Md: Genealogical Publishing Co., Inc., 1980.

Aurand, Harold W. *From the Molly Maguires to the United Mine Workers.* Philadelphia, Pa: Temple University Press, 1971.

Bogdanovich, Peter. *John Ford.* Berkeley, California: University of California Press, 1968

Catton, Bruce. *This Hallowed Ground.* New York: Doubleday & Company, Inc., Pocket Books, 1961.

Catton, Bruce. *A Stillness at Appomattox.* New York: Doubleday & Company, Inc., Pocket Books, 1973.

Clayton, Lawrence A. *Grace -- W. R. Grace & Co., The Formative Years -- 1850-1930.* Ottawa, Illinois: Jameson Books, 1985.

Clum, John. *The Angel of Tombstone.* Reprinted from the *Arizona Historical Review,* 1931.

Collier, Peter and David Horowitz. *The Fords, An American Epic.* New York: Summit Books, 1987.

Davin, Nicholas Flood. *The Irishman in Canada.* Introduction by D.C. Lyne. (2nd ed.) Shannon, Ireland: Irish University Press, 1969.

Edwards, Ruth Dudley. *An Atlas of Irish History.* (2nd ed.) London and New York: Routledge, 1981.

Elliott, Bruce S. *Irish Migrants in the Canadas, Kingston and Montreal.* McGill-Queen's University Press, 1988.

Fink, Gary M. ed-in-chief. *Biographical Directory of American Labor.* Westport, Connecticut: Greenwood Press, 1984.

Francis, Diane. *Controlling Interest, Who Owns Canada.* Toronto: Macmillan of Canada, 1986.

Gray, Earle. *Wildcatters -- The Story of Pacific Petroleums and Westcoast Transmission.* Toronto: McClelland and Stewart Ltd., 1982.

Herm, Gerhard. *The Celts.* (2nd ed.)
London and New York: Routledge, 1981.

Houston, Cecil J. and William J. Smythe. *Irish Emigration and Canadian Settlement, Patterns, Links and Letters.* Toronto: University of Toronto Press, 1990.

"Irish Impact on Toronto." *The Toronto Star*, March 17, 1992.

Jackman, S.W. *Portraits of the Premiers.* Sidney, British Columbia: Gray's Publishing Ltd., 1969.

Jones, Mary Harris. *The Autobigraphy of Mother Jones.* Chicago: Charles H. Kerr and Company, 1990.

Keddell, Georgina. *The Newspapering Murrays.* Toronto: McClelland and Stewart, 1967.

Lazarus, Morden. *Years of Hard Labour -- Trade Unions and the Workingman in Canada.* Toronto: An Ontario Federation of Labour Publication, 1974.

Longford, Lord. *Nixon, a Study in Extremes of Fortune,* Great Britain: Butler and Tanner, Ltd., 1980.

MacKay, Donald. *Flight from the Famine.* Toronto: McClelland and Stewart, Inc., 1990.

MacManus, Seamus. *The Story of the Irish Race* (22nd ed.). New York: The Devin-Adair Company, 1972.

Maguire, John Francis Maguire. *The Irish in America.* London: Longmans, Green & Co., 1868.

Mangan, James J. *The Voyage of the Naparima.* Ste-Foy, Quebec: Carraig Books, 1982.

Mattimoe, Cyril. *North Roscommon, Its People and Past.* Boyle, Ireland: Roscommon Herald, 1992.

McAvoy, Thomas T. *The History of the Catholic Church in the United States.* Notre Dame, Indiana: University of Notre Dame Press, 1969 and 1970.

McCaffrey, Lawrence J. *The Irish Diaspora in America.* Bloomington: Indiana University Press,1976.

McClung, Nellie. *Clearing the West.* New York: Fleming H. Revell Company, 1936.

McClung, Nellie. *The Stream Runs Fast.* Toronto: Thos. Allen & Son Ltd., 1965.

"Microsoft Mourns the Loss of Frank Gaudette." *MicroNews*, April 30, 1993.

Morris, Richard Knowles. *John P. Holland: 1841-1914.*
　　Inventor of the Modern Submarine. Annapolis, Md:
　　United States Naval Institute, 1966.

Nasmith, George G. *Timothy Eaton.*
　　Toronto: McClelland & Stewart Ltd., 1923.

O'Brien, Pat. *The Wind at My Back.*
　　New York: Doubleday, 1964.

O'Brien, Michael J. *Irish Settlers in America.* Baltimore, Md:
　　Genealogical Publishing Company, 1979.

Oursler, Fulton and Will, *Father Flanagan of Boys Town.*
　　New York: Doubleday & Company, Inc., 1949.

Persico, Joseph E. *Casey -- The Lives and Secrets of William J.*
　　Casey: From the OSS to the CIA. New York:
　　Viking Penguin, 1990.

Phelan, Josephine. *The Ardent Exile, The Life and Times of*
　　Thomas D'Arcy McGee. Toronto: The MacMillan
　　Company of Canada, 1951.

Reagan, Ronald. *Ronald Reagan, An American Life.*
　　New York: Simon and Schuster Pocket Books, 1990.

Robinson, Archie. *George Meaney and His Times, a*
　　Biography. New York: Simon and Schuster, 1981.

Sarris, Andrew. *The John Ford Movie Mystery.* London: Secker
　　and Warburg/British Film Institute, 1976.

Shannon, William V. *The American Irish.* New York:
　　MacMillan Publishing Co., Inc., 1961.

Sheehy, Terence. *Ireland and Her People.* New York:
　　Greenwich House, 1983.

Sinclair, Andrew. *John Ford -- A Biography.*
　　New York: Dial Press/James Wade, 1979.

Sloan, Irving J. ed, *Ronald W. Reagan, 1911-,*
　　New York: Oceana Publications, 1990.

Steel, Edward M. ed. *The Correspondence of Mother Jones,*
　　Pittsburgh, Pa: University of Pittsburgh Press, 1985.

Taylor, Philip. *The Distant Magnet, European Emigration to U.S.A.*
　　London: Eyre & Spottiswoode, Ltd., 1971.

Vincent, Isabel. "Fordlandia. Toronto." *The Globe and Mail,*
　　March 20, 1993.

White, Randall. *Ontario 1610-1985, A Political and Economic History.* Toronto and London: Dundrum Press, 1985.

"William Clark and Marcus Daly." Montana Historical Society, Helena, Montana.

Woodham-Smith, Cecil. *The Great Hunger, Ireland 1845-1849.* New York: Harper & Row, 1962.

Index

351

Frank Keane

FRANK KEANE was born in Garryowen, Limerick City. He joined the British Army during World War II, serving in the Parachute Regiment.

He immigrated to Canada in 1954 and worked for the Financial Post Corporation and Richardson Securities. He moved to the Vancouver area in 1967 where he worked in the investment business and owned and published a community newspaper.

Keane is the author of several books, including *How to Get Yourself a Job, Independent Schools of British Columbia, Canadian Gold Companies, Pezim-Tales of a Promoter* and a travel book, *Down the I5 and Up the 101.*

Patrick Lavin

PATRICK LAVIN emigrated from his native County Roscommon to Canada in 1954. He moved to Los Angeles in 1960 where he attended California State University, Northridge, graduating with a Bachelor of Arts degree. He studied government administration and congressional affairs at the National Institute of Public Affairs in Washington, D.C.

Patrick retired in 1990 from a career with the United States government. Active in Irish-American affairs, he was the founder and first president of the Sheridan Circle, a Washington, D.C. forum for the exchange of information relating to American and Irish cultural, economic and public service matters.

Patrick now lives in White Rock, British Columbia with his wife, Joan.